THE RESEARCH PROCESS

Canadian Edition

Gary D. Bouma
Rod Ling
Lori Wilkinson

OXFORD
UNIVERSITY PRESS

OXFORD
UNIVERSITY PRESS

70 Wynford Drive, Don Mills, Ontario M3C 1J9
www.oupcanada.com

Oxford University Press is a department of the University of Oxford.
It furthers the University's objective of excellence in research, scholarship,
and education by publishing worldwide in

Oxford New York

Auckland Cape Town Dar es Salaam Hong Kong Karachi
Kuala Lumpur Madrid Melbourne Mexico City Nairobi
New Delhi Shanghai Taipei Toronto

With offices in

Argentina Austria Brazil Chile Czech Republic France Greece
Guatemala Hungary Italy Japan Poland Portugal Singapore
South Korea Switzerland Thailand Turkey Ukraine Vietnam

Oxford is a trade mark of Oxford University Press
in the UK and in certain other countries

Published in Canada by Oxford University Press

Library and Archives Canada Cataloguing in Publication

Bouma, Gary D.
The research process / Gary D. Bouma, Rod Ling and Lori Wilkinson.
— 1st Canadian ed.

Includes bibliographical references and index.
ISBN 978-0-19-542615-1

1. Social sciences—Research. I. Ling, Rod II. Wilkinson, Lori, 1972– III. Title.

H62.B675 2008   300.72   C2008-903578-X

2 3 4 – 12 11 10 09
Printed in Canada

Contents

Acknowledgements

To Donald H. Bouma

This book is dedicated to my father—sociologist, community leader, and opinion shaper. I learned research as a child. I learned the importance of having evidence to support an argument and how evidence-based argument could be a powerful tool for liberation. For him, it was used in support of the black civil rights movement in the United States. For me, it has been used to advance other liberations and the analysis of the shape and management of religious diversity in post-modern societies.

We would like to thank all those who have attended workshops and seminars on 'research methodology'. The questions you raised, the ideas you shared, and the enthusiasm you had for the topic led to the writing of *The Research Process*. Particular thanks are due to Mary Sinclair for her assistance in opening her classes to learning about research, using early versions of this material, and for her general support.

We are grateful to the hundreds of students who have taken the research process course at Monash University. Their comments on the text, its examples and shortcomings, have greatly helped to shape the progress of new editions.

I am deeply indebted to the many PhD, masters, and honours students who have come to me for supervision. I hope that they have learned as much about research from me as I have from them.

I also wish to thank the thousands of people who participated in the research projects I have conducted. Whether it was quantitative or qualitative research, I depended absolutely on their willingness to tell me about themselves in some way.

Gary D. Bouma

I send my deepest thanks and love to my parents, Rex and Heather, who gave me everything.

Rod Ling

I would like to thank my graduate students Farzana Quddus and Fadi Ennab for providing assistance in the creation of the tables for this book. Their dedication to my various research projects over the past two years has been greatly appreciated. Yvonne Hébert of the University of Calgary and Mehrunissa Ali of Ryerson University have provided immeasurable support throughout this and other academic activities. Jennifer Charlton at Oxford University Press greatly facilitated the exchange of information across provincial and international borders. Many thanks to three anonymous reviewers as well for their helpful and insightful comments. Their suggestions have greatly strengthened this book. My sincere appreciation goes to Dorothy Turnbull for her careful copyediting of the manuscript. Finally, thanks to my family and numerous friends who have always supported me throughout my academic endeavours. John, I couldn't have made it this far without you!

Lori Wilkinson

Preface

If you want to know what social science research is all about and how to do it, this book is for you. In accessible language, it will lead you into the world of research and give you confidence that you know how to design a research study, how to carry it out, and how to report on your research. You will become aware of the range of possible approaches and what each offers. You will learn how to decide what approach suits the issue you want to study, the question you want to answer. You will also become aware of some of the pitfalls as well as learning 'tricks of the trade'.

The logic of research is presented in such a way as to enable the novice to prepare research proposals and to conduct research. The essential logic of scientific research is the same for physicists as it is for sociologists. It is the same for beginners as for masters of the art. This book introduces the essential logic of research—that is, the kind of disciplined thinking that scientific research requires. Designing and conducting a research project also requires clear and disciplined thinking, and this book is intended to serve as a brief, easy-to-digest introduction to the research process. More advanced students are strongly encouraged to consult other methodological texts, particularly once they have decided on a research design, mode of sampling, and method of data analysis.

While there are many kinds of research, and research projects seem at first to take many forms, it is a mistake to assume that there is no pattern to the process. A second mistake is to mindlessly follow one pattern.

This first Canadian edition of *The Research Process* is aimed at post-secondary students who are enrolled in an introductory research methods course or who want to learn how to do the kinds of research required for jobs in marketing, social policy, social work, politics, communication, and community work. It assumes that readers have only an introductory understanding of 'social science' and little knowledge about doing research. The text begins in a leisurely way, introducing concepts one at a time with examples. It takes a non-statistical approach, presenting the essentials of the research process in an easily understood manner. Both quantitative and qualitative methods are introduced. While the methods differ in some ways, there are many issues common to both of these important ways of gathering evidence for understanding the social world we live in.

This is not a book on the philosophy of science or social science. The past few decades have witnessed hotly contended debates about the aims, the achievements, and the very possibilities of the sciences. In the meantime, researchers have carried on with their basic task of describing the way aspects of our world work and testing theories by relating evidence to propositions about the state, nature, and operation of the universe. The essential philosophical questions apply to all research—whether conducted by chemists, physicists, social psychologists, demographers, or other researchers.

THE APPROACH

We approach research methodology as a process involving a sequence of activities, each step preparing students for the next. When doing social science research, some questions are best answered before others are raised. We explain the reasons for this sequencing of questions and point out several common pitfalls. The process of social science research is divided into three phases. Phase 1 involves:

1. selecting a problem (including narrowing and clarifying the problem) and restating it as a hypothesis for quantitative research or as a research objective for qualitative research;
2. defining variables and determining ways of measuring them;
3. choosing a research design;
4. choosing a sample.

Phase 2 is the data collection stage. We discuss researchers' ethical responsibilities in this regard; understanding these responsibilities will help you to secure the approval of a human research ethics committee for conducting your research.

Phase 3 involves the analysis and interpretation of data and writing the report.

Several examples in each chapter demonstrate how the research process progresses. In addition, exercises and questions throughout the text provide you with practice in the methods discussed. Each chapter ends with questions to test your comprehension of the material.

This Canadian edition contains critical updates on ethical policies in relation to conducting research with human subjects, secure storage of data and personal information, and new guidelines on obtaining informed consent. While legislation for the protection of personal information varies from province to province, the intent is similar across Canada. Our aim is to give students a good understanding of how to navigate the ever-changing contexts of ethics. This edition also contains additional readings, tips on computer programs, and up-to-date examples using Canadian statistics.

The Research Process is designed to develop research skills important for living and working in our world—a world in which information is becoming one of the most valuable commodities and in which the ability to handle information is one of the most valued and marketable skills—a skill that is critical to getting a job today.

Gary D. Bouma
Rod Ling
Lori Wilkinson

February 2008

INTRODUCTION

How We Know What We Know and How We Know We Know

Have you ever had an argument with someone? She said one thing, and you said another. She claimed she was right because she read it in a book. You defended your position by pointing out that a doctor told you and a doctor should know. So arguments go. But how do they stop? How can these points of view be tested to determine which is correct? How do we know when we are right or wrong? How do we know what we know?

We are confronted by questions all through life. What is the best diet for weight loss? What is the impact of job loss on the rate of marital breakdown? What is the solution to child poverty or homelessness? Is post-secondary education worthwhile? Is coeducation better for males than it is for females? We may spend a lot of time debating the issues raised by these and similar questions, but how do we find reliable answers to our questions? How do we get the knowledge we seek?

Knowledge can be defined as a description of the state or operation of some aspect of the universe upon which people or groups are prepared to act. If I 'know' that it will rain, I am likely to take my umbrella or wear a raincoat. If I 'know' that completed post-secondary education is reliably associated with higher levels of income, I am more likely to make some effort to attend and graduate from a post-secondary institution.

Knowledge does not hang in space; it is a product of social processes. The production of knowledge usually begins when the public, governments, or groups of experts recognize that the state of knowledge in a particular area is inadequate.

Next, funding bodies, corporations, and universities accept research proposals and decide which are the most relevant and deserving of support. Successful proposals are carried out by teams of researchers who produce findings through their combined experience and skills. Research findings are communicated and endorsed by professional organizations that decide what research should be published and how it should be presented. Finally, communities and governments 'have a say' in how new knowledge is applied by debating and legislating for its appropriate uses. In this way, knowledge is both a product and the property of social groups.

ANSWERING OUR QUESTIONS

One of the first issues facing us is whether to answer questions ourselves or rely on others for the information we need. If we want to know whether it is raining outside, we can look for ourselves or ask someone else. If we want to know what Canadians think about politicians, we can either ask Canadians ourselves or look at the recent polls. Whatever the question, we are faced with roughly the same choice. We can do research—that is, collect the evidence ourselves—or consult an authority.

CONSULTING AN AUTHORITY AS A WAY OF KNOWING

Usually when we have a question, we look up the answer in an encyclopedia, 'surf' the Internet, ask a friend who 'knows', or ask an expert—a medical practitioner, a professor, a religious leader, a police officer, a lawyer, or an umpire, as appropriate. We refer to articles in journals or newspapers or look for a book, a website, or a CD-ROM on the subject. The most common way by which we get answers to our questions is to consult authorities. As long as the authority consulted knows the answer, this is the most efficient way to answer a question.

People can have at least two kinds of authority: authority because of position and authority because of knowledge. The kind of authority most useful for answering our questions about the nature and operation of the world—particularly the social, biological, and physical world—is authority derived from knowledge.

The problem with consulting authorities is selection. On what bases do we select authorities? When we are looking for an answer to a question or problem, the essential guideline should be that the authority has the knowledge we need. However, other factors sometimes influence our choice.

We are sometimes influenced by a person's position, popularity, or appearance. The critical point is that no matter how prominent the person, no matter how much authority or power they have, their opinion on a subject is of no more value than any other person's unless they have expertise in the area. A bishop, a physician, a judge, or an Olympic gold medallist may hold opinions about unemployment, taxation, the way families should be raised, or the role of government in foreign aid. These opinions, unless based on special knowledge of the issue in question, are no more valid than those expressed on the same topic by anyone else.

Inevitably, a problem with consulting authorities will arise—two recognized authorities in the same field disagree. For example, it is very common to encounter conflicting opinions regarding the extent of unemployment, gender discrimination, and racial discrimination; the benefits and costs of domestic welfare programs, foreign aid, and affirmative action policies; and the incidence of infections and work-related injuries. Authorities also fail us when they cannot answer questions with assurance. Sometimes their opinions are unconvincing. On many issues that are or appear to be new, there may be no authorities at all.

RESEARCH AS A WAY OF KNOWING

To evaluate the opinions of authorities, we review their research. For this, we need to understand the 'research process'—the generally adopted approach to doing research. Then we can make informed inquiries and judgments of authorities. Has the authority chosen the most appropriate research method? Have all stages of the research been conducted properly? Does the authority's research address the relevant aspects of the question? Has the authority made a valid interpretation of the research findings? What are the limitations of the research?

When authorities cannot answer our questions or we are dissatisfied with their opinions, we conduct research ourselves. To obtain findings in which we can have confidence, we must be familiar with the research process.

The research process is guided by rules and principles for making confident statements about knowledge of the world based on our observations. As the rest of this book will show, the research process is not an activity that we know intuitively and can just 'go and do'. It is an activity that others have spent much time developing through practice and critical discussion. You will not become familiar with the research process unless you study and practise it.

The following list contains examples of the types of important questions that face groups in today's societies. To pursue valid answers to such questions, it is essential that you have knowledge of the research process.

1. Corporations need to have an informed idea of public preferences for products or services. Will the public accept changes in packaging or product performance?
2. Social workers need to know what it is like to live under certain conditions, with certain levels of ability, or in certain ethnic groups and subcultures in order to design appropriate service delivery systems.
3. Professionals such as doctors need to assess the validity of theories that have consequences for the way they practise. Does taking a regular low dose of aspirin reduce the incidence of cardiovascular disorder?
4. Governments need to know about the effects of policies. What have been the consequences of the immigration policies of the past two decades? What are the consequences of prison terms for juvenile offenders?

If the subject of the research is controversial, it will come under considerable scrutiny. The researchers will be challenged to provide solid and carefully collected evidence. If the results of their research are clear, they may be able to settle the controversy, not by appeal to authority, but by appeal to the evidence they have collected and are able to show to others.

SUMMARY

Research is done to settle disputes about the nature and operation of some aspect of the universe. The research process is a disciplined way of coming to know something about our world and ourselves.

QUESTIONS FOR REVIEW

1. When is research carried out?
2. In what ways is the expertise of an authority limited?
3. Discuss some of the problems involved in consulting authorities in order to answer questions. Who would you consult about child-raising techniques? Who would you consult about the impact of explicitly violent television on the play routines of children?
4. List the authorities you regularly consult. How do you know they know? What characteristics of these authorities are important to you? Gender? Age? Social position?
5. Is it possible to live without accepting the word of authorities?

Suggestions for Further Reading

Chalmers, A.F. 1999. *What Is This Thing Called Science?* 3rd edn. St Lucia: University of Queensland Press.
Denzin, Norman K., and Yvonna S. Lincoln, eds. 2000. *Handbook of Qualitative Research.* 2nd edn. London: Sage.
Wallace, W. 1971. *The Logic of Science in Sociology.* Chicago: Aldine.
Waters, Malcolm, and Rodney Crook. 1993. *Sociology One*, chapters 1–3. Melbourne: Longman Cheshire.

Research as a Way of Knowing

Science can be defined as a discipline that collects, weighs, and evaluates the empirical evidence for accepting a particular theory or explanation. The *goal of science* is to produce a widely acceptable description of the nature or operation of some aspect of the universe. Science, whether social, psychological, biological, or in the field of physics, does this by collecting and analyzing sensory evidence in such a way that others looking at the same evidence in the same way would draw the same conclusions or at least understand that it is possible to see what the researcher was examining. *Scientific research* involves the attempt to gather evidence in such a way that others can see why particular evidence was gathered, how that evidence was gathered, and what the findings were; they can then draw their own conclusions on the basis of that evidence.

This chapter explores the practical meaning of this definition of science. How does scientific research go about trying to produce knowledge that is supported by empirical evidence—that is, by physical, tangible evidence? What are the several kinds of disciplined activities involved in the research process?

Scientific research is done to find ways of understanding, describing, and making more predictable, or controlling, the behaviour of some aspect of the universe. The results of research may be used to develop remedies for problems, strategies for projects, and plans for action. Problems like youth homelessness, projects to improve levels of education, and plans to combat or contain diseases like sars all require information that does not exist and must be researched.

We also engage in research to settle conflicting claims or differences of opinion or to test ideas about the world we live in. Take the following simple case:

Georgina: Relationships between people over the age of 65 are more stable. The longer people are married, the more satisfied they are with their spouse.

Frank: You are wrong. People in long-term marriages are more likely to be dissatisfied.

The conflict between Georgina and Frank can be settled by scientific research. They both have 'theories' about the marital satisfaction of older people. It is possible to collect evidence to test their competing 'theories'. This example will be developed through this chapter.

RESEARCH AS A PROCESS

Doing research involves a process or a series of linked activities moving from beginning to end. The research process is not absolutely rigid, but it will be weakened or made more difficult if the first steps are not executed carefully.

Those who have done a lot of research develop their own style of going through the phases of the research process. Each researcher will be able to describe a pattern or a regular way they do their research. When their patterns are compared, a 'normal' sequence begins to emerge—normal not in the sense of a strict set of steps but as an order of basic phases, with related issues considered at each phase.

The following outline of the research process has helped many students to learn the necessary skills and avoid the major pitfalls involved in research. It is not the only way of doing research, just one useful way.

Outline of the research process

Phase 1: Essential first steps
The researcher clarifies the issue to be researched and selects a research method.
Phase 2: Data collection
The researcher collects evidence about the research question.
Phase 3: Analysis and interpretation
The researcher relates the evidence to the research question, draws conclusions about the question, and acknowledges the limitations of the research.

Phase 1 of the research process involves five essential steps, each concerning a separate issue. Failure to satisfactorily address these issues will render the rest of the research process more difficult or impossible—therefore, the steps are essential. While qualitative and quantitative research designs both follow these steps, there are differences in the way they do. These differences will be noted as we go along.

Phase 1: Essential first steps
1. Select, narrow, and formulate the question to be studied.
2. Select a research design.
3. Design and devise measures for variables.
4. Set up tables for analysis.
5. Select a sample.

Step 1: Focus and narrow the research problem. Initially, a research problem may start with an observation like 'Most people who are unemployed seem to be young.' One approach to developing a research problem from this observation would be to ask, 'What is it like to be young and unemployed?' This would probably lead to qualitative research guided by a research objective. Another approach would be to test the validity of this observation. To do this, it is necessary to be clear about what has to be tested. The observer claims that there is a relationship between two varying aspects (variables) of their general social experience, 'unemployment' and 'age'. They are really saying that according to their general observations, 'The lower a person's age, the more likely the person is to be unemployed.' This is one way of moving from the observation to articulating a relationship to be tested. Each of these approaches clarifies the focus of the research. At this point, it is important to review the literature on youth unemployment. This will assist you in identifying the major findings and the research questions asked by other researchers. It is also the first step in situating your own research findings within the existing research debates. More will be said about the literature review in Chapter 3.

Step 2: Select a research design. The first choice here is between qualitative and quantitative research. Your observation might motivate you to ask, 'What is it like to be young and unemployed?' or 'Is being unemployed different for young men compared to young women?' Such questions are usually answered using qualitative research methods.

On the other hand, you might want to test a more quantitative question, such as 'What percentage of youth are unemployed?' or 'Is youth unemployment greater now than in the 1980s?' or 'Is youth unemployment more prevalent in Vancouver than in Victoria?' The first question about the relationship between 'age' and 'unemployment' could be tested in a single social environment such as a social club or a suburb. The results would be based on information gathered in one environment. The subsequent questions require that the relationship be examined in several social environments, such as different points in time or several suburbs, and that the results for each be compared, providing the desired results.

Step 3: Select ways of measuring changes in variables. If you choose to take a quantitative approach, you will select variables and find measures for them before you gather evidence. For example, to measure changes in 'unemployment', you might select the government's official 'unemployment rate'. However, if you take a qualitative approach, you will decide which prompts to use to enable your interviewees to tell their stories or select certain aspects of human behaviour to observe and record. Consulting the literature is an important step here as well. How have other researchers defined unemployment? How have other researchers defined youth? Does the existing literature define youth as being between the ages of 15 and 24, or do they define youth differently? This is an important aspect to consider when situating your research and is further discussed in Chapter 3.

Step 4: Set up tables for analysis. If you choose to take a quantitative approach, you will design tables to be used in summarizing your data in a manner that makes later reporting and analysis straightforward. If you take a qualitative approach, you may have a set of tentative themes in mind that you expect to explore, but you remain open to your experience in data collection to shape the approach you take in analyzing your observations or interview transcripts.

Step 5: Select a sample. Research is almost always done on a sample; very rarely is everyone included. The extent to which you wish to generalize your findings will shape your selection of a situation or a group of people for your research. In qualitative research, situations or people are selected to represent dimensions of interest to the researcher. To learn what it is like to be young, unemployed, and female/male, it makes sense for you to talk to some young males and females who are unemployed. On the other hand, if you wish to test the relationship between age and unemployment in your local area, then you will want a sample that represents the population of the area—a more systematic sample is required.

These steps provide a basis for the successful conduct of the research in three ways. First, they articulate the problem and narrow the focus of the research. This allows the researcher to undertake the practical aspects of the project with a clear awareness of what has to be tested or studied. Second, these steps immediately introduce discipline to the research procedure. This discipline is necessary to keep the project focused and to maintain rigour in data collection and analysis. Last, the steps provide a structure to evaluate the progress of a research project. If something goes wrong or the project gets bogged down, revisiting the steps will probably tell the researcher where the project went off the rails.

A quantitative example

We now return to the argument about whether or not older married couples are satisfied with their relationships. Both Georgina and Frank have a hunch, or a 'theory'. Let's test these theories. We commence with step 1 of Phase 1 by focusing the question and narrowing it to a specific set of circumstances. For this particular problem, consideration must be given to the following issues:

- Do participants need to be married, or can they be in long-term relationships?
- Will those living in common-law relationships be considered for inclusion in the study?

- What will be the geographical context of the study? All Canadians? Only those living in a particular province? A particular city?
- What will be the age of participants? What is our definition of elderly? Age 60? Age 65? Age 70?
- How do we define 'satisfaction'?
- How long must couples be in a relationship before they can be considered for inclusion in the study? One year? Ten years? Twenty years?
- What aspects of satisfaction will be considered? Financial satisfaction? Happiness with partner?
- Will arguments between the partners be taken into consideration?
- Will any allowances be made to consider the effects of unpleasant life events, such as the death of a child, on satisfaction in the relationship?

Step 1 requires us to focus, clarify, and narrow the research problem. Let's say that the study is limited to adults aged 65 years and older who have been in their present relationship for 20 years or longer. This will be a national study, so participants may be drawn from samples collected in any city or province in the country. It will include married and common-law couples who have been living together for at least 20 years. Marital happiness is our main area of interest, so financial well-being and other factors relating to satisfaction will not be considered as part of marital satisfaction. We may, however, still ask about these outside factors to learn more about marital relationships among the elderly. As with quantitative studies, it is imperative that we consult the existing research literature on the subject. It will help us to formulate the appropriate research question and to situate our findings within the existing research debates.

The research question is no longer simply 'What is the relationship between length of marriage and marital satisfaction?' It has become 'What is the relationship between years of marriage/common-law relationship and marital satisfaction among Canadians aged 65 and older?'

We also define our variables. The first variable is 'marital satisfaction'. A number of studies have tested questions dealing with the measurement of marital satisfaction. We select some recent research conducted by Kira Birditt and her associates (2008) and the list of questions they asked in a similar study conducted on American adults. The second variable is 'length of relationship'. This information can be obtained by asking the couples to report the number of years they have been in their current relationship. This is one way of considering the relationship we have to test.

In step 2, we select a research design. We are going to use a basic research design in which we compare the marital satisfaction among married and cohabiting couples by means of a simple survey. Here an examination of the research literature may be helpful in determining an appropriate research design. Research design also entails the way the research question is phrased. This topic is discussed further in Chapter 7.

In step 3, we select the measures for each variable. The measure for marital satisfaction is less straightforward because it involves asking the couples a series of questions relating to their marital happiness. Based on their answers to the questions on marital satisfaction, some couples will be defined as 'satisfied' while others will be defined as 'dissatisfied'. Length of relationship is measured by asking the couples to report the number of years they have been in their relationship. Again, consulting the literature is important. Other researchers have likely studied this phenomenon, and it will be important to review their findings. They may have asked questions or defined the variables in a similar way.

In step 4, we design a table for easy analysis and data collection, such as Table 2.1.

TABLE 2.1 A simple table designed for easy collection and analysis of research results

	20–39 YEARS IN RELATIONSHIP	40+ YEARS IN RELATIONSHIP
Marital satisfaction		

In step 5, we select a sample. In this case, we need to select a random sample of older adults in marital or common-law relationships. We discuss sampling strategies in a later chapter. For now, let us assume that we have a list of 20 couples who fit the criteria for our study (being in marital or common-law relationships for at least 20 years).

Phase 2: Data collection
1. Collect data.
2. Summarize and organize data.

Data collection is a major enterprise in research but not the only factor in producing a good research study. Preparation (Phase 1) takes the most time, and drawing conclusions and writing the report often take more time than data collection. Data collection may not be time consuming, especially in quantitative research.

In step 1, we collect data about the couples and their satisfaction in their current relationship, which is the measure for the variable 'marital satisfaction'. Let's say that couples married for between 20 and 39 years score 3.5 on our marital satisfaction measures while those married for 40 years or more score, on average, 4.25 on the same measures. A discussion on calculating the findings can be found in later chapters.

For step 2, we summarize the data (see Table 2.2).

Now we are ready for Phase 3, analysis and interpretation. In this phase, we relate the data collected to the research question and draw conclusions. It is really quite simple, as long as the research problem is articulated and made clear in Phase 1.

TABLE 2.2 Completed table

	20–39 YEARS IN RELATIONSHIP	40+ YEARS IN RELATIONSHIP
Average marital satisfaction score	3.5	4.25

Phase 3: Analysis and interpretation
1. Relate data to the research question.
2. Draw conclusions.
3. Assess the limitations of the study.
4. Make suggestions for further research.

In step 1, ask yourself, 'How does the data relate to the research question? What can the data tell us about marital satisfaction?'

In step 2, we draw conclusions. Given the data in Table 2.2, what would you conclude? Is Frank right in his assertion that marital satisfaction decreases as the length of the relationship increases, or is Georgina's belief that martial satisfaction increases as length of relationship increases correct?

In step 3, we acknowledge the limitations of the research. You may be able to see some limitations in our study. It applies only to couples living in Canada aged 65 or older in relationships of 20 years and over. Measurements were taken at one point in time, so changes occurring over months and years were not quantified. The outcome might have been influenced by the time of year the study was conducted. In this study, the data were collected during January and February, traditionally the coldest months of the year. Satisfaction surveys indicate that happiness is generally lower among all people during the colder winter months. What might have happened if we had conducted the survey in the summer months? Different questions on marital satisfaction might have produced different results. What might have happened if we had used the questions from another research study on marital satisfaction? What other limitations should be mentioned in the research report?

In step 4, we suggest further research that should allow us to answer the research question in more detail. You should propose and plan another piece of research that would clarify any questions raised by the limitations. For example, the research was conducted with only 20 couples. This raises the question 'Would the results be the same with a larger number of couples participating?' To research this question, the test should be repeated among a larger sample of married and common-law couples.

At this juncture, a return to the literature review is important. How do your findings differ from the existing research on this topic? Do your findings support certain aspects of the debate or refute them?

As shown in this quantitative example, research is a process by which ordinary questions are focused upon and in which data is collected in such a way that the research questions are answered on the basis of observable evidence.

Most research projects raise new questions, and in this sense the research process is a continuous one, with the end of one project becoming the beginning of another. The steps for conducting qualitative research are similar. The following section outlines the process.

A qualitative example

Phase 1: Essential first steps. The first step requires that we decide what to observe and state what it is in the form of a research objective. This is necessary to focus our attention and to screen out what is only of incidental or passing interest. In practice, we all tend to get distracted by things that have some personal interest.

Take the observation mentioned above about youth and unemployment. You might decide to take as your research objective 'How does it feel to be unemployed for young men as compared to young women?'

In step 2, you decide to do an in-depth interview study involving young men and women from one social club. This will keep a number of background characteristics similar while allowing access to both genders. This is a case study.

In step 3, you decide to ask interviewees to tell you about being unemployed. What is it like? How do other people respond when they learn of their situation? Do they try to pretend to be employed? If one topic gets them going, let them follow it—it is probably important to them.

Step 4 involves identifying themes for analysis. These might include parents' reactions, friends' reactions, dealing with employment agencies, and other themes. For the most part, you will wait until your informants have told their stories before you code the responses.

Step 5 involves selecting those whose stories you will collect. This will depend on who is available and willing to participate. It will also depend on characteristics that you may have identified as potentially important—length of unemployment, marital status, or whether they live at home or on their own.

Phase 2: Data collection. You go to the club and put up a poster saying you want to talk to people about their experiences of being unemployed. You sit in a corner and people talk with you. You may audio-record what they say, or you may make notes and write it up afterwards. Whichever way, your data will be conversations with unemployed young people, male and female.

Phase 3: Analysis and interpretation. This is where the really hard work begins in qualitative research. You pore over the interviews and begin to code them and identify themes. As you read and re-read the interviews, you will begin to appreciate and understand what it is like to be young and unemployed. You will also begin to detect differences between males and females. They may not be what you expected, but that is why we do research—to find out what we do not already know. The process is time-intensive and very detailed. Chapter 12 discusses analysis and interpretation more thoroughly.

RESEARCH AS A DISCIPLINE

Research requires discipline, clear thinking, and careful observation. The first and probably the hardest discipline required by the research process is learning to ask the right questions. The problems that motivate us to do research are often enormous. How to prevent nuclear war? How to save the economy? How to prevent sudden infant death syndrome? How to improve the quality of life for all people? The first discipline is to move from these 'global' questions to researchable questions.

Researchable questions have two basic properties. First, they are limited in scope to certain times, places, and conditions. A researchable question is usually a small fragment of a larger question. One of the hardest things for a researcher to do is to confront a large issue by tackling only one small, manageable part of it. Failing to take a focused approach to an issue, of course, would doom the work to failure because the greater issue is much larger than the time, energy, or other resources available to the researcher. It is better to answer a small question than to leave a large one unanswered. Perhaps by piecing together a number of small answers, a large answer may be discovered.

For example, the question 'What factors affect decision-making within Canadian families?' is very large. Many factors are involved, and these factors may vary depending on the type of family observed. A more manageable question would be 'Among single-parent families in Halifax, are choices of breakfast food influenced by the parent's gender?' Similarly, in order to be researched, the question 'Does parents' education affect scholastic achievement of children?' would have to be focused, narrowed, and limited.

The best and probably the only way to learn the skill of narrowing and focusing a broad issue so that it becomes a research question is to practise. Try limiting the question 'Does parents' education affect scholastic achievement of children?'

To help you get started, let us look at the question. As it stands, it looks like a simple question requiring a 'yes' or 'no' answer. To become a research question, it needs to be made more specific. It helps to ask, 'What are the main things, ideas, or activities in the question?' The question asks something about the *relationship* between 'parents' education' and 'scholastic performance'. What do we mean when we use the term 'parents' education'? In what aspects of 'parents' education' are we specifically interested?

- the stage at which they finished their education (secondary school, technical college, university)?
- their standards of academic achievement at school, technical college, or university?
- the types of schools (public/private) they attended?
- the prestige of the schools or universities they attended?

Similarly, we should ask ourselves, 'What do we mean by "scholastic performance"?'

- final grades in all subjects?
- consistency in high grades across subjects? Overall grades?
- quality of their school report cards?
- level of participation in important school activities such as student councils and sports?

The process results in some focused research questions incorporating the focused versions of our original concepts, 'parents' education' and 'scholastic performance':

- Does the type of school attended by parents affect children's final grades?
- Does the stage at which parents finish their education affect children's overall place in class?
- Do parents' levels of academic achievement affect the quality of children's school report cards?

Now try your hand at limiting the following questions:

1. What factors are important in family decision-making? (Hints: Try listing some factors—for example, economics, social life, extended family commitments. Limit the area of decision-making.)
2. Can we promote the development of a positive self-image among handicapped teenagers? (Hints: What do you know about self-image? What are key factors that lead to a healthy self-image or to a negative self-image?)

The first property of a researchable question is that it is limited in scope, narrowed in focus, and confined to a certain time, place, and set of conditions. While frustrating and difficult, the discipline required to focus the research question is one of the most important in the research process.

The second property of a researchable question is that it identifies some observable, tangible, countable evidence or data that can be gathered. There must be something that can be observed by you and others. That is, the question must be answerable through observation of some aspect of the universe we live in. Some refer to this as 'empirical research'. Empirical research can only deal with the observable, measurable aspects of the questions we want to answer. For example, questions about morals are not answerable by the kind of research we are talking about. Research cannot determine whether an action is 'right' or 'wrong'. The question 'Is it morally right to allow terminally ill patients to die?' is not answerable by empirical research. Empirical research can be either qualitative or quantitative. Empirical research only seeks to answer those questions that can be answered by reference to sensory data. Sensory data are data that can be seen, heard, touched, recorded, measured, or counted.

empirical Based on, guided by, or employing observation and experiment rather than theory. From the Greek word *empeirikos* meaning experience, skilled.

Shorter Oxford English Dictionary

While empirical research cannot answer the moral question 'Is it right or wrong to allow terminally ill patients to die?', it can answer the question 'How many students in a particular university seminar think that it is right or wrong to allow certain types of terminally ill patients to die?' One of the disciplines associated with doing research is learning to ask questions to which there are measurable, sensory, countable answers—that is, questions that can be answered in terms of observations and experiences.

There are other kinds of questions to which there are no empirical answers—for example, questions of beauty or faith. Are the Rocky Mountains more or less beautiful than the Gatineau Hills in Quebec? Is St John's, Newfoundland, more beautiful than Montreal? Is the Canadian Museum of Civilization in Ottawa more interesting than the Hockey Hall of Fame in Toronto? Does God exist? These are questions of aesthetics, taste, and spirituality, not empirical questions.

Of course, they can be turned into empirical questions. For example, we can make up an empirical question relating to one of the above aesthetic questions. And while empirical research cannot answer questions of religious faith, it can answer questions such as 'How many professors at Dalhousie University believe that God exists?' or 'What social characteristics are found among believers in God?'

The same issues can be raised about other questions of taste, fashion, etiquette, morality, religion, and political ideology. Empirical research cannot determine which table setting is 'most tasteful' or which jacket is 'most fashionable' or whether or not God exists. These are not empirical questions. Empirical research can answer such questions as 'Which table setting is judged the most tasteful by a sample of interior decorators?'

In summary, the first discipline required by the research process is to ask the right kind of questions. Researchable questions are limited in scope and very specific. It can be a real challenge to devise a clear, specific, narrow question. This skill can be learned. You can learn to take a general question and formulate a research question from it. You will get more practice in doing this in the next chapter.

Honesty and accuracy

The second major discipline required by the research process is to be honest and accurate. Honesty and accuracy should be characteristics of any intellectual enterprise and require a degree of self-control. We often have in mind an outcome we wish to arrive at. For example, we might believe that a majority of Dalhousie

University students believe that God exists. But discipline in doing research compels us to be as objective as possible; we must make sure that there is no bias in the way we ask questions, and ensure that we correctly record the data and are honest in reporting the results. What is wrong with the following examples?

- 'Here are two descriptions of God. You really don't think that the Christian God is more inviting, do you?' Write an unambiguous version of this question.
- 'Only 70 per cent of those asked thought that the Buddhist interpretation of God was correct.' Write an unbiased statement of this research finding.

If we are disciplined and accurate in our reporting of research findings, then we increase the reliability of the research process. Some research has fallen into disrepute because researchers have not been disciplined, accurate, and honest. Have you ever read about controversy over scientific work in which bias has been suggested? An example would be Hwang Woo-Suk's research on cloning human embryos (2005). Some people have forced their data to fit their theory by falsifying results, by not recording data accurately, or both. Research is useful only to the extent that the researchers have been disciplined, accurate, and honest.

Record-keeping

The third discipline is recording what was done in such a way that someone else can see exactly what was done and why. There are two reasons for this kind of discipline. First, it safeguards the reliability of the research process. If what was done is reported accurately and in adequate detail, then another person can repeat the research. If they get the same results, then what was originally found becomes even more certain. If they do not get the same results, then the original findings are less certain.

The second reason for this discipline is to provide a record for yourself. It is amazing how quickly we forget what we did and why. At the end of a research project, you need to be able to refer to your research notes and refresh your memory. This is a great help when you are writing about the limitations of the study.

Assessing limitations

The fourth and final discipline of the research process involves assessing the limitations of the research. If you study only one family, you cannot apply your findings to all families. If you study a group of 10-year-old boys, your findings apply to that group and that group only. It is a great temptation to over-generalize, to make claims that apply beyond the data collected.

Similarly, if you did your research on an empirical question derived from a non-empirical question, your conclusions apply only to the empirical question. For example, if your initial question was 'Does God exist?' but your research question was 'How many Dalhousie University students believe the Buddhist definition of God', the data you collect will answer the empirical question, not the question of interest. Keeping your conclusions at the level of the question asked is part of the discipline of accepting the limitations of the research process.

In summary, doing research requires discipline. First, the right kind of questions must be asked. Questions must be narrowly defined, because only empirical questions can be answered by empirical research. Second, honesty and accuracy in asking questions and reporting findings are required. Third, careful record-keeping and accurate reporting are needed. Finally, you must assess the limitations of the research process and your particular research question.

THEORY AND DATA

A research question can come from anywhere. We may just be curious: I wonder how that works? I wonder why some people do this or that? Does it make any difference? Curiosity can begin the research process.

On the other hand, a problem may motivate us to ask a researchable question. How is the problem of teenage malnutrition best handled? How can I make my father understand me? How can I improve my health? How can the incidence of drunk driving be reduced? Problems such as these, and many others, motivate people to ask researchable questions.

Arguments are a frequent starting point. The example of Georgina and Frank is typical. I might have one idea about how things are, and you might have another. It may be possible to design a piece of research to see whose idea is supported by evidence. Research is often started by controversy.

Magellan sailed around the world. Was this evidence uniformly accepted as proof that the Earth was not flat and that sailors who ventured too far would not fall off the edge? No. Even after Magellan's circumnavigation of the Earth, many people continued to believe that it was flat. Perhaps satellite photographs of the Earth taken from great distance provide the most compelling evidence available to date that the Earth is not flat.

As with Magellan and the flat-Earth theory, evidence does not always stop the controversy that motivated research. Some people do not accept the evidence. Some argue that the research was not properly conducted. Some argue that the research questions were not properly defined. In such cases, the research process usually continues, with more evidence being collected to test more carefully defined questions. Part of the fun of doing research is to see how each question leads to more questions. The research process is continuous.

The research process is a disciplined process for answering questions. Another way of putting this is to say that the research process is a disciplined process for relating theory and data. At this point, we will try to clarify and simplify the terms 'theory' and 'data'.

Theory

Put most simply, a theory is a guess about the way things are. Georgina had a theory about marital satisfaction among elderly Canadian couples. A theory is an idea about how something works, or what it is like to be something, or what will happen if . . . . It may be an idea about what difference will be made by doing or not doing something. Theories are ideas about how things relate to each other.

There are many ways of expressing theories. Some are very formal, others are informal. Some theories are very elaborate and complex, yet simplicity and clarity are often desirable features of theories. Put simply, theories are ideas about the way other ideas are related. Theories are abstract notions about the way concepts relate to each other. This will become clearer as you proceed through this book. Here are some examples of crude theories:

- a hunch about marital satisfaction among elderly couples in long-term relationships;
- a guess that the more reassurance you give to small children that they are valued, cared for, and wanted, the more likely they are to develop healthy images of themselves;
- the idea that more education produces more reliable, more productive, more contented people.

A theory asserts a relationship between concepts. It states that some 'things' are related in a particular way. It is a statement of how things are thought to be. A theory is an idea, a mental picture of how the world might be.

The research process is a disciplined process for answering questions. It is a way of testing theories, a way of determining whether there is any evidence to support a mental picture of the way things are. The evidence collected in the research process is called data.

Data

datum (singular), *data* (plural) Latin, neutral, past participle of *dare*, to give. A thing given or granted; something known or assumed as fact, and made the basis for reasoning or calculation.

Shorter Oxford English Dictionary

Data are facts produced by research. Data, like facts, by themselves are meaningless. They acquire meaning as they are related to theories. For example, the fact that a couple living in Winnipeg who have been married for 28 years scores higher on the marital satisfaction scale than a couple living in Hamilton who have been married for 37 years is meaningless. The fact takes on meaning when it is related to the two theories about how marital satisfaction develops among elderly couples. The fact becomes part of the data by which these theories can be tested.

Data are empirical facts. They are scores on a number of questions (degree of marital satisfaction). They are counts (100 students thought the Buddhist definition of God was more viable than the Christian definition). They are tapes of conversations or transcripts of interviews. They are written observations. Data are records of the actual state of some measurable aspect of the universe at a particular point in time. Data are not abstract; they are concrete, they are records of events, they are measurements of the tangible, countable features of the world. While theories are abstract mental images of the way things may be, data are measures of specific things as they were at a particular time.

Two kinds of data are used in social science: quantitative and qualitative. Quantitative research tends to answer questions such as: How much? How many? How often? Quantitative data are usually expressed in numbers, percentages, or rates. In contrast, qualitative research tends to answer questions such as: What is it like to be a member of that group? What is going on in this situation? What is it like to experience this or that phenomenon? Hence, qualitative data tend to be expressed in the language of images, feelings, and impressions; they describe the qualities of the events under study. The research process is somewhat different for each type of research. Quantitative styles of research are dealt with first because they require the most preparation during Phase 1, while the efforts in qualitative research tend to be concentrated in the data collection and interpretation phases.

The challenge of the research process is to relate theory and research in such a way that questions are answered. Both theory and data are required. When we are faced with a question, we formulate a theory about its answer and test it by collecting data—that is, evidence—to see if our theoretical answer works. Data cannot be collected without some theory about the answer to the question. Theories alone are unsatisfactory because they are unproven, untested. To answer our questions, we need both theory and data.

The result of the research process is neither theory nor data but knowledge. Research provides answers to researchable questions with evidence that is collected and evaluated in a disciplined manner. This is how we know. We ask questions, propose answers to them, and test those answers. We ask what it is like and go and find out. Doing research in a disciplined way is 'how we know we know'.

QUESTIONS FOR REVIEW

1. Why do we undertake research?
2. It is claimed that research is a process. What is a process?
3. What is the normal sequence of the research process? In what way is it normal?
4. What are the essential first steps of the research process? Why are the first steps so important?
5. What is done in Phase 2 of the research process?
6. List the four major disciplines involved in the research process.
7. What are the two major properties of a researchable question?
8. What are theory and data? What role does each play in the research process?
9. What are the two major kinds of research? What is the main difference between them?
10. Find a newspaper article or an article in a recent magazine that reports a controversy over research findings. What was the nature of the criticism of the research?

Suggestions for further reading

Babbie, E.R. 2003. *The Practice of Social Research*. 10th edn. London: Wadsworth.

Chalmers, A.F. 1999. *What Is This Thing Called Science?* 3rd edn. St Lucia: University of Queensland Press.

de Vaus, D.A. 2002. *Surveys in Social Research*. 5th edn, chapter 2. St Leonards, NSW: Allen and Unwin.

Denzin, Norman K., and Yvonna S. Lincoln, eds. 2000. *Handbook of Qualitative Research*. 2nd edn, Introduction. London: Sage.

Giddens, Anthony. 2001. *Sociology*. 4th edn, chapter 20. Cambridge: Polity Press.

Kumar, Ranjit. 1999. *Research Methodology: A Step by Step Guide for Beginners*, chapters 1–2. London: Sage.

Minichiello, Victor, Rosalie Aroni, Eric Timewell, and Loris Alexander. 1995. *In-Depth Interviewing: Principles, Techniques, Analysis*. 2nd edn, chapter 1. Melbourne: Longman Cheshire.

Wallace, W. 1971. *The Logic of Science in Sociology*. Chicago: Aldine.

Waters, Malcolm, and Rodney Crook. 1993. *Sociology One*, chapters 1–3. Melbourne: Longman Cheshire.

PHASE 1
Essential First Steps

Selecting a Problem

The first step in Phase 1 of the research process is selecting and focusing a research problem. This step involves decision-making, sorting, narrowing, and clarifying. It requires clear thinking and at times the discarding of favourite topics for more focused ideas. This chapter describes the skills involved in developing an initial question into a practical research problem.

STARTING POINTS

The research process begins when our curiosity is aroused. When we want to know something, we begin formally or informally to engage in research. An observation, something we read, a claim someone made, a hunch about something—each may be a stimulus to begin the research process. This chapter presents several examples to develop your skills for moving from starting points to focused researchable questions.

Here are some examples of starting points for research projects.

An observation
Some students get better marks than others.

An observation like this may prompt someone to ask the following questions: Why? Which students? Is it the way papers are marked? An observation may trigger the inquiring mind to ask questions, and the research process has begun.

An important family decision

The Wright family has to decide whether to send their daughter to a public school or a private school.

Someone who knows of this situation might be prompted to ask such questions as: What difference would it make? Is there a difference in terms of her chances of being accepted into university? What kinds of factors do the Wrights consider important as they arrive at their decision? A situation like an important family decision may stimulate the asking of questions, and the research process is underway.

A news report

News reports often raise questions for research. Read your daily newspaper, or tune into radio and television news, and pay attention to the headlines that may lead to research projects: 'Divorce rate steady for a decade', 'Crime rate on increase', 'Single moms in poverty trap', '1 in 10 unemployed seriously depressed', 'Teenage suicide rate increases', 'Plight of homeless worsens', 'More females studying law'. Each of these headlines could lead to a research project to expand knowledge about some aspect of social life or to test some idea about what is happening in the world.

News reports usually contain a lot of 'facts' about patterns in society but few clear and explicit interpretations of those 'facts'. You may be prompted to ask questions: How does the pattern presented in this report compare with the situation 5, 10, or 15 years ago? Why is this pattern developing? What factors might be affecting changes in things such as the career choices women make, the teenage suicide rate, age at first marriage, or the effects of unemployment? Questions like these, prompted by your reading of news reports, can be the start of research projects.

A policy issue

The provincial government is concerned about the provision of proper care in homes for elderly people.

Think about this issue. What questions does it raise? What is the current state of affairs in homes for elderly people? What do elderly people need? Again, the inquiring mind is prompted to ask questions that might lead to research.

It makes little difference where you begin the research process: the first step is to narrow the focus and clarify the issues involved in the problem. None of the above starting points provides a sufficiently focused research question. The first step in the research process is to move from an ordinary everyday question to a research-able question by focusing on one aspect of the issue arousing your interest.

THE LITERATURE REVIEW

An important step in the research process is embedding your research question and your subsequent findings within the existing literature. The literature review has several purposes. At the conceptualization phase, it can assist in identifying and preparing a good research question, be helpful in identifying appropriate theoretical and research design approaches, and assist in defining central variables. At the data analysis stage, it is important for embedding your findings within the larger research debates and in advancing knowledge on a particular topic. It can also assist policy-makers in determining new directions for existing programs. The literature review is a central component of the research process, and it is worthwhile to examine some of its uses here.

At the beginning of the research, when you may not yet have a clearly defined research question, the literature review will assist you in identifying the studies that have been conducted. It is best to become familiar with these studies to get a sense of the research results and to identify the prevailing debates in the literature. This process can take a while, especially for topics that have been subject to a large number of studies. However, it is a crucial first step. It is not worth your while to replicate a study that has already been conducted. Funders will not want to support research questions that have already been answered. For this reason, becoming familiar with the existing literature will save you time and money. Throughout the literature review process, look for gaps in the literature. What questions have not been asked? This information is important because it increases the chance that your research will receive funding and it increases the value of your research findings, since you will be contributing new knowledge to our understanding of existing social problems.

Reviewing the literature can also assist in the selection of theoretical approaches. A good deal of social science literature outlines the major theoretical approaches. What is your theoretical approach? How can it help you to answer your research question? What does your theoretical approach have to say about the problem you are investigating? This review of theoretical approaches will help you to identify important factors to consider in your study. Similarly, it may give you clues about an appropriate research design. How have others conducted research on similar questions? What research designs best capture the answers you need to answer your research question? Perhaps there are new research designs that you can use to answer your research question. From a theoretical and research design standpoint, the literature review is a useful tool.

The literature review can be central to identifying factors that you may not have considered including in your research project. Reconsider the planned research on the causes of youth unemployment. A small but growing part of the literature on this topic reveals that family contexts, such as the presence of both father and mother plus the birth order of siblings, are a major determinant of post-secondary school attendance. Youth who live in two-parent-headed households and who are the youngest siblings have the greatest chance of attending and completing university. If you do not review the existing literature on youth unemployment, you may forget to include questions about family context and birth order, making your research open to criticism and much less valuable once it is completed.

Once your data have been collected and analyzed, return to your literature review. How do your findings contribute to existing research? Say you discovered in your study of youth post-secondary education completion that birth order of siblings matters only if they live in families headed by a single father. In families headed by a single mother or those headed by two parents, birth order does not determine university completion. Knowing about this debate makes it easier for you to discuss your research findings and make a valuable contribution to the literature on a particular topic. Since you have already done all the 'hard work' prior to collecting data, the literature review at this stage is more easily accomplished. All you need to do is update yourself on the research literature that may have been published between the time you conducted your initial review in Phase 1 and the analysis of your data in Phase 3.

In short, while it may seem as though you are not accomplishing much by reviewing the literature at the beginning of the research project, a good knowledge of the existing literature on a topic is essential to research planning and dissemination.

NARROWING AND CLARIFYING THE PROBLEM

Our goal in this step in the research process is to produce a clear statement of the problem to be studied. A statement of a problem must explicitly identify the issues on which the researcher chooses to focus. How do we do this? There are no rules or recipes. The skill is best learned by practice.

Once we examine most starting points, we quickly realize that they suggest research problems that are too unclear and unfocused for practical research. To clarify and focus a problem, we have to 'unpack' it—that is, list the issues that make up the problem. We can then choose the issues on which to focus our attention.

The following general questions can be used to unpack a problem:

- What are the major concepts?
- What is happening here?
- What are the issues?
- Is one thing affecting, causing, or producing a change in something else?
- Why is this so?

Such questions may isolate issues of interest. As an example, take the observation 'Some students get better marks than others.' Begin with the question 'What might lead to this observation?' Here are four possible explanations:

1. Some students are smarter than others.
2. Some students study more than others.
3. Some students eat better meals than others.
4. Some students enjoy study more than other students do.

Relying on your own experience, write down four other possible reasons for some students getting better marks than others.

Did you think of factors such as exercise, parents' education, social life, family income? If so, you have begun to unpack the issue. You have begun to isolate factors and possible explanations.

You now have eight possible factors. You can begin narrowing the research question by selecting just one. However important other factors may be, it is usually necessary to focus on very few.

Our general observation of the differences in student marks can now be focused to create a variety of research problems. These problems can be described in direct questions about the issues they address:

- Are students' marks affected by the amount of time spent studying?
- Are students' marks affected by the nutrition of the meals they eat?
- Are students' marks affected by their enjoyment of school?
- Are students' marks affected by the status of their parents' occupations?

Another way to narrow and clarify a problem is to consult research relevant to issues raised by the starting point—in other words, review the literature. What have others found? Look at previous research for factors and approaches to the problem that you have not considered.

In unpacking the observation 'Some students get better marks than others', you might consult your professor. A reference librarian might be able to suggest a few articles or books for you to read. This documentation may include reports of previous research in the area. More ideas will come to you. Reading about the topic of your research will help to clarify your thinking.

Since this step in the research process is so important, let us take another example. Remember, the goal is a clear question for research. To do this, you unpack your starting point. List everything that comes to mind about the subject. Do some reading. Consult some people who know—the more ideas, the better. Then select one factor, one idea, and one small problem for your research.

Take the example of an important family decision. The Wright family has to decide whether to send their daughter to a public school or a private school. Remember that the aim is to isolate a question for research, not necessarily to find an answer to the problem facing the Wright family. What issues are suggested? There are no right or wrong answers here. You are working towards a research question.

Here is a list of some of the issues raised by this particular starting point:

1. Is one system of education demonstrably better than another:
   - in terms of sport?
   - in terms of test results?
   - in terms of social life?

2. How do families make decisions like this?
   - What factors do they consider?
   - Do the children participate?
3. Do socio-cultural factors shape these family decisions?
   - Is sex or gender an issue?
   - Do ethnic groups differ?
   - Is social class a factor?

What issues, further questions, and factors occurred to you? Write them down. What resources do you have that might help you with this question? Do you know someone who might have ideas on the subject? You could ask your librarian for material on family decision-making, or you could ask for information on public versus private education. Are there other things you can use to help identify the issue here? List some other resources.

At this point, the key tasks are to identify issues, select one to pursue in depth, and leave the rest behind.

We have seen that there are many issues, ideas, and factors involved in the decision to send a daughter to a public school or a private school. You will probably be able to direct your research to only one of them. The rest must be left for other studies. The mark of a clear thinker and a good researcher is the ability to identify and note the many issues and to choose to study one. People reading your report will recognize that you are aware of the complexity of the issues involved but are sufficiently disciplined to address yourself to only one.

STATING THE PROBLEM

The next task is to restate the issue as a researchable question. This is a skill in itself. Two basic forms will be discussed: *hypothesis* and *research objective*. Most other forms can be seen as variations of either a hypothesis or a research objective.

The hypothesis

A hypothesis is a statement that asserts a relationship between concepts. A concept is an idea that stands for something, or that represents a class of things or a general categorization of an impression of something. If we watch a chess game and decide that chess is an 'intellectual activity', we are describing, both to ourselves and to others, our impressions of chess in terms of the concept 'intellectual activity'. Concepts are categories or descriptions of our world and experience. We use concepts to make sense of the world for ourselves and others.

The key feature of a hypothesis is that it asserts that two concepts are related in a specific way. Usually a hypothesis takes the form 'Concept X causes concept Y' or 'Concept X is related to concept Y'. Return to the example of students' grades that we have been using. We began with the observation 'Some students get better marks than others'. We have unpacked this observation by listing

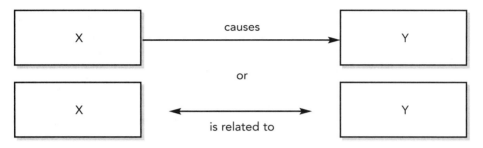

The usual form of a hypothesis

issues that come to mind. We thought of the possible impact of factors such as amount of study, nutrition, and students' enjoyment of particular subjects. We talked to our professor and read material given to us by the librarian. When all that was done, suppose that we decided to do some research into the impact of the amount of study on marks. We have two concepts: 'study' and 'marks'. We also have an idea about how these two concepts are related. We suspect that the more somebody studies, the better their marks will be.

Having done our preparation, we are in a position to write a hypothesis to guide our research. For example:

The more a student studies, the better the student's academic performance will be.

Note that a more general concept, 'academic performance', has been selected in place of 'marks'. Our observation was of a difference in marks, but the general issue or problem is variation in 'academic performance'. It sometimes helps to become more general before focusing on concepts. In our example, this will enable you to consider a wider variety of measures of academic performance.

This hypothesis states that two concepts—namely, amount of study and academic performance—are related in such a way that more of one (study) will produce or lead to more of the other (academic performance). This hypothesis could be represented or 'diagrammed' as follows:

The two concepts are in boxes. The boxes are linked by an arrow going from one concept to the other. The arrow indicates that one concept (amount of study) does something to the other concept (academic performance). The plus sign indicates that the relationship is seen as a positive one—that is, that more of the one will lead to more of the other.

Diagramming hypotheses is a very useful device to promote clear thinking. If you cannot diagram your hypothesis, it may be because it is not yet clear to you.

Take a different example. We have diagrammed a positive relationship between two concepts. How about a negative relationship—that is, when more of one concept leads to less of the other and vice versa. Look over your list of factors that might affect academic performance. Would you say that increases in any of them lead to lower academic performance? How about the number of parties attended? The hypothesis would be stated:

> The more parties a student attends, the lower the student's academic performance will be.

It would be diagrammed as follows:

A hypothesis states that there is a relationship between two concepts and specifies the direction of that relationship. The above hypothesis states that there is a negative relationship between parties attended and academic performance. The greater the number of parties attended, the lower the academic performance.

Continue with the 'factors affecting marks' example. Suppose that in doing your literature review on the factors affecting marks, you came across an article that claimed that the kind of breakfast students ate had an effect on their academic performance. Write a hypothesis derived from this article.

Now diagram this hypothesis in the form below:

* Is the relationship proposed by the hypothesis postive or negative? If it is positive, place a plus sign in the blank. If it is negative, place a minus sign in the blank.

The best way to develop skill in deriving hypotheses is to practise. Do the following exercises, and then derive hypotheses relevant to other topics and issues.

1. Here is a hypothesis: 'As fewer people have involvement with churches, there will be an increase in the number of couples choosing to live in common-law marriages'. What are the concepts?
   • church involvement
   • common-law marriages

What relationship between these concepts does this hypothesis assert? Diagram the hypothesis here:

* Is the relationship proposed by the hypothesis postive or negative? If it is positive, place a plus sign in the blank. If it is negative, place a minus sign in the blank.

2. Suppose you decide to compare the happiness of couples in common-law relationships and formal marriages. You might propose the following hypothesis:

   Couples who are formally married enjoy more marital satisfaction than couples in common-law relationships.

In this example, the relationship between the concepts cannot be described as positive or negative because the independent concept, 'relationship', is a special type, the categorical concept. A *categorical concept* is one that is rigidly divided into two or more exclusive categories. Examples of categorical concepts include:

- marital status (formal marriage vs common-law marriage)
- gender or sex (male vs female)
- social class (upper class vs middle class vs lower class)
- occupational status (white collar vs blue collar)
- school education (public school vs private school)
- wealth (poor vs rich)
- spiritual belief (atheist vs believer)

Changes in categorical concepts are not described as 'more' or 'less' of the variable but as 'one category' or 'another category'. You don't usually classify people as 'more female' or 'less female' but as either 'male' or 'female'.

In the above example, we cannot say that more or less of the independent concept 'relationship' leads to more or less 'marital satisfaction'. The independent concept does not vary in terms of 'more' or 'less'. It takes the form of either of its categories, 'formally married' or 'common-law'.

Diagram this hypothesis here:

3. If you read some of the literature on marital satisfaction, you would discover that there are many factors in reported marital satisfaction. Some of these factors are:
   - values shared
   - emotional health of partners
   - common backgrounds
   - number of friends
   - economic security
   - length of the relationship
   - security in the relationship

One hypothesis that could be derived from these factors is this:

   Couples in formal marriages feel more secure in their relationships than common-law couples.

Diagram this hypothesis:

4. Derive another hypothesis from the above list of factors and write it out concisely.

   As you can tell from doing these exercises, developing a hypothesis requires that you identify one concept that causes, affects, or has an influence on another concept. The concept that does the 'causing' is called the *independent concept*. An independent concept 'causes', produces a change in, or acts upon something else. The concept that is acted upon, produced, or 'caused' by the independent concept is called the *dependent concept*.

   Writing a hypothesis requires that you identify an independent concept and a dependent concept. In the examples where we examined students' grades, amount of study, parties attended, and nutrition were independent concepts. These concepts were seen as 'causes' of changes in academic performance.

   List the independent concepts in the exercises you have just done. For example:

Exercise 1: church involvement
Exercise 2: marital status
Exercise 3:
Exercise 4:

In terms of the diagram, the independent concept is the one from which the arrow is drawn.

The dependent concept is the thing that is caused, acted upon, or affected—the thing in which a change is produced by the independent concept. List the dependent concepts in the exercises you have just done. For example:

Exercise 1: common-law marriages
Exercise 2: marital satisfaction
Exercise 3:
Exercise 4:

In the pattern of diagramming introduced above, the dependent concept is the one to which the arrow is drawn:

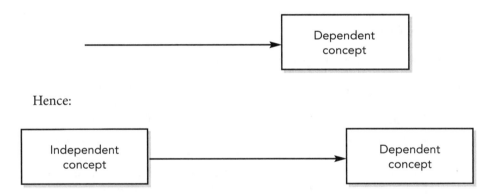

Hence:

In its usual form, a hypothesis states that something about the independent concept produces a change in the dependent concept.

Some of the confusion about independent and dependent concepts arises from the fact that it is possible for the same concept to take the *independent* role in one hypothesis and the *dependent* role in another. Just because a concept is independent in one case does not mean that it should always be treated as independent. For example, here are some concepts:

- academic performance
- nutritional adequacy of breakfast
- study
- party-going
- intention to go to university

These concepts can be linked in a variety of ways. Many hypotheses can be derived from this list. We can ask the following questions:

Which of the above concepts is the independent concept? Which is the dependent? We have also seen that:

Which of the above concepts is the independent concept? Which is the dependent? But it also makes sense to derive the following hypothesis using two of the concepts in the above list:

The greater the academic performance of a high school student, the more likely it is that the student will intend to go to university.

This hypothesis would be diagrammed as follows:

In this case, what had been a dependent concept (academic performance) in one hypothesis becomes an independent concept, because going to university is dependent on academic performance, whereas, earlier, academic performance was dependent on study. Whether a concept is independent or dependent depends on your theory. Focusing and diagramming hypotheses helps to clarify theories.

The research objective

Not all research is best guided by a hypothesis. Some research, such as qualitative research (see Chapters 4, 12), is done to find out what is 'going on' in a situation. Sometimes it is not possible or desirable to specify the relationship between concepts before making observations. There are times when developing a *research objective* is a more desirable way to focus a research project. For example, if the general area of your study relates to child development or skill acquisition, you might use the following research objective to guide your research:

Objective: To observe a particular child, four years of age, for a specified period of time, in order to observe patterns of skill acquisition through play.

When the goal of the research is descriptive rather than explanatory, a statement of an objective can serve to guide the research. Consider this example:

Objective: To describe what factors the Wright family took into account in deciding whether to send their daughter to a public school or a private school.

The intent of this research is to describe what happened, not to explain what happened. At the end of the study, the researcher will be able to specify the factors that emerged in this family discussion. Who raised which issues? Who responded and in what ways? These observations can lead the researcher to formulate a hypothesis that attempts to explain the family's actions, to be tested later.

A starting point dealing with the policy issue of care for the elderly might prompt research that is primarily descriptive. When you want to describe what is 'going on', an objective will help to focus your efforts. Here are some examples of research objectives related to care for the elderly.

Objective: To determine the number and percentage of elderly people in a particular community who require special accommodation.

The goal of this study is to ascertain a community need. There are no influencing factors under study. There is no attempt to test the impact of anything or to ascertain whether special accommodation is needed.

Objective: To discover the existing policy on admission to homes for elderly people.
Objective: To discover the government's policy on funding for homes for elderly people.

As long as your aim is to describe what is, rather than to test explanations for what is, a research objective is the preferred guide to your research. Chapters 5 and 6 show how to convert a research objective into a statement that can guide your research effectively, whether you adopt a qualitative or quantitative approach. Chapter 12 describes the way that qualitative research is done.

SUMMARY

The research process may be started from many points. Curiosity, claims of others, reading, problems—all these can begin the process. Once begun, the first step is to clarify the issues and to narrow your focus.

In order for your research to succeed, a clear statement of the problem or issue must guide it. The two most common forms of such statements are the hypothesis and the research objective. A hypothesis is developed to guide research intended to test an explanation. A research objective states the goal of a study intended to describe. Without a clear statement of the problem, the research will be confused and ambiguous. It is impossible to satisfactorily proceed to the next stage of the research process without such a statement.

QUESTIONS FOR REVIEW

1. List six common starting points for the research process.
2. What are the reasons for reviewing the literature on a particular subject?
3. Why is it essential to identify the issues or factors involved in a subject, topic, or problem being considered for a research project?
4. Why is it necessary to select one issue from among the issues identified?
5. What is a hypothesis? Give an example. Diagram a hypothesis.
6. What is a negative relationship? Give an example. How is it diagrammed?
7. What is a positive relationship? Give an example. How is it diagrammed?
8. What is an independent concept? What is a dependent concept? Which of the following are independent concepts? Which are dependent concepts?

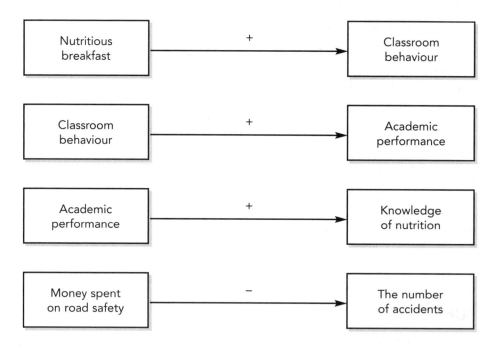

9. Fully write out each of the above diagrammed hypotheses.

10. Diagram the following:
- The greater the proportion of sweets in the diet, the greater the incidence of dental cavities in children.
- The introduction of a module on management theory will improve the quality of decision-making among students.
- The greater the age gap between parents and children, the greater the degree of difficulty in communication they experience.

11. What is a research objective? How is it different from a hypothesis? For what kinds of research is it appropriate?

Suggestions for further reading

Babbie, E.R. 2003. *The Practice of Social Research*. 10th edn, chapter 3. London: Wadsworth.

Bessant, Judith, and Rob Watts. 2002. *Sociology Australia*, chapter 3. St Leonards, NSW: Allen and Unwin.

de Vaus, D.A. 2002. *Surveys in Social Research*. 5th edn, chapter 3. St Leonards, NSW: Allen and Unwin.

Giddens, Anthony. 2001. *Sociology*. 4th edn, chapter 20. Cambridge: Polity Press.

Judd, C.M., E.R. Smith, and L.H. Kidder. 1991. *Research Methods in Social Relations*, chapters 1–2. Fort Worth, TX: Holt, Rinehart and Winston.

Kumar, Ranjit. 1999. *Research Methodology: A Step by Step Guide for Beginners*, chapters 3–4. London: Sage.

Wallace, W. 1971. *The Logic of Science in Sociology*, chapter 3. Chicago: Aldine.

Waters, Malcolm, and Rodney Crook. 1993. *Sociology One*, chapters 1–3. Melbourne: Longman Cheshire.

4

Qualitative or Quantitative Research? Where Do I Begin?

A significant debate exists in the social science literature with regard to the relative value of qualitative and quantitative data collection strategies. In our opinion, much of this debate is false. A guiding principle of all good research is to let the research question determine the data collection strategy rather than the other way around. Good researchers will use the method that best answers the research questions posed. It is our belief that researchers who declare themselves as strictly qualitative or quantitative methodologists do a disservice to their research agendas. It is important for all researchers, no matter what they are studying, to approach their research questions critically, with the aim of obtaining the best possible answers. This means being flexible in your approach. Even if your career does not involve much research, it is important to be able to distinguish between qualitative and quantitative research and to become knowledgeable about the benefits and problems associated with each method.

This chapter examines the differences between qualitative and quantitative research to give you an overview of each method. This may help you to review existing studies more critically and to determine an appropriate approach to your own research projects.

WHAT IS QUALITATIVE RESEARCH?

Qualitative research sets out to provide an impression: to tell what kinds of 'something' there are; to tell what it is like to be, do, or think something. Qualitative researchers exercise great discipline to find out 'what is going on here' from the perspective of those who are in the situation being researched. By comparison, quantitative research sets out to find numerical results that can be reported in tables and graphs. It answers questions about situations in terms of 'how many?' or 'what proportion?' Drawing an absolute line between qualitative and quantitative research is never satisfactory, because they have similarities, and researchers often combine the approaches.

For example, one of the co-authors of this book is conducting a study of the job-search experiences of racialized youth in Winnipeg, in conjunction with a similar study conducted by colleagues in Vancouver. First, the researchers wanted to know how many first and second-generation youth and racialized youth live in Winnipeg compared to Vancouver. They also wanted to know about their educational attainment and employment rates. Most of this information could be gained from the census and other government statistics. However, the researchers also wanted to find out 'what it is like' to be a racialized first- or second-generation young adult looking for work in Winnipeg or Vancouver. This could not be ascertained by reference to census data. To find out 'what it is like' to be a racialized youth in Canada, it was necessary to listen to these young people describe their lives.

The fundamental obstacle was that the co-author could not assume that she perceived or appreciated the most outstanding issues in the lives of people of a different age and with migration backgrounds different from her own. If she had already understood the dimensions of living as a member of a racialized minority in Canada, she might have been able to construct a questionnaire along the lines of those described in Chapter 5. But she had only limited experience, and many of the issues that were important to her were not important to racialized youth living in Canada. If she had embarked on the research with preconceived ideas, she would not have found out what it is like to be young and racialized in Canada, because she would have been appreciating their lives in the context of her own experience.

While it helps to declare preconceptions at the start of a project, it also helps to share them with others in order to uncover potential biases that the researcher may not be aware of. In designing this study, the co-author declared her preconceptions to members of a community liaison group, who then directed her attention to their concerns and their view of things.

She chose to use two qualitative techniques, in-depth interviewing and focus groups, so that the subjects of the research would feel free to tell her what was important to them, free to tell their stories and to describe their perceptions and their feelings. She did not attempt to take a random sample, nor would it have been relevant. Rather, people were selected as 'windows' into, or 'listening posts' on, some aspect of racialized youth in Canada. Male and female youths from a variety of national backgrounds, who had been in Canada a short time, a moderate length of time, a long time, or were born in Canada, were interviewed. The interviews, each of which took about one hour, were conducted by young university students who were about the age of the target group. These interviews were conducted according to an interview schedule that essentially helped to produce an 'employment biography' for each participant.

This research used both qualitative and quantitative research techniques because it was designed to answer both 'what is it like?' and 'how many?' questions. Once the data were collected, further questions of 'qualitative versus quantitative research' arose. The data could be analyzed in a 'qualitative way' or a 'quantitative way'. It is important to remember this when discussing the differences between qualitative and quantitative research. These issues arise at each phase of the research process, and decisions are made at *each phase* about which to use. Sometimes quantitative options will be used at one phase and qualitative at another. It is possible to collect qualitative data and to subject them to quantitative analysis, just as it is possible to collect quantitative data in a way that makes it possible for them to be analyzed qualitatively.

WHEN TO USE QUALITATIVE RESEARCH

As with all decisions that arise during the research process, deciding whether to use qualitative or quantitative approaches depends on what the researchers want to know—it depends on the questions they are asking. If the researchers want to know how many first- and second-generation youth live in certain neighbourhoods of Winnipeg, it will be necessary to do quantitative research. Counting households, citizens, adults, women, men, and children and recording ages may be some of the tasks involved in the census required to answer 'how many?' This is why the census is conducted every five years in Canada (and many other countries). If there were no census, researchers would have to rely on sample surveys to estimate features of the population. Qualitative approaches will not answer questions such as 'how many?', 'how often?', or 'what proportion?' because qualitative research is not concerned with such questions.

Qualitative approaches, such as visiting a neighbourhood, may give an impression, provoke a feeling about the place, or enable the researcher to describe the look of the neighbourhood. For instance, while driving through certain commercial districts in the Vancouver suburb of Richmond, a researcher will see many shops with Vietnamese and Chinese signs offering foods from Southeast Asia, and may form the impression that this is a Vietnamese and Chinese neighbourhood. The shopping strip gives that impression, but it does not reveal how many Vietnamese and Chinese live in that area or what proportion of the businesses are owned or run by Vietnamese and Chinese. But asking, 'What impression does a particular shopping area give?' is a perfectly valid research question. It may also be a very important question for market or ethnic-relations research. And that question cannot be answered by information on how many people of a particular ethnic background live in the area.

In addition to providing impressions and feelings about a particular situation, qualitative research often seeks to answer the question 'what is going on here?' Often, the aim of qualitative research is to describe in detail what is happening in a group, in a conversation, or in a community—who spoke to whom, with what message, with what feelings, with what effect.

Sometimes researchers apply qualitative methods as a preliminary to quantitative research. For example, you may want to know how many or what proportion of users of a particular service are satisfied with it. You could ask a simple 'yes/no' or 'much/some/little' question of each user over a few days. This would give a lot of quantitative information about levels of customer satisfaction, but it is probably not all you really want to know. You would soon become curious about the aspects of the service the users do and do not like, what users expect, and why they use the service. Unless you already know why people use the service and what their problems are, you will find that you need some qualitative research to answer your questions.

In this case, you may wish to interview a range of users to learn what they expect from the service and their range of perceptions of its performance. Having listened to users of the service, you will know what using the service feels like because respondents will have told you 'what is going on here'. You will be able to appreciate the range of reactions to the service, and you will have gained impressions about the users. You may even be able to identify types of responses to the service, themes in the comments, or other patterns in the users' responses. But you will not know how many or what proportion of users react in each way or how many come away with certain types of feelings. In order to answer such questions, you will need to survey representative samples of the clients with a quantitative measure. Having already identified certain types of users and certain perceptions or themes in the users' responses in the qualitative research, the quantitative survey will enable you to discover the frequency with which these types or themes occur.

What separates qualitative from quantitative research is its approach to the study of human nature. For qualitative methodologists, there is no single unified truth. The search for truth is meaningless, since truth is shaped by individuals. What I believe is true differs from what you believe is true. This is part of being human. For this reason, qualitative research is very focused on the individual rather than on generalized social trends. In order to understand a phenomenon, it is best to take a lived-experience approach. For example, how does a person with a terminal illness such as cancer make sense of their mortality? This would be a difficult question to research with a quantitative approach. Qualitative researchers value the individual voices of the participants in their study. In a study of cancer patients in palliative care, for instance, researchers would be interested to hear the stories of both cancer survivors and cancer sufferers in order to better understand their life outlooks. Asking cancer survivors and sufferers a battery of impersonalized questions intended to generalize the 'cancer experience' would be demeaning and would not shed light on the experience of living with terminal cancer.

The idea that individuals have voice and that their stories should be central to understanding a social issue is called phenomenologism. According to Palys (2003, 9), 'any effort to understand human behaviour must take into account that humans are cognitive beings who actively perceive and make sense of the world around them, have the capacity to abstract from their experience, ascribe meaning to their behaviour and the world around them, and are affected by those meanings'. Approaches that try to assign numbers to people's opinions are artificial and do not fully explain the human experience. In order to fully understand the issue, researchers must work hard to learn about all aspects of a social problem. In the above example study of terminal cancer patients, good researchers would not only interview cancer sufferers, they would also get to know their family, friends, and caregivers in order to get a full picture of the end of life. In the process of talking with all stakeholders, researchers often uncover other questions and ideas that they had not previously considered. This process is called inductive understanding. By building on information provided by all informants and stakeholders, the researcher obtains a fuller explanation of the phenomenon.

Often, the best and most innovative research uses both qualitative and quantitative approaches. Well-executed qualitative research is often essential preparation for worthwhile quantitative research and vice versa. This does not mean that qualitative research should be regarded as secondary to quantitative research. In many cases, the relationship between the two is symbiotic. Quantitative research presumes that the researcher knows 'what is going on'. Having discovered the range of issues confronting certain people, it is often highly desirable to find out how these themes or issues are distributed among those people, demonstrating the close relationship that exists between quantitative and qualitative research techniques.

WHAT IS QUANTITATIVE RESEARCH?

In contrast to qualitative research, the purpose of quantitative research is to describe trends and large-scale social processes. Sample sizes in quantitative research are much larger than in qualitative research. Sometimes the studies include millions of people, such as in the Canadian national census. In 2006, the date of the last census, more than 33 million people participated in the survey. Its goal is to give the government and researchers access to a large pool of data from which to draw conclusions—such as an assessment of the size of the city of Winnipeg or the number of females living in the Yukon. But sample sizes may be much smaller, some as small as 200 people. The idea is to draw a representative sample from which to draw conclusions about social trends. For example, the General Social Survey, conducted annually by Statistics Canada, surveys a few thousand people about such issues as their use of time, reported victimization, and Internet usage. In this case, the idea is to collect information about a small number of people in order to understand more about a particular social phenomenon. It is not necessary to survey all the people; a small sub-sample of the population is usually enough to reveal accurate, truthful information about a particular phenomenon.

A common concern of quantitative research is the way the sample is selected. One of the issues that differentiates quantitative from qualitative research is the sampling method. Since quantitative research is concerned with generalizing the results to a larger population and does not involve asking everyone for their opinion (which would be too time-consuming and costly), samples must be selected using random means. Since sampling is discussed in Chapter 8, we will not go into detail here. For now, we will simply say that the idea of sampling is to give every person in a population an equal or near-equal chance of being selected to participate in the study.

In contrast to qualitative research, quantitative research designs cannot give detailed in-depth information about a social problem. It can only provide data on general trends and patterns. This is because participants are asked only a small number of questions that are closed-ended. For example, we might ask participants questions about whether or not they support the building of an electrical line along the eastern shore of Lake Winnipeg. We ask the participants a series of short questions, such as 'How likely or unlikely are you to support the construction of a new electrical line along the shore of Lake Winnipeg?' This may be followed by five choices (very unlikely, unlikely, neither likely nor unlikely, likely, and very likely). At no time are participants asked to tell us why they feel this way. For instance, one participant may be very likely to support the initiative because she believes that it may create more jobs for people working in the construction industry. Another respondent may also support the initiative, but for different reasons, such as favouring hydroelectricity over nuclear-powered generators. Unless the surveyors ask, we will never know why the respondents feel the way they do. It is tempting to ask respondents 'why' in large-scale quantitative research, but such questions are generally avoided because they prolong the research process and cost too much in terms of recording and analyzing the answers. Remember that surveys are large, aimed at capturing information from hundreds or thousands of participants.

Another difference between the quantitative and qualitative approaches has to do with perspective. Most quantitative researchers feel that the social sciences should adopt scientific methods to mirror the kind of research conducted in the natural sciences. In this regard, quantitative methodology encompasses a positivist approach. Positivists believe that there are real and truthful answers to any social question. The purpose of social research, according to this paradigm, is to uncover facts and truth. The best way to accomplish this, according to most positivists, is to measure the attitudes, beliefs, and experiences of as many people as possible. Using scientific methods such as statistical modelling, researchers can begin to understand social causes and effects. While social science does not directly deal with cause and effect, those following the positivist paradigm want to follow the model as closely as possible. Students interested in learning more about positivism and quantitative standpoints should consult Palys (2003) or Neuman (1997).

WHICH IS BETTER: QUALITATIVE OR QUANTITATIVE?

By now, it should be clear that the difference between qualitative and quantitative research is not a matter of 'better' or 'worse' but rather of appropriateness to the question. However, since the mid-1960s, when the importance and value of qualitative research became an issue in the conduct of social science, some people have taken staunch ideological positions on the relative merits of quantitative and qualitative research. This has resulted in an artificial and politicized conflict between those who practise one method and those who subscribe to the other. Fortunately, this conflict is subsiding as it becomes increasingly obvious that such polarized views do not coincide with what researchers are actually doing. However, some traces of the conflict persist, and some people still resolutely cling to one side or the other.

For example, some argue that each individual, family, or situation is unique, so it is impossible—indeed immoral—to group them for purposes of analysis and generalization. To do so, they contend, is to fly in the face of reality. For them, the only valid research is individual case studies, in which the uniqueness of each subject or group is appreciated. This is a difficult position to maintain, because someone will eventually begin to identify patterns within and between groups: the stories of women share certain themes, as do those of people with a common lifestyle or of a particular age group; villagers recount different experiences from those of urban dwellers. The original careful attention to the details of individual stories is valuable in itself, but through these details it may be possible to begin to see patterns that can be tested by quantitative approaches, demonstrating again the need for both qualitative and quantitative research methods.

Both qualitative and quantitative approaches are absolutely essential to the research process in the social sciences. They require some common and some different skills. Neither approach sets the standards for the other, since each has its own rules of practice and requires various disciplines on the part of the researcher. Neither is easier than the other, nor is one approach more creative than the other.

QUESTIONS FOR REVIEW

1. How do the questions asked in qualitative research differ from those asked in quantitative research?
2. Why is it not helpful to ask whether quantitative or qualitative research is better or which is more important? What question should be asked?

Suggestions for further reading

Neuman, W. Lawrence. 1997. *Social Research Methods: Qualitative and Quantitative Approaches*. 3rd edn. Toronto: Allyn and Bacon.

Palys, Ted. 2003. *Research Decisions: Quantitative and Qualitative Perspectives*. Scarborough, ON: Nelson.

5

Selecting Variables

As you will recall from Chapter 2, the act of doing research involves reducing conceptual problems to empirical questions—that is, questions about 'things' that can be measured, counted, recorded, or in some way observed. Finding ways of measuring concepts demands creativity and skill. It is one of the more challenging aspects of doing research.

CONCEPTS AND VARIABLES

Concepts are categories into which ideas, impressions, and observations of the world can be placed. So far, we have dealt with concepts such as academic performance, study, nutrition, and marital happiness. While concepts are critically important in the initial stages of research, they have limited use when they are difficult or impossible to measure. Some are elusive to define, mean different things to different people, and lack definite boundaries. Often, concepts are not perceived by touch, sight, smell, or hearing, and direct measurements are not possible.

Take the concept 'happiness'. How could you define or describe the essential aspects of happiness? The problem is that an infinite number of experiences, observations, and impressions are included in the concept. A simple definition that includes all your impressions of happiness is impossible to produce. This task becomes even more difficult to imagine when you attempt to account for other people's impressions of happiness. Finally, what are the boundaries of happiness? When does happiness become its opposite, unhappiness? Often, we feel that we are neither happy nor unhappy. If we don't know, then there must be 'in-between' emotional states in which we cannot be sure whether we are measuring happiness or unhappiness.

It is clear that the concept of happiness has a wide range of meanings, is not readily measurable, and is difficult to observe. How then can happiness be observed and measured in a way that is acceptable to you and to most other people? The same problems are encountered when you try to research most concepts.

Variables

If we are going to do empirical research that others can follow and evaluate, we have to make our abstract concepts observable and measurable. The conventional procedure for doing this is to replace abstract concepts with measurable concepts, referred to as 'variables'. What is a variable? A variable is a type of concept, one that varies in amount or quality. A variable is something that it is possible to have more or less of, or something that exists in different 'states' or 'categories'. The variables that interest us are those that not only vary in amount or kind but are also measurable.

For example, the concept 'heat' can be measured by measuring the variable 'temperature'. To measure temperature, we read a thermometer and document the measurement it indicates. We generally take the measurement of temperature to be an indicator of the level of heat.

Someone might say that 'love' is a variable—you can have more or less of it, and there are different kinds of love. However, love is not directly measurable. If we want to measure love, we have to find suitable and measurable variables to use. Some might choose such measurable variables as the number of kisses received from their lover or spouse, the frequency and quality of flowers received, the number of hugs, or the failure to remember important dates such as birthdays and anniversaries. Although love itself is not directly measurable, we can use measurable variables to assess whether we are loved or not.

Specifically, the primary function of any variable is to enable measurement of changes in its corresponding abstract concept. When we pose a hypothesis, we argue that changes in one abstract concept occur as a result of changes in another. When we test a hypothesis, we use variables to allow us to measure changes in the abstract concepts. To be measurable substitutes for abstract concepts, variables must have the following characteristics:

1. Variables must validly represent an abstract concept being studied. This means that changes in variables validly represent changes in abstract concepts. A valid variable for the concept 'academic performance' is 'final grades', because most people would be confident that changes in final grades

represent changes in academic performance. Generally, though, the concept of academic performance does not extend to 'batting average' or 'popularity rating', which, in this case, would not be valid variables for detecting changes in academic performance. We will expand on this point later in the chapter, in the section 'The question of validity'.

2. Variables must have at least one range of 'possible states'. For example, a range of possible states for the variable 'final grades' is 'distinction', 'credit', 'pass', and 'fail'. (Another range is 0–100 per cent. Some educational institutions use the range A, B, C, etc.) Since a variable has a range of states, it can change, and these changes can be taken to indicate change in the abstract concept represented by the variable. A positive change in a student's final grades (variable), from credit to distinction level, indicates a positive change in academic achievement (abstract concept).

3. Variables have 'states' that are observable and measurable. You can only detect changes in a variable if you can observe and measure it. For example, the variable 'final grades', which represents the abstract concept 'academic performance', can be observed and measured by checking students' reports or asking their teacher. If you cannot observe and measure a variable, then you cannot detect changes in the variable, and you cannot detect changes in the abstract concept it represents. Say the abstract concept 'happiness' is given by the variable 'inner peace'. This would be unsatisfactory, because you cannot observe or measure 'inner peace'. Consequently, it would be a useless variable for the concept 'happiness'.

The activity of finding measurable variables for concepts is called 'operationalization'. An operational definition of a concept goes beyond a usual dictionary definition. It defines a concept in terms that can be measured—that is, it defines a concept in empirical terms.

The basic question that guides this activity is 'How can I measure that?' That is, what can I take as an indicator of what is going on? Let's continue our sample hypothesis about academic performance. When we last left it, it looked like this:

This hypothesis says that two concepts, study and academic performance, are related in such a way that the more there is of one (study), the more there will be of the other (academic performance). The question we now face is, 'How shall we measure study and academic performance?' or 'What measurable, tangible, observable things can we take as indicators or variables of study and academic performance?'

Take academic performance first. We are so familiar with ways of measuring academic performance that we often forget the concept being measured. The measures with which we are most familiar include:

- final grades
- test results
- essay marks
- examiners' reports
- project assessments

Academic performance is the abstract concept. Marks and test results are variables related to the concept of academic performance.

What about study? How shall we measure study? What variables can be taken as indicators of study? It is hard to measure such things as concentration or the absorption of material. But we can measure the amount of time a student spends 'studying'. Hence, an operational definition of the concept 'study' might be:

- time spent studying
- time spent practising

It is now possible to state our hypothesis in two forms, in a conceptual form and in an operational form.

Conceptual form of the hypothesis

In its conceptual form, the hypothesis describes a relationship between the concepts 'study' and 'academic performance'. Study is the independent concept, and academic performance is the dependent concept.

Operational form of the hypothesis

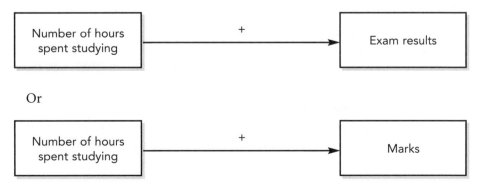

The operational form of the hypothesis asserts that there is a relationship between variables—that is, the number of hours spent studying and exam results or grades. Number of hours spent studying is the independent variable, and exam results, or marks, is the dependent variable.

Any hypothesis can be stated at both the conceptual (abstract or theoretical) level and the operational (empirical or measurable) level. At the conceptual level, a hypothesis asserts a relationship between concepts, and at the operational level it asserts a relationship between variables. We will practise deriving variables as appropriate measures of concepts, then we will discuss the problem of the relationship between concepts and variables.

FINDING VARIABLES FOR CONCEPTS: HYPOTHESES

There are no set ways or even useful guides for finding variables that are appropriate measures for concepts. This is an area for creativity and experimentation. Doing research involves a great deal of inventiveness and a willingness to think in new ways. You have to search for variables. Variables must be measurable and relate in some accepted way to the concept in question. Beyond those two rules, the task (or fun) of finding variables is up to you. Here is another conceptual hypothesis:

Better nutritional status leads to better academic performance.

Diagrammed, the hypothesis looks like this:

If we are to test this hypothesis, we must find a variable that relates to nutrition and another that relates to academic performance. We already have some ideas about academic performance—test results, marks, examiners' reports, etc. What variables might give an indication of a student's nutritional status? What about:

- how many meals per week include vegetables;
- whether breakfast includes fruit;
- the percentage of recommended daily allowance of nutrients in foods eaten each day.

List others you can think of.

Taking one of the variables associated with nutrition and one of those associated with academic performance, restate the hypothesis in operational form.

Higher nutrition of meals leads to higher final grades.

Now in diagram form:

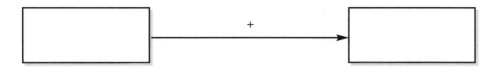

In this case, what is the independent variable, and what is the dependent variable?

For further practice, take two other variables, one related to nutrition and another related to academic performance. Develop an operational hypothesis and write it out. Then diagram it.

Now let us try an entirely new hypothesis. Take the area of family life. We are concerned about the relationship between the abstract concepts 'family resources' and 'family happiness'. We may have the theoretical hypothesis:

The more resources available to a family, the happier that family will be.

Diagram this theoretical hypothesis:

Think of variables that might be useful indicators, or specific measures, of family resources—things such as:

- family income
- relatives
- time
- social status
- quality of housing

Now, what variables might be taken as indicators of family happiness? Happiness is one of those concepts that are not directly measurable. But we can get some indication. How? How about:

- absence of divorce
- presence of observable signs of affection—hugs, kisses
- self-reported happiness
- the result on a test of marital happiness

Think of other indicators of family happiness. One operational hypothesis that can be derived from the above lists of variables is:

Greater family income leads to less divorce.

This would be diagrammed as follows:

Note that although the conceptual hypothesis asserts a positive relationship between two concepts, this operational hypothesis asserts a negative relationship between two variables. This is not a problem. Divorce is taken as a negative indicator of marital happiness. Here is another possible operational hypothesis:

The more time a family spends together, the more likely members of the family are to report that they are happy with the family.

This hypothesis would be diagrammed:

Gain some practice by deriving other operational hypotheses from the above lists of variables, and diagram them.

Let us take a final example, this time with a categorical variable. Some family researchers believe that intimacy between parents and their infants is a very important factor in successful infant development. The independent concept in this example is 'parent–infant intimacy', and the dependent concept is 'infant development'.

A variable for 'parent–infant intimacy' could be 'feeding intimacy', a categorical variable with two states, 'breastfed' and 'bottlefed'. The first half of a diagram of an operational hypothesis, the part showing the independent variable, would look like this:

The problem now becomes selecting some measure of 'infant development'. Infant development is a very wide concept. To arrive at a suitable variable, let's consider some 'sub-concepts' of infant development that might be affected by feeding preference:

- infant growth
- motor development
- physical health
- emotional health

Add some of your own.

Let's take 'infant growth' as a substitute for infant development. The developed conceptual hypothesis would be:

Greater feeding intimacy leads to increased infant growth.

This would be diagrammed:

But this is still at the conceptual level. It is now necessary to think of variables that are indicators of infant growth. What variables might be associated with infant growth? There is weight accumulation. You can have lower or higher weight accumulation. 'Weight accumulation' is a variable. The operational hypothesis could now be phrased as follows:

Feeding intimacy influences infant weight accumulation.

This hypothesis would be diagrammed:

Alternatively, you might have preferred to use the sub-concept 'physical health' instead of 'infant development'. In that case, the conceptual hypothesis would be stated:

Parent–infant intimacy influences a baby's physical health.

How can this hypothesis be operationalized? What variables can you think of that relate to physical health? Here are a few:

- absence of colic
- absence of infectious disease

- normal growth pattern
- appropriate development
- physician's report

Add to this list.

To gain more practice in selecting variables, look through your notes, identify some issues, formulate conceptual hypotheses, and then try to identify appropriate variables.

FINDING VARIABLES FOR CONCEPTS: RESEARCH OBJECTIVES

When developing research to meet our objectives, it is still necessary to clarify our concepts and to select variables appropriate to these concepts. For example, the research objective might be:

To learn about infant growth and development.

'Growth' and 'development' are the concepts. The question that needs to be answered is 'What variables relate to growth and development?' Growth is fairly easy—weight, height, and length of limbs are all variables that relate to growth. By observing changes in these variables, we can measure growth.

What variables relate to development? We can now see that the above objective is still very broad. What kind of development—social, behavioural, psychological? For each of these and other kinds of development, there are well-established variables to observe. Specific abilities or patterns of behaviour are taken as evidence of certain kinds of development.

Research objectives are used to guide research that seeks to *describe* rather than *explain* what is happening. While this means that there will not be independent and dependent concepts and variables, it is still necessary to operationalize the concepts in the research objective. Variables must be selected to serve as indicators for the concepts being studied.

An objective presented in Chapter 3 was:

Objective: To discover the existing policy on admission to homes for elderly people.

'Policy' is a fairly general concept. How might admission policy vary from home to home? How do policies relate to:

- age;
- health;
- financial status;
- family status?

All of these are variables related to the concept 'policy'. Put differently, they are aspects of admission policies of homes for the elderly, which can vary. By thinking through these issues before beginning your data collection, you ensure that the research is focused and clarified. Some background reading—reviewing the relevant literature—will help you to identify variables that might be related to the concepts being studied.

Another example of a research objective may help to further demonstrate the idea that both hypotheses and research objectives deal with concepts.

Objective: To observe the classroom behaviour of school students.

What aspect of the concept 'classroom behaviour' is to be observed? What are some variables related to the classroom behaviour of students? Some of the following might be considered:

- attention span of each student
- noise level in the classroom
- frequency of discipline
- attention span of the whole class
- frequency of disruptive behaviour
- length of time taken to settle down at the beginning of a lesson

Before beginning an observational study, it is necessary to decide what is to be observed. This involves selecting a few variables related to the concepts being studied.

THE QUESTION OF VALIDITY

The most critical consideration in choosing variables is 'validity'. When measured, does the variable adequately reflect our understanding of the concept? This is the issue of validity. We must question all the variables we use to provide indicators of our theoretical concepts. How good is a possible indicator? Does it adequately represent our concept? Is it not quite the same thing?

Many arguments arise over the issue of validity. Take the case of IQ testing. Are such tests valid indicators of intellectual ability? Or do they test something else? Take the issue of academic performance. Do exam results validly reflect academic performance? Or do they measure something else? Can the absence of disease be taken as an indicator of health, as one of our hypotheses suggested? Can the absence of divorce be taken as an indication that a family is happy? Were you satisfied with the variables suggested as measures of love—number of kisses or hugs, flowers, and anniversaries remembered?

Whenever we feel dissatisfied with the variables chosen to measure a concept, we raise the issue of validity:

- Is a low noise level a valid indicator that a class is learning? Or is the class just well disciplined?
- Is the fact that a baby gains a great deal of weight quickly a valid indicator of the baby's health, or does it simply indicate the kilojoule content of its diet?

- Is an expressed opinion a valid indicator of the way a person will act?
- Is church-going a valid indicator of depth of spirituality? Or is it an indicator of conformity? Or of something else?

These are examples of issues regarding the validity of chosen variables. Such issues are inevitable, because the act of choosing variables involves finding a concrete expression of abstract (i.e., conceptual) ideas. Not everyone will agree with your choice of variables. Some people will question your research based on your variable choices.

Another problem raised by questions of validity is that concepts are often multidimensional and impossible to represent with a single variable. For such concepts, a single variable has to be chosen on the basis of its being the 'least inadequate' option. For example, 'social class' is a concept with a range of dimensions—income, wealth, education, ownership/control of the factors of production, gender, etc. When choosing a variable for 'social class', you can select only one of these factors. Obviously, any single factor is inadequate as a variable. Therefore, you have to choose the variable that is the 'least inadequate'. The inadequacy of your chosen variable is a limitation of your research. The only thing that can be done about it is to describe the inadequacies of your chosen variable in your research report.

Usually, you cannot find the 'perfect' variable for a given concept. There are no perfect variables. Variable selection is a matter of finding an adequate variable and being honest about its shortcomings.

AN OVERVIEW OF THE RESEARCH PROCESS

What have we learned so far? It is important that we keep the various threads of development together.

When we encounter a problem, or a question about which we want to do some research, we first try to express that concern in a research objective or a hypothesis. This activity focuses our attention. It clarifies our interest. When stated as a hypothesis, our focal question or statement of concern asserts a relationship between two or more concepts. When stated as a research objective, our focal question defines, using concepts, our area of interest. We examined sample hypotheses such as:

More study leads to better academic performance.
Better nutrition leads to better academic performance.
Greater family wealth leads to greater family happiness.

These hypotheses are all stated at the conceptual level. Each hypothesis states a relationship between ideas.

By now we can see that regardless of whether our research is guided and focused by a hypothesis or by a research objective, we select variables as observable indicators for the concepts we are studying. One of the more challenging and creative tasks in the research process is the discipline of finding measurable, observable, sensory variables that relate to the concepts that concern us. The following may help to clarify the steps in the research process that we have learned so far:

Step 1
Select, narrow, and focus the problem to be studied.
State the problem as either a hypothesis or a research objective.

Step 2
Select variables that relate to the concepts in the hypothesis or research objective.

As we go along, we will fill in the additional steps that have to be taken. Table 5.1 lays out some of the examples we have developed.

TABLE 5.1   Concepts and their related variables

CONCEPT	VARIABLES RELATED TO CONCEPT
Academic performance	Marks
	Exam results
	Essay evaluations
	Examiner's reports
Nutritional adequacy	What is eaten for breakfast
	Contents of lunch
Growth	Height
	Weight
	Length of limbs
Classroom behaviour	Attention span
	Degree of disruption

For each concept, we have identified several related variables. For each idea, we have suggested two or more measurable, observable indicators.

If a variable relates appropriately to the concept being studied, it is said to be a valid variable. The problem of validity deals with the success of our efforts to find measurable indicators of our theoretical concepts. One of the limitations usually discussed in research reports is the validity of the variables selected. How valid is this variable as an indicator of that concept? For example, how valid are test results as indicators of intelligence? How valid are changes in height and weight as indicators of growth, or the contents of someone's lunch as an indicator of the nutritional adequacy of their diet?

QUESTIONS FOR REVIEW

1. What is a concept? Give three examples.
2. What is a hypothesis?
3. What is a variable?
4. Why are variables selected?
5. Table 5.2 lists a number of concepts. For each one, think of at least two variables.

TABLE 5.2   Finding variables for concepts

CONCEPT	RELATED VARIABLES
Health	
Marital happiness	
Nutritional adequacy	
Maturity	
Socio-emotional development	

6. What is the difference between a hypothesis and a research objective? Why must variables be selected for both?
7. To what does the question of validity refer?
8. What is an operational definition? State the following hypothesis in an operational form:

The better a student's nutritional status, the better that student's classroom behaviour will be.

Suggestions for further reading

de Vaus, D.A. 2002. *Surveys in Social Research*. 5th edn, chapter 3. St Leonards, NSW: Allen and Unwin.

Giddens, Anthony. 2001. *Sociology*. 4th edn, chapter 20. Cambridge: Polity Press.

Judd, C.M., E.R. Smith, and L.H. Kidder. 1991. *Research Methods in Social Relations*, chapter 2. Fort Worth, TX: Holt, Rinehart and Winston.

Juredini, Ray, and Marilyn Poole. 2003. *Sociology: Australian Connections*, chapter 12. St Leonards, NSW: Allen and Unwin.

Kumar, Ranjit. 1999. *Research Methodology: A Step by Step Guide for Beginners*, chapter 5. London: Sage.

Wallace, W. 1971. *The Logic of Science in Sociology*, chapter 3. Chicago: Aldine.

Finding a Variable's Measurements

The general task of empirical research is to 'observe' for changes in variables. When testing hypotheses, we observe for changes in at least two variables to see whether they change together in the manner we predict. When pursuing research objectives, we focus our attention on certain variables, observing either how they appear or how they change.

So how do we know whether variables have or have not changed? We 'measure' variables in different situations, such as two points in time. If the measurements are different, then we recognize that a change has occurred. If the measurements produce the same results, then we recognize that no change has occurred. But how do we 'measure variables'? That is the main subject of this chapter.

THE LOGIC OF MEASUREMENT

The logic of measurement is something we take for granted. For instance, we frame many of our everyday perceptions in standard systems of measurement—thinking of distances in kilometres, the outdoor temperature in degrees Celsius, and the cost of gas in cents per litre. Also, we constantly use measuring instruments such as watches, speedometers, thermometers, rulers, and gas meters. Generally, we don't question the validity of these measuring systems and instruments—we tend to take their validity for granted.

In a research situation, where we set out to measure variables, we need to be more conscious of the logic of measurement. In deciding how variables should be measured, we face three major issues that require careful consideration:

1. What is it that varies in the variable?
2. By what instrument are we going to measure the way(s) the variable varies?
3. In what units are we going to report our measurements of this variation?

Table 6.1 uses the example of physical growth to show the relationship between concept, variable, measuring instrument, and units of measurement. This relationship is basic to all empirical research. To measure a variable, we need both a measuring instrument and units of measure in which to report variations in measures taken of the variable.

TABLE 6.1   Measurement: the example of physical growth

CONCEPT	VARIABLE	MEASURING INSTRUMENT	UNITS OF MEASUREMENT
Physical growth	Length	Metre stick Ruler Tape measure	Metres, centimetres
	Weight	Scales	Kilograms, grams

Figure 6.1 clearly shows the order in which the problems facing you, as a researcher, should be handled. First, clarify the problem by defining the concepts to be studied. Second, identify variables associated with each concept. Select one or two variables for each concept. Third, for each variable, devise or select a measuring instrument. Fourth, select or devise units of measurement.

FIGURE 6.1   The logical order of issues to be decided in measurement

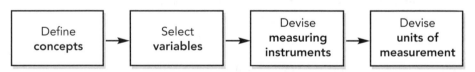

Some additional examples may help to clarify the logical flow of the issues related to measurement. As you look at the examples in Table 6.2, try to think of other ways of measuring each variable or of other units of measurement.

TABLE 6.2   Examples of the logical order of issues to be decided in measurement

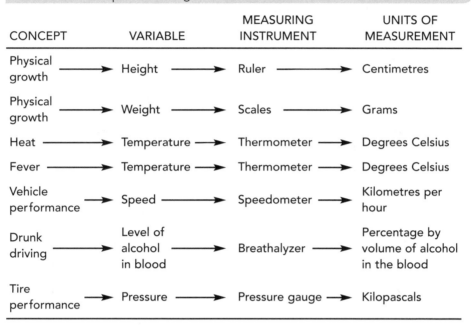

CONCEPT	VARIABLE	MEASURING INSTRUMENT	UNITS OF MEASUREMENT
Physical growth	⟶ Height ⟶	Ruler ⟶	Centimetres
Physical growth	⟶ Weight ⟶	Scales ⟶	Grams
Heat ⟶	Temperature ⟶	Thermometer ⟶	Degrees Celsius
Fever ⟶	Temperature ⟶	Thermometer ⟶	Degrees Celsius
Vehicle performance	⟶ Speed ⟶	Speedometer ⟶	Kilometres per hour
Drunk driving ⟶	Level of alcohol in blood ⟶	Breathalyzer ⟶	Percentage by volume of alcohol in the blood
Tire performance	⟶ Pressure ⟶	Pressure gauge ⟶	Kilopascals

VARIABLE MEASUREMENT IN THE SOCIAL AND BEHAVIOURAL SCIENCES

For most variables studied in the 'natural sciences' (physics, chemistry, and biology), there are generally accepted units of measurement and measuring instruments. Length is measured in metres, volume of sound in decibels, time in seconds, and the strength of an electric current in amps. Clocks are standard instruments for measuring time, speedometers commonly measure speed, and so on. This is because natural scientists have established some agreement on the nature of many of their common variables, like velocity, current, and salinity. Since they generally agree on *what* they are measuring, they have general agreement on *how* variables are to be measured.

Agreeing on what is to be measured makes agreement on how to measure easier. For example, if you and your friends generally agree that the variable 'height' is the physical distance from the floor to the top of a standing person's head, then agreeing on how to measure 'height' is not so difficult, because at least there is general agreement on what has to be measured to obtain a value for 'height'.

In the social and behavioural sciences, however, researchers do not enjoy the same level of agreement about the nature of common variables such as class, status, and poverty. Consequently, they have not reached general agreement on how common variables ought to be measured.

For example, any two social researchers will probably agree that there is such a variable as 'standard of education'. However, many would disagree about the nature of this variable. One researcher might think of 'standard of education' in terms of a scale of the highest level of formal education a person has completed (none/primary/secondary/post-secondary). Another might think of it in terms of the number of years in full-time education. Different ideas about the nature of the variable would lead different researchers to adopt different measures, because they would have different notions about *what* they were measuring.

Life as a researcher would be simpler, although perhaps less interesting, if there were generally accepted and standard ways of measuring the following common social and behavioural variables:

- social class
- academic performance
- political preference
- quality of teaching
- marital satisfaction
- sexuality
- ethnicity
- motivation
- race
- racial tension
- status
- social integration

Given this situation, researchers need to take great care when devising their own measures for variables. This process is one of the challenging aspects of doing research in the social and behavioural sciences.

The importance of measuring variables in the social and behavioural sciences

The practice of adopting measures for variables strengthens several areas of the research process. First, it focuses data collection. Most variables are vague and might be measured by a large number of empirical phenomena. Marital satisfaction might be measured by frequency of sexual activity each month, average amount of time spent together, number of incidents of infidelity, and so on. Given the confusion that can occur as a result of having so many choices, researchers need to clarify variable measures for their own benefit. Researchers must limit their choices and focus their data collection on those choices. If they do not, they will lack direction in their data collection and have less chance of carrying it out coherently.

Second, when data collection becomes focused, it can also become more streamlined and efficient. Data collection devices such as interview schedules and tally sheets can be designed so that the data is collected clearly and easily organized for analysis.

Third, selection of measures allows for disciplined and consistent observation of variables in different situations and, therefore, disciplined and consistent observation of changes in variables. If you apply the same measure of the variable 'unemployment', such as the official national unemployment rate, in two consecutive years, you can compare the measurements and ascertain whether 'unemployment' has changed. If you take different measures of unemployment for two consecutive years—for example, the official national rate in the first year and an unofficial rate in the second—you cannot compare those measurements to ascertain whether unemployment has changed.

Fourth, variable measurements create a context in which data analysis and findings can be expressed clearly. A report on the findings of a study into unemployment that has no consistent measure for unemployment could read: 'Given what they observed in welfare offices, job agencies, and the newspapers, the researchers judge that the level of unemployment has increased significantly over the past two years.' This statement gives little indication of how the researchers analyzed the data or how the finding was reached. It is vague because it lacks a rigorous context.

Alternatively, the report might say: 'The national level of unemployment increased significantly during the period investigated. At the beginning of year 1, the official national unemployment rate was 8.2 per cent. Subsequently, the rate increased by an average of 0.1 per cent every three months for the next two years. By the end of year 3, the official unemployment rate had increased to 9 per cent.' These findings are expressed in a context that readers should be able to understand—that is, the context of the official unemployment rate, which is the measure for unemployment. Readers have a clear, rigorous context in which to consider the researchers' analysis and findings.

Measuring variables through data collection

Once a measure for a variable has been identified, data collection for the measure can be organized and conducted. The collection of such data is the process of variable 'measurement'. Imagine you have decided to research the variable 'patriotism' among male and female adults in your street. You decide that the measure of patriotism for each group will be the 'percentage of males/females who can sing the national anthem'. When you collect data on this measure, you are taking measurements of the variable 'patriotism' among males and females. Therefore, such directed data collection is variable measurement. From this point, the term 'data collection' will be used to signify 'variable measurement'.

There are three basic data collection techniques that researchers use for measuring variables. The first is 'observation', when researchers observe what is 'going on' and record what they observe. The second technique is interviewing, when researchers ask people questions and record the responses. The third technique is examining records and documents. Each technique provides quantitative data for variables—that is, data that can be counted or measured.

As described above, the measurement of variables has two major steps, which occur in the following order:

1. choosing an appropriate measuring instrument;
2. choosing units of measurement.

In the social and behavioural sciences, this procedure is often less rigid. After selecting a variable, social and behavioural scientists often develop their measuring instruments and units while they interact with their subjects. This process can be seen in the following descriptions of data collection techniques.

USING OBSERVATION TO MEASURE VARIABLES

To conduct 'observation' is simply to 'watch what happens'. However, all research observation is guided by a research question. Researchers do not just go and 'have a look' at their subjects—they look for something in particular that is stated or alluded to in their research hypothesis or objective. More important, what the researcher is looking for is best determined before the observation commences. Let's examine the requirements of a proper observational study for which the measure of the variable has been decided before data collection commences.

First of all, decide what to observe and state what it is. This is necessary because in practice, we all tend to get distracted by things that have some personal interest. The following experiment should demonstrate this tendency.

Take a look
This exercise is best done with a group. It can be fun for three or more people. Go with the group to some place: a coffee shop, a classroom, a playground, a street, an intersection, a football game—almost any place will do. Let everyone look at the scene selected for two minutes. This should be done quietly, with no sharing of views. Then ask each person to write down everything they observed. After each person has finished writing, share your observations. Then ask:

- What did you find?
- Was there much similarity in what was seen?
- Were there many differences in what was seen?

The results of your exercise will probably show that different observers focused their attention on different things. If observation is not directed by the hypothesis or research objective, then we are likely to become distracted and gather irrelevant data. Therefore, we need to discipline ourselves—and any other researchers we are working with—to observe only those 'things' that are relevant to the hypothesis. We do this by identifying the focus of our observations before we begin observing.

Next is an example of an observational study in which the observation is directed by the research hypothesis. You are assigned the task of studying the behaviour of car drivers in the pre-Christmas period. As a good researcher, you have decided to focus on the concept of 'illegal driver behaviour' to keep the study manageable. Further, you have decided to study this concept at a busy city intersection for the weeks of December leading up to Christmas Day. Your research objective is clearly stated as follows:

To observe 'illegal driver behaviour' at one city intersection over a four-week period.

You have decided to use 'traffic light infringements' as the measurable variable to indicate changes in illegal driver behaviour. Hence, the operationalized restatement of your research objective would be:

To observe 'traffic light infringements' at one city intersection over a four-week period.

You would not just occasionally look at the traffic and guess whether more or fewer drivers were 'running the red light'. Rather, you would observe the intersection at specified times and ask, 'How many motorists are driving through red lights?' The measure of your variable would be 'the number of motorists who drive through red lights at specified times'.

You might observe the intersection each Thursday during December (assume that 1 December is a Thursday). Each observation session takes place during the peak traffic period, 4 pm to 7 pm. You could record the data for each observation session on a data collection sheet such as that shown in Figure 6.2.

FIGURE 6.2 A data collection sheet

ILLEGAL DRIVER BEHAVIOUR—DATA COLLECTION SHEET

Date: 1 December   **Time:** 4 pm–7 pm

Traffic light infringements (place a check mark for each observation):

✓✓✓✓✓✓✓✓✓✓

Daily total: 10

Next, you would place the totals for each observation session on a data summarization form, which might look like Table 6.3.

TABLE 6.3   A data summarization form

WEEKLY OBSERVATION	DATE	TOTAL TRAFFIC LIGHT INFRINGEMENTS
1	1 December	10
2	8 December	16
3	15 December	22
4	22 December	30

This summarization form provides a systematic record of observations. It shows a steady increase in traffic light infringements from week to week, which would support the hypothesis that drivers become increasingly reckless as Christmas Day approaches. From the table, you can construct graphs, charts, tables, or other presentations of your data.

If you studied more than one intersection, you would have a separate summarization form for each. You would also keep a different set of weekly tally sheets for each intersection. It would be essential to record data separately for each intersection in order to make comparisons later.

From the above example, you can see that to prepare for data collection, you need to:

1. select concepts;
2. select variables;
3. select a means for measuring those variables;
4. design a means for recording the measurements you will make.

If all this is done before you begin to collect data, then data collection and analysis will proceed more smoothly and easily. Failing to measure and record your data properly will jeopardize the rest of the research process. Think back over the above example. Ask yourself the following questions:

- What concept was studied?
- What variable was selected?
- How was the variable measured?
- In what unit of measurement was variation in the variable reported?
- What data-recording devices were developed?

The concept was 'illegal driver behaviour'.
The variable was 'traffic light infringements'.

The variable was measured by observing traffic at a given intersection, at a given time, and by noting the total number of drivers who had driven through the intersection when the red light was showing.

The unit of measurement was 'traffic light infringements'.

Two recording devices were developed. The first was a 'data collection sheet', on which daily traffic light infringements were recorded and later totalled. The second was a 'data summarization sheet', on which the total observed infringements at every observation session were recorded so that comparisons for each week could be made.

The research process has a set of steps. The first two steps—defining concepts and selecting variables—must be done in the order shown in Figure 6.1. However, in the social and behavioural sciences, the fourth step of the process—devising units of measurement—often occurs while data is being collected. This is demonstrated in the next example.

You may hear teachers make the following statement about the students at their school:

Boys behave better in the classroom than girls.

You decide to research this claim. The concepts of the hypothesis are 'sex' (independent) and 'classroom behaviour' (dependent). The independent variable can remain as 'sex'. The dependent variable can be 'disruptive behaviour'. 'Sex' is easy to measure; our problem will be to find measures for 'disruptive behaviour'.

This is a difficult variable to measure, because there are many types of disruptive behaviour, which occur spontaneously, and we cannot know for certain which ones will occur when we conduct our observation. Therefore, deciding on a single measure before entering the class could result in a waste of time.

A possible approach would be to devise a checklist of disruptive behaviours before observing the class. The total occurrences of all such behaviours would be the measure for this variable. Data could be collected separately for each group. Each time any such behaviour is observed in a class, we would place a check mark after the behaviour in the appropriate column, 'boy' or 'girl'. If girls exhibited more total disruptive behaviours than boys, the hypothesis would be supported by the data collected. Our completed observation checklist might look like that shown in Figure 6.3.

The data, which are now organized to clearly represent measurements of the variables, indicate that in this particular class, our measurement for disruptive behaviour was greater for girls than for boys. The hypothesis that 'boys behave better in the classroom than girls' is supported by measurements of the variables.

As can be seen from Figure 6.3, an observation checklist focuses observation of the indicators of change in the variable and enables the researcher to record these observations as data, rendering them 'countable'.

The results make it possible to move from an impression to facts when describing observations. Instead of saying, 'It was my impression that the girls were more disruptive in class than the boys', you would be able to say, 'The girls were observed to engage in a greater number of disruptive acts than the boys.'

FIGURE 6.3   An observation checklist for classroom behaviour

Class: 10A	Date: 13/4/2007
Observer:	Reece Ercher
School:	Canadian High
Teacher:	T. Cher
Subject:	Social Etiquette

Behaviour	Boy	Girl
1 Pokes neighbour	1	0
2 Talks out of turn	1	3
3 Whispers	0	6
4 Interrupts	5	0
5 Gets out of desk	2	3
6 Dozes	1	0
7 Throws something	2	2
8 Teases	1	3
9 etc.	etc.	etc.
10 etc.	etc.	etc.
Total disruptive behaviour in this classroom	24	32

To recap: observation is the most basic data collection technique available to researchers. The first difference between casual observation and scientific observation is that scientific observation is guided by a clearly stated question. The second difference is that researchers systematically measure and record their observations in ways that make the phenomenon being studied countable. Instead of impressions, researchers record numerical data:

Not: I think that drivers are breaking the rules more often in the month before Christmas.

But: In observations conducted at a certain intersection between 4 pm and 7 pm on each Thursday of December, the number of motorists who drove through red light signals increased from 10 to 30.

Not: It is my impression that boys are better behaved in the classroom.

But: In one-hour observations conducted in each of six classrooms at such-and-such school, girls were found to exhibit an average of 32 disruptive acts per hour while boys exhibited 24 such acts.

Thus, one way of measuring a variable is by systematic observation.

Some further examples of research using systematic observation to measure a variable may help to develop your skills in observation. Suppose you were interested in the area of sex-role differences. Your background reading in this area has indicated that the opinions of women are frequently given less weight, ignored, or ridiculed by men. Moreover, you suspect that this occurs frequently in discussions involving family members. You decide to observe a family interacting in order to test the hypothesis that:

The evaluation of contributions to a conversation within a family will be affected by the sex of the contributor.

This can be diagrammed:

Sex is a categorical variable. A person is either 'male' or 'female'. The dependent variable poses a greater challenge. But you, the researcher, have decided to focus on the evaluation of opinions expressed in a family context. You will explore the variable by asking the following questions while observing a family conversation:

- Is the opinion ignored?
- Is the opinion discussed further?
- Is the opinion ridiculed or scorned?
- Is the opinion discounted?
- Is the person expressing the opinion interrupted?
- Is the person expressing the opinion ignored?

This is a list of indicators of a negative evaluation. You will measure each during the family conversation.

How can you conduct the study? Assume that you have received a family's permission to record its mealtime conversation.

The Sloan family consists of father, mother, and two children: John, who is 18, and Helen, who is 16. Once you have the tape of their conversation, you and perhaps others can observe what was going on and fill out an observation checklist (such as Figure 6.4) for each person in the conversation.

FIGURE 6.4   An observation checklist for analyzing a conversation

Person: Helen

Type of conversation: Mealtime   Fate of opinion

	Location on tape	Opinion	Rejected	Ridiculed	Ignored	Interrupted	Discussed	Praised	Adopted	
1	137	re: Weather	✓							
2	236	re: Football match		✓						
3	etc.	etc.								

The question is 'What happens to each member's contribution to the conversation?' On the checklist, note where on the tape the contribution began (using the counter on the tape recorder). Note the speaker. Then note what happened to the opinion.

By using a tape recording, you can go back over the event and check it. You can also have other people observe the event and compare assessments. For example, let us assume that you recorded a family mealtime conversation.

Part of the conversation might have gone:

Helen   (Trying to get a word in) I've got a problem.
John   You always have problems. (He continues speaking about Saturday's football match.)

In this instance, Helen's comment was ignored. The conversation continues:

Helen   Look, I've got to talk to you about . . .
Father   Be quiet and let John finish.

Here Helen is interrupted and stopped by her father. If this pattern continued throughout the conversation, there would be some evidence to suggest that male members of the family did not take Helen seriously.

Once you have filled out a checklist for each person in the conversation, you can compare the fate of each family member's contributions. You can compare parents with children, males with females, mother with father, and son with daughter. By comparing the number of negative fates (being ignored, discounted, ridiculed, or interrupted) to the number of positive fates (discussed further, praised, adopted, or taken seriously), you can assess differences in the variable 'evaluation of contributions to a conversation'.

Thus, one way to measure a variable is by systematic observation. The following questions should be answered in order to ensure that the proposed observation will yield useful results.

A checklist for research involving observation

1. Have you clarified and narrowed your hypothesis or research objective? What are the key concepts?
2. What variables are to be studied?
3. How is each variable to be measured?
4. Have you devised an observation checklist or some other means of systematically recording your observations?
5. Have you practised using your checklist?
6. In what units will the results be reported?

If you can answer these questions, you are probably ready to conduct your observations. You are not ready until you can do so.

USING INTERVIEW SCHEDULES AND QUESTIONNAIRES TO MEASURE VARIABLES

The second common data-gathering technique involves asking people questions— that is, interviewing. In an interview, the researcher asks the respondent (the person being questioned) questions in a face-to-face situation or on the telephone using an 'interview schedule'. A 'questionnaire' is used when the respondent reads and answers the questions on their own. Interview schedules and questionnaires measure variables by gathering answers to questions.

Interview schedules and questionnaires must collect data that are measurements of variables. This is extremely important. Each question must be relevant to one of the variables being studied. These techniques are not 'fishing' expeditions in which all sorts of 'interesting' questions are asked.

There are two practical issues concerning the relevance of interview questions. First, remember that you are selecting questions for the purpose of measuring variables, not to satisfy simple curiosity. Resist the temptation to include a question just to satisfy your curiosity. Such questions do not generate useful data and often confuse respondents.

The second issue concerns your planning and preparation. Never attempt to compensate for inadequate preparation by including questions that have only potential relevance to your variables. You must be honest with yourself about this. Before including a question, always ask yourself, 'What do I plan to do with the data collected with this question? Which variable am I measuring?' If you cannot answer, then your preparation is inadequate, and even if you get reliable data, you will have no framework for data analysis. You will not be able to articulate *what* you have measured, and your analysis will be very weak. If you realize that your preparation is inadequate, repeat the steps of the research process, and ask yourself the above questions again.

When consideration is given to what must be asked to measure the variables in a study, the choice of questions becomes straightforward, and the number of questions can be kept within an acceptable limit. It is hardly necessary to say that a short questionnaire is easier to answer and analyze than a long one. Identify which questions must be asked in order to measure a variable adequately, and discard the rest.

It is important to realize that most hypotheses and research objectives can be researched using more than one technique of data gathering. For example, the observational study of driver behaviour discussed earlier could have been done using interview techniques. The same data-recording form would be used, but each week the interviewer would visit or telephone the relevant police station and ask, 'How many traffic light infringements were recorded by the cameras this week at "X" intersection?'

Take another example. Remember this hypothesis:

More study leads to greater academic performance.

One of the operational forms of this hypothesis developed in Chapter 5 was:

Increased studying leads to more satisfactory exam results.

This hypothesis was diagrammed as follows:

You have been assigned to do some research related to this hypothesis. How are you going to measure the variables? The problem is straightforward in this case. You can count hours of study easily and examination results can be recorded. You need to have a record, for each student involved, of only two things—the number of hours they spent studying and their examination marks.

Assume that your history tutorial group is to have a one-hour examination in a month's time. You could ask each student to keep a record of the time spent studying history. Then get each student's examination mark. One way of doing this would be to give each student a mini-questionnaire such as the one in Figure 6.5.

This questionnaire measures the variable 'hours spent studying' by asking each student to keep a record. It assumes that students will be honest in reporting both the time spent studying and marks. You could check with the tutor to ensure that the marks were honestly reported. One problem of using questionnaires is that you depend on the honesty of the respondents.

FIGURE 6.5   A questionnaire on time spent studying

Student name (or identification number*): 2155260
I would be most grateful if you could help me with my research project. It will not take much time.

We are to have an examination on 8 May. During the month between now and then, please keep an account of the time you spend studying.

	hrs	mins			hrs	mins
April	_____			April	_____	
8	1____10____			24	_____	
9	1____10____			25	_____	
10	etc._____			26	_____	
11	_____			27	_____	
12	_____			28	_____	
13	_____			29	_____	
14	_____			30	_____	
15	_____			May	_____	
16	_____			1	_____	
17	_____			2	_____	
18	_____			3	_____	
19	_____			4	_____	
20	_____			5	_____	
21	_____			6	_____	
22	_____			7	_____	
23	_____					

Total time spent studying: 45 hrs 30 mins
After the examination place your result in this blank.
Examination result: 49%
Return the questionnaire to me.
Thank you.
Harry Doolittle
History 101
Canadian University

*Researchers sometimes assign numbers to people or to groups to preserve anonymity or to organize their data when names are not important.

Once you have collected all the questionnaires, create a form to summarize your data. In this case, you have data on two variables, 'time spent studying' and 'examination result', for each student. Using a form like the one in Table 6.4 may be useful to summarize and organize your data. It will be particularly helpful when it is time to analyze your data. The data summarization form preserves all the data required by this study for later analysis.

TABLE 6.4 A suggested data summarization form

STUDENT NAME OR NUMBER	HOURS SPENT STUDYING	EXAMINATION RESULT (%)
2155	45.5	49
2156	47.5	51
2157	48	53
etc.	etc.	etc.

Here are some helpful hints for writing questionnaires that ask the respondent questions of fact rather than questions about opinions or attitudes:

1. Clarify exactly what it is you want to know. It is also important to ask yourself why you are asking the question. How does this question relate to your hypothesis and your variables?
2. Be direct and simple when asking questions. For example, if you wish to ask some people about the number of vacations they have taken in the past two years, you could design your question in this very indirect and complex way:

> In the past 24 months, on how many occasions have you taken a leave of absence from your usual activities in your home and your place of work to take up temporary residence in another locality for the purposes of recreational activities, relief of stress, and a conscious perception of a change in environment?

This question is very comprehensive, but the basic theme of its inquiry is not directly stated or easy to understand. A simple, direct question would be much more likely to get a clear answer. For example:

> In the past two years, how many times have you taken a vacation away from your home and paid job?

3. In most research, some questions are asked in order to obtain background information. They are often referred to as 'face-sheet' questions because they often appear on the front page of questionnaires. These questions request information about such things as the respondent's age, sex, religion, marital status, education, income, and number of children. Only ask face-sheet questions that are directly related to your project.
4. Make sure that each question is clear and elicits a simple response of fact and not one of evaluation as well. Rather than asking a mother how she feels about the amount of television her child watches, a question such as 'How

many hours did your child spend watching television last night?' will provide a clear and simple factual answer.

5. Address questions to the right person. If you wish to know how many hours a worker spends doing their job in their workplace, do not ask the employer or co-workers, who might not know. Ask the worker—the person you are researching.

6. If you are asking for a response about a quantity of something, discourage the respondent from giving vague, general answers such as 'often', 'a great deal', or 'quite a lot'. Give a clear indication that the response should be in terms of your choice of variable measurement. For example:

> How much time per week do you spend watching television?
> (in hours)_____
> How often do you watch the news? (Circle your answer.)
> once a day   three times per week   once per week   never

7. Be sure that respondents are willing to answer your questions. Questions that are deeply personal, are offensively worded, or ask respondents to give secrets or unpleasant information are not likely to be answered. For example, respondents are often uncomfortable about revealing their income.

8. Avoid informal terms, informal titles, and abbreviations. The question 'Who would you vote for at the next election, the CPC or the liberal parties?' contains a set of initials, 'CPC', and an informal title, 'the liberal parties'. Don't assume that respondents are familiar with such expressions. Formal terms, formal titles, and unabbreviated names are more likely to be familiar to respondents.

9. Avoid asking questions that raise more than one issue. Take the question 'Should there be an increase in income tax, and if so, should the increase in tax revenue be spent on arts projects?' This question raises two issues: 'Should there be an increase in income tax?' and 'Should an increase in revenue be spent on arts projects?' If you wish to research two issues, then ask two separate questions, and you will collect clearer information about respondents' positions on each issue.

10. Try not to use colourful or emotional language in writing questions. Here is an example:

> Do you agree that white sugar is 'white death'? Yes/No

This is an emotionally written question and should be stated in a more balanced way that does not attempt to motivate a 'No' response. For example:

> Sugar is bad for health. Do you agree or disagree? ____

11. Do not word questions in such a way that the respondent is placed in an impossible situation—for example, 'Have you stopped beating your wife?' or 'When did you stop cheating on your exams?'

12. Examine your questions for assumptions that may be wrong. If you asked a group of schoolchildren, 'What does your father do for a living?', you would be making the assumption that each child in the group knows a person whom they think of as their father. Of course, many children grow up without knowing such a person, and others have experienced the death of their father. For them, the question would be inappropriate or hurtful.

13. It is always a good idea to test your questionnaire or interview schedule. Conduct a trial with people who are not in your sample but are like the people you plan to study. If respondents give you the wrong information or cannot answer or understand your questions, then your questions and interviewing method need refining. Ask for their comments on the relevance and coherence of each question. This will help to ensure that your questionnaire gives you the information you want. When you do the real survey, the number of questionnaires containing useless responses will be reduced.

Attitudes

The questions examined to this point have been designed to gather facts from the respondent. How much does your baby weigh today? How long have you studied? What was your result on the history examination? Questionnaires and interviews are often also used to assess the respondent's attitudes, values, beliefs, or opinions. The construction of a questionnaire to measure opinions, attitudes, beliefs, and values is much more complex than simply asking questions of fact. Consider the following hypothesis:

> Males who have gone to single-sex schools are more sexist in their attitudes than males who have attended coeducational schools.

The concepts involved in this hypothesis are:

- social development environment of school;
- sexism.

Note that the first concept emphasizes the social development aspect of the schooling situation. Students experience social development 'only among boys' or 'among boys and girls'. This is what the researchers were thinking about when they constructed the hypothesis. The concept does not emphasize the enrolment policy of the school attended, which is the most obvious essential difference between 'all boys' and 'coed' schools. The essential difference considered by the researchers was 'social environment'. The variables are:

- independent variable—school social environment (single-sex vs coeducational);
- dependent variable—sexist attitudes.

The independent variable is a categorical variable and easy to measure. Respondents' school social environment is either single-sex or coeducational.

Those who have experienced both contexts can either be put in a third category (mixed) or eliminated from the study.

One of the first questions to be included in an interview schedule or a questionnaire designed to measure this variable would be:

Have the schools you have attended from the time you began school until now been (check one):

___ a coeducational?

___ b single-sex?

___ c both (coeducational and single-sex schools)?

Now comes the more difficult part. How do you propose to measure the dependent variable—sexist attitudes? This is a very complex variable. The abstract concept 'sexism' refers to the idea that one sex is in some way inferior or superior to the other. You could not measure this variable by asking the direct, simple question 'Are you sexist?' This approach would only measure the respondent's self-perception. What is required is a series of questions or statements (called 'scales') designed to evoke reactions from the respondents that, taken together, provide an indication of the respondent's sexist attitudes. While there are other kinds of scales, the attitude scale is one of the easiest to construct and analyze.

In this case, the respondent is presented with a series of short statements and is asked to agree or disagree with each statement. The questionnaire shown in Figure 6.6 is an example.

Why is this called an attitude scale? It is a device to measure variation in an attitude. Its values range between two points, and all respondents can be placed on that scale according to their responses to the questionnaire. It is also called a Likert scale, after the person who invented it. In a Likert scale, the respondent is asked to indicate agreement or disagreement with a series of short statements on a given (usually five-point) range of responses.

How does a Likert scale work? The responses are turned into a numerical scale by assigning numerical values to each response and summing up the results. The scale can be made to run from a low number (indicating a low degree of sexism) to a high number (indicating a high degree of sexism) by assigning low numerical values to those responses indicating non-sexist responses and high values to sexist responses. In Figure 6.6, agreement with statements **a**, **b**, **d**, and **e** indicates a sexist attitude; so does disagreement with **c**. The numerical values assigned to each response in this case would be:

For **a**, **b**, **d**, **e**: SA = 5, A = 4, U = 3, D = 2, SD = 1
For **c**: SA = 1, A = 2, U = 3, D = 4, SD = 5

The highest numerical value on this scale would be 25. To get 25, a respondent would have to indicate strong agreement with items **a**, **b**, **d**, and **e** and strong disagreement with item **c**. If this scale accurately measures sexist attitudes, such a

FIGURE 6.6   A questionnaire designed to test for sexist attitudes among males

Name/identification number: _____

Date: _____

1 Have the schools you have attended since you began
   school been (check one):

   | Do not write
   | in this area
   | 1

   _____ a coeducational?

   _____ b single-sex?

   _____ c both (coeducational and single-sex schools)?

2 Please indicate your agreement or disagreement with   2
   the following statements by circling the response that
   most closely coincides with your own.
   SA = Strongly Agree; A = Agree; U = Uncertain;
   D = Disagree; SD = Strongly Disagree

   a A women would never make
      a good judge.   SA A U D SD   a

   b Women are not as good at
      sports as men.   SA A U D SD   b

   c Women should be encouraged
      to seek leadership positions.   SA A U D SD   c

   d Men should not have to wash
      dishes.   SA A U D SD   d

   e Men should be left to make
      money decisions.   SA A U D SD   e

                                              Total

person would be sexist indeed. The lowest score on this scale would be five. To
get a score of five, a respondent would have to indicate strong disagreement with
items **a**, **b**, **d**, and **e** and strong agreement with item **c**. Respondents who failed to
answer all the items would have to be eliminated from the analysis. By adding the
numerical equivalents to each response, the respondent's total score can be calculated. Each respondent will have a score between 5 and 25.

   If you were satisfied that responses to the statements you used gave an adequate
indication of whether a person held sexist attitudes, this scale would be all you
would need to test the hypothesis above. You now have a measure for each variable. The measure for the dependent variable is an attitude scale. The measure for
the independent variable is provided by a single question related to the respondent's schooling. If you were to use a data summarization sheet, it might look like
the one in Table 6.5.

TABLE 6.5   A data summarization sheet for a study of sexist attitudes among

NAME OR IDENTIFICATION NUMBER	TYPE OF SOCIAL SITUATION IN SCHOOL	SCORE ON SEXISM SCALE
David	Single sex	20
Johnny	Coed	10
etc.	etc.	etc.

Remember to ask only questions that are expected to collect data that measure variables. It may be intriguing to ask other questions, but they are not relevant to your study. For example, it may have occurred to you that other questions could be included in a study on sexism. You might have wanted to know such things as:

- Does the respondent's mother work?
- Has the respondent any sisters?
- What does the respondent's religion say about sexism?
- Have all the respondent's teachers been males or females?

While these are useful questions in themselves, because of the limitations of time and energy and the need to focus the study, the sole independent variable was the type of educational context. Questions dealing with other issues were not raised. The fact that you considered these factors potentially relevant but were not able to include them in your study should be noted in the limitations to your study.

Scales like the one above can be developed for nearly everything. Some basic rules should be followed in designing attitude scales. The following suggestions state an ideal approach and include compromises that are acceptable for student projects, which must be kept manageable so that skills can be learned:

1. The usual procedure is to begin with hundreds of items and, through testing and critical feedback, to narrow the number to between 20 and 50. Student projects should have no more than 15 items.
2. Each item should clearly state one issue. Here are some examples of what not to do. The following items have more than one key element:
   - Women are smarter and better behaved than men.
   - Men should not do the dishes, and women should not do car maintenance.
   - Men are stronger, but women are more spiritual.
   It would be much better if each item were split:
   - Women are smarter than men.
   - Women are better behaved than men.
   - Women are better at washing dishes.
   - Men are better at doing car maintenance.
   - Men are stronger than women.
   - Women are more spiritual than men.

3. For a group of items to constitute a scale, each item must be related to a single theme. Each item should pick up a different aspect of the theme. For example, the above items all relate to the theme of the respective abilities of males and females. It would add a totally different dimension to the scale to add items on respective social roles.

4. The range of response categories must be designed very carefully. They must be in one dimension (e.g., 'agreement') and provide responses across the whole range of the dimension. Although research is done using a wide variety of response categories, several conventions have emerged. The five-point Likert-type response category is the most frequently used. These response categories are strongly agree, agree, undecided, disagree, and strongly disagree.

5. The more specific the response categories, the more accurate and precise the information gathered will be. For example:

Canada should support the creation of more nuclear power plants.
SA   A   U   D   SD

How often do you go to church?
Never   Yearly   Monthly   Weekly   Daily

How long did you study for this quiz?
Two hours   One hour   Half-hour   Quarter-hour   Not at all

Next are examples of unspecific response categories. These are examples of what not to do.

Canada should support the building of additional nuclear power plants.
Agree   Maybe   Perhaps   Not sure   Possibly not

Immigrants should be allowed to express their unique cultures.
In principle   Sometimes   Only on Sundays   As long as no one is offended

Here is a method for constructing a list of items. First, select and list a large number of items arbitrarily. Include any items that you believe to be even partially relevant to your variables. Then, begin sifting through the list by eliminating or rewriting items and retaining those that you believe to be relevant. Sift through the list with friends or other students. Also, give the whole list to a group of people similar to those for whom the questionnaire or interview is being designed. Talk to them afterwards about what you are trying to measure. They may have useful suggestions.

Try the following exercise to gain more experience in constructing a scale to measure an attitude. Suppose that you have been asked to do a study related to the creation of additional nuclear power plants. Your dependent variable is 'attitude towards nuclear power plants'. Assignment: construct a five-item scale measuring attitude towards additional nuclear power plants. Remember that you must not only write the items but also decide what attitude dimension to measure and the range of responses to offer. Then you will be able to specify the highest and lowest possible scores. Now ask yourself:

1. How did I measure my dependent variable? How did I measure attitude towards the building of nuclear power plants? List the items.
2. What range of responses do I want to offer?
   a. Simple agree/disagree or a broader range?
   b. Will I include a neutral position, or will I force the respondent to make a choice?
3. Should the statements be collectively designed so that 'agreement' responses indicate an anti–nuclear power plant attitude or a pro–nuclear power plant attitude? Alternatively, should the statements be collectively designed so that agreement indicates an anti–nuclear power plant attitude for some and a pro–nuclear power plant attitude for others? Compare the following examples:

   a. There is no need for Canada to invest in new nuclear power plants.
      SA   A   U   D   SD

   b. Canadians should not mine uranium.
      SA   A   U   D   SD

   c. Nuclear-powered electricity should be used as an alternative to burning coal.
      SA   A   U   D   SD

   d. Development of nuclear power plants is a good public investment.
      SA   A   U   D   SD

   Agreement with **a** and **b** would be taken to indicate an 'anti–nuclear power plant' response. However, agreement with **c** and **d** would indicate a pro–nuclear power plant response. It is usually better to vary the response pattern in this way. This prevents people from getting into the habit of checking the same column. It helps to keep respondents awake and thinking.
4. What is the highest possible score on the scale constructed from the items you listed for question 1? What is the lowest? This will depend on the number of items you included and the number of response categories you used. If you had five items and five response categories (SA/A/U/D/SD), then the highest possible score would be 25, and the lowest would be five.

Here is how the highest and lowest possible scores are calculated for the scale formed by responses to the four items relating to nuclear power plant creation listed in question 3.

Say that you wanted your scale values to run from high (indicating strong pro–nuclear electricity attitudes) to low (indicating low pro–nuclear electricity attitudes). In this case, the numerical values assigned to each response would be as follows:

For **a** and **b**

SA	A	U	D	SD
1	2	3	4	5

For **c** and **d**

SA	A	U	D	SD
5	4	3	2	1

The reason for this is that agreement with **a** and **b** indicates an anti–nuclear power plant position. When agreement indicates the reverse position (pro–nuclear power plant, as in **c** and **d**), the numerical values assigned to the response categories are reversed. In this case, the highest possible score would be given to the person who made which responses? What is the highest possible score? What is the lowest?

A scale is a set of values among which respondents can be positioned on the basis of their response to items on a questionnaire or an interview schedule. A scale is a device for measuring variation in a person's commitment to an attitude or the strength with which an attitude is held. Although there are many complicated issues in the measurement of attitudes, values, and beliefs, you should now be familiar with the basic logic.

There is one more form of questionnaire to be considered. This involves ranking options. Ranking is often used in research into values and preferences. Canadian voters are asked to rank candidates. Respondents can be asked to rank options, candidates, preferences, commodities, or values. Ranking forces respondents to express the relative strength of their attitude to all the options. It is important that all the options be of the same kind. Here is an example:

Rank the following values from highest (1) to lowest (7) in terms of their importance to you:

loyalty	_____	independence	_____
excitement	_____	equality	_____
peace	_____	creativity	_____
security	_____		

Here is another example:

Rank the following qualities from most important (1) to least important (8) in terms of how you would assess a potential marriage partner:

_____	appearance	_____	sensitivity
_____	honesty	_____	ability to earn money
_____	integrity	_____	religiosity
_____	sense of humour	_____	flexibility

Respondents, or groups of respondents, can be compared in terms of the way they ranked options. For example, you might find that a group of girls on average ranked sensitivity higher than appearance, while a group of boys on average ranked sense of humour above flexibility. Ranking options provides another way of measuring respondents' values and preferences.

The questionnaire and the interview schedule are data-gathering techniques by which a researcher can measure the variables being studied. Questions are asked in order to gain information. This information can be factual: 'How did you vote?', 'How old are you?', 'How much does your baby weigh?' Or questions may be asked in order to determine respondents' attitudes, beliefs, or values: 'Would you support Canada becoming a republic?', 'Do you believe in heaven?', 'What is the most important thing in a relationship?'

EXAMINING RECORDS AND PUBLICATIONS TO MEASURE VARIABLES

The third common data-gathering technique is to measure variables by using the information kept in records or official reports of organizations, government agencies, or persons. Possibly the most familiar example of this kind of data is the Census of Canada. Government departments keep records of marriages, divorces, deaths, and financial transactions. Organizations keep records. Hospitals have records of admissions, discharges, and types of surgery performed. Some churches retain documents about members, marriages, baptisms, and amounts of money received and paid. Schools archive information about student numbers, student–teacher ratios, and subjects taught.

The basic problem with using records to gather data is gaining access. Census material is available from Statistics Canada and in many libraries and on the Internet. The yearbooks or annual reports of many organizations often give information on various aspects of the organization. However, sometimes researchers do not know the location or nature of records—whether they are computer files, bound annual reports, or uncollated documents in filing cabinets. There are often occasions when a researcher does not know whether records are available or even exist. Finding and gaining permission to access records can take a great deal of time.

The second problem is that the records often do not contain the exact information you want. They may be for the province of Alberta when you are interested in the city of Edmonton. Or they may be for the city of Toronto, and you want only the records for the Jane and Finch neighbourhood. Information may be collected in one way in 1996, in another in 2000, and in yet another in 2006, making comparison difficult.

If you are interested in such information as trends in divorce, birthrate, population growth, the proportion of people of a certain age in the population, average age at first marriage, average age at divorce, the number of children affected by divorce in a given year, the incidence of teenage pregnancy, or the percentage of weddings performed by civil celebrants, you can find answers in documents available from Statistics Canada.

If you attend a post-secondary institution, these kinds of documents will be available to you in or through your library, or you can make direct inquiries to Statistics Canada, which has a website and publishes census data on the Internet, by CD-ROM, and on paper.

Content analysis

Content analysis is a different way to examine records, documents, and publications. It is very like an observation study. In a content analysis, a checklist is developed to count how frequently certain ideas, words, phrases, images, or scenes appear. However, in a content analysis, what is being observed is a text, a film, or a radio or television program.

Recently, some of our students conducted a study of the perception of the aged in our society. This involved the researchers watching a night's television to observe the roles played by the elderly in television commercials. Another approach required that the researchers deduce the needs of the elderly on the basis of advertisements aimed at the elderly.

The procedure for a content analysis of a television or radio program follows the same lines as an observation study. Recording the program allows the researcher to go back over the material several times to complete and check the accuracy of the content analysis. It provides an opportunity for several people to do a content analysis of the same material, and it helps them to examine the material to see what things can be observed and counted. The steps for preparing a content analysis of television or radio material are as follows:

1. Clarify and narrow your hypothesis or research objective. What are the concepts involved?
2. Identify variables related to the concepts under study. This may involve watching some television programs or listening to radio programs to become familiar with what there is to be observed.
3. Devise a way to measure the variables. Develop a checklist to count how often the things you have selected to observe appear—for example, the number of advertisements featuring the elderly or the number of advertisements in which women play roles of authority.
4. Decide what programs to examine. Decide whether your unit of analysis is a time period (e.g., two hours of Wednesday-night prime-time television) or a specific program, or a number of advertisements over a period of time (e.g., the first 10 advertisements screened after 6 pm on channel 9 on Friday nights).
5. Devise a data summarization sheet.
6. Collect your data by doing the observations you propose.
7. Summarize the results on the data summarization form.

The content analysis of published material

Published material is a storehouse of material for content analysis. Magazines, periodicals, books, novels, and textbooks—all can be subjected to content analysis. The logic of research using content analysis of published material is the same as the logic of other kinds of research. The first step is to clarify your hypothesis or research objective. Once the concepts under study have been identified, variables that are related to the concepts can be selected. Then the problem of how to measure and record variation in the variables can be tackled. Once measurement problems are settled, the units of measure in which to report findings can be decided upon. Remember this flow:

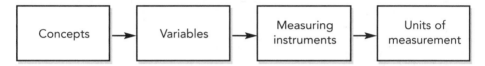

This same flow of issues occurs in designing research using the content analysis of written material. Let us assume that you are interested in the area of sex-role stereotyping. You are interested in the origin of sex-role stereotypes—where do they come from? One possible source would be children's books. This might lead you to ask whether there has been a change in the amount of sex-role stereotyping in children's books. How could you measure change in the amount of sex-role stereotyping over a number of years?

One possible way would be to examine the reading material used to teach reading to Grade 1 students. What are Grade 1 children reading today compared to 20 years ago? To do this, you need access to the material used 20 years ago and the material used now. Next, you need to develop a set of indicators of role stereotyping. What roles do girls and boys play? What roles do men and women play? What activities characterize each sex? Do the illustrations promote sex-role stereotyping? Once you have begun to identify countable features, you can devise a checklist on sex-role stereotyping in Grade 1 books.

Or you might devise a set of questions like the ones in Figure 6.7.

In this way, a scale of sex role stereotyping in literature can be developed. By applying it to literature from different times, changes can be observed and systematic comparisons made.

Here is an example of research using content analysis of published material. Since the Second World War, an increasing proportion of Canadian married women have been employed. Has this movement into paid work outside the home had an impact on the publications directed at women? The hypothesis could be this:

As the proportion of women who are employed outside the home increases, there will be an increase in the attention paid to working women in the publications aimed at women.

FIGURE 6.7 A content analysis questionnaire

	Check the appropriate column				
	Always	In over half the stories	Half and half	In less than half the stories	Never
1 Are boys shown to dominate girls?					
2 Are girls shown to win against boys?					
3 Is unisex clothing used?					
4 Are women shown in traditionally male roles (e.g., a female physician or a female priest)?					
5 Does a male ask a female for help or directions or information?					
6 Are females shown to be helpless?					

This can be diagrammed as follows:

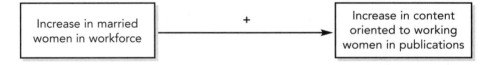

Since we know that there has been an increase in the proportion of married women who are employed, we only need to find variables to provide an indication of change in the dependent concept—change in content of material published for women. Several approaches are possible.

First, the number of magazines published for women may have changed between 1945 and the present. Are there more or fewer now? Are some of the new ones directed mainly at employed married women? You might gain help from your library on the number and kind of women's magazines that have come and gone since 1945.

A second approach would be to select one title that has been published continuously through this time. For example, *Chatelaine* and *Vogue* have been published continuously. It would be interesting to see whether the number of articles that appeal to working women, or address the problems faced by working women, has changed. Here you must decide what to count. Do you count articles or the number of pages? Do you take just one issue or an entire year of issues? It would be better to select more than one issue in each year in case the issue you chose for a given year is atypical. The results would be reported as the number of articles or pages per year appealing to working women.

A third approach would be to see whether the magazine's attitude to the idea of married women working has changed. It is possible that over the years, *Chatelaine* has devoted roughly the same number of articles or pages or proportion of space to the subject of employed married women but that its attitude has shifted from disapproval to approval. This would require not only counting articles or pages devoted to the subject but deciding whether each was favourable, unfavourable, or neutral. Your record of research might look like Figure 6.8.

Let us say that 12 issues for each of the years 1945 and 2006 were read. There would be 24 record sheets, one for each issue. The analysis would be by year.

The classification of the content of the articles as favourable, unfavourable, or neutral would proceed on similar lines. Additional categories might need to be introduced after all the material has been read.

Content analysis can be fun. Popular music, movies, and magazines are interesting to analyze.

FIGURE 6.8 A record sheet for a content analysis of articles dealing with employed married women

Magazine: _____   Issue: _____

Year: _____   Total no. of pages: _____

Total no. of articles: _____

Title of article	Number of pages	Orientation expressed
Total no. of articles	Total no. of pages	

Before you begin content analysis, refer to the following checklist:

1. Clarify the hypothesis. What concepts are involved?
2. What variables can be used to indicate changes in or differences between the concepts?
3. How can this variable be measured using content analysis? What is to be counted—pages, words, articles, pictures, or something else? Devise a record sheet for recording your data.
4. In what units are the results to be reported—pages per issue, words per year, articles per issue, or something else? Devise a data summary sheet for reporting your data (for example, Table 6.6).

TABLE 6.6   A data summarization sheet for content analysis

	1945	2006
Total pages		
Number of pages devoted to employed married women		
Proportion of total pages devoted to employed married women		
Total number of articles		
Number of articles devoted to employed married women		
Proportion of articles devoted to employed married women		

VALIDITY

At the end of Chapter 5, the problem of validity was discussed. This is concerned with how accurately a variable fits a concept. For example, is 'absence of disease' a valid indicator of health? Is a history test a valid way to test a student's grasp of historical material? Most variables can be questioned in one way or another.

The problem of validity is most acute in the construction of questionnaires or interview schedules to 'measure' a person's attitudes, beliefs, or values. For example, it is necessary to ask whether the items used to measure variation in a person's attitudes to the building of additional nuclear power plants, developed earlier in this chapter, are valid. On reflection, one of the items does not deal with nuclear power plants but with the mining of uranium. It is quite possible for someone who is very much against nuclear power plants to favour the peaceful use of nuclear material in other ways, such as medical diagnostics. This item does not focus clearly on the variable to be measured. Therefore, it lacks validity.

It is important to be aware of the problems of validity. In professional research, a great deal of time and effort is spent ensuring validity. As a student, there are things that you can do too. In addition to being very careful in your construction of measuring devices, record sheets, questionnaires, and checklists, you can ask your friends and your professor to comment on your measures. This may help to increase their validity. Moreover, you can pre-test scales using individuals known to exhibit extremes of the dimensions you are trying to measure. For example, what would it mean for the validity of your scale if someone whom you knew to be very sexist got a low score on a sexism scale that you had devised? Clearly, you would have to rework your scale! It is very important to pre-test your research instrument to ensure that it is working properly before actually doing your research.

RELIABILITY

The question of reliability is different from the question of validity. When someone asks whether a measure is reliable, they are asking whether different researchers using the same measuring device would get the same results when measuring the same event. For example, will a group of 10 students who weigh the same baby, one after another, record the same weight? Is a baby-weighing scale reliable? This may depend on how difficult it is to hold the baby still, which is relevant to the reliability of a weighing scale. The basic question is whether the measurement device employed provides the same results when repeated. This is called test-retest reliability.

The reliability of observation techniques is often questioned. Will a group of observers report the same observations? This is also a problem in content analysis. Will several people agree that article X dealt with a topic related to the needs of working married women? Will they agree that it recognizes the right of married women to work? The more agreement there is in coding observations on content analysis, the more reliable the instrument is.

A feature of recorded or published materials that facilitates the testing of their reliability is that others can review the exact material. When there are differences, it is possible to sort them out with those who are evaluating the material. Was the daughter's comment ignored, or was it ridiculed? If you are unsure, you can go back to that section of the tape and check. The challenge to the reliability of a measure is that different researchers using the same measure may record different results.

Questions of reliability refer to problems in the accuracy of the measuring device. Questions of validity refer to the appropriateness of the measuring device. It is important for you to be aware of both these problems. It is appropriate to include questions about validity and reliability in any discussion of the limitations of your research.

SUMMARY

Once you have clarified your hypothesis and selected variables for study, the issue of measurement must be considered. Three basic techniques for measuring variables have been discussed: observation techniques, questionnaires or interview schedules, and content analysis. The importance of developing systematic data-recording forms and data summarization forms has been emphasized. The fact that you collect data to measure variables in a hypothesis is the major emphasis of this chapter. Data are gathered to measure variables you have clarified beforehand.

QUESTIONS FOR REVIEW

1. What are the basic steps in preparing to do research involving observation as a data-gathering technique?
2. What is the purpose of a checklist for observation?
3. What is the purpose of a data summarization sheet?
4. What are the basic steps in preparing research involving the use of a questionnaire or interview schedule?
5. What is the difference between an interview schedule and a questionnaire?
6. How do you determine the highest and lowest possible scores on a scale framed by responses to items designed to measure a respondent's attitudes, values, or beliefs?
7. What does it mean to reverse the polarity of response for an item? What impact does this have on the way the responses are scored for scale construction?
8. What are the steps involved in preparing to do research involving the use of content analysis?
9. What is the problem of validity?
10. What is the problem of reliability?

Suggestions for further reading

Babbie, E.R. 2003. *The Practice of Social Research*. 10th edn, chapter 5. London: Wadsworth.

Bryman, A., and J.J. Teevan. 2005. *Social Research Methods*. Canadian edn, chapter 2. Don Mills, ON: Oxford University Press.

de Vaus, D.A. 2002. *Surveys in Social Research*. 5th edn, chapters 4, 6, 7. St Leonards, NSW: Allen and Unwin.

Foddy, William. 1993. *Constructing Questions for Interviews and Questionnaires: Theory and Practice in Social Research*. Cambridge: Cambridge University Press.

Judd, C.M., E.R. Smith, and L.H. Kidder. 1991. *Research Methods in Social Relations*, chapters 3, 7, 10. Fort Worth, TX: Holt, Rinehart and Winston.

Kumar, Ranjit. 1999. *Research Methodology: A Step by Step Guide for Beginners*, chapters 9–11. London: Sage.

Minichiello, Victor, Rosalie Aroni, Eric Timewell, and Loris Alexander. 1995. *In-Depth Interviewing: Principles, Techniques, Analysis*. 2nd edn, chapters 2, 4, 6. Melbourne: Longman Cheshire.

Wallace, W. 1971. *The Logic of Science in Sociology*, chapter 2. Chicago: Aldine.

Selecting a Research Design

QUALITATIVE OR QUANTITATIVE?
WHICH APPROACH SHOULD YOU USE?

Even the most accomplished researcher must decide what method to use. Good researchers will utilize the approach that best fits the research question. Some research questions are best answered by gathering rich, deep, descriptive data from a small number of participants. Other research questions are more amenable to more large-scale, numerical data gathered from a larger number of participants. The first step for students is to decide what kind of data is needed to answer the research question. This chapter provides researchers with the basic information necessary to make that decision by providing an overview of selected modes of data collection. There are many other ways to collect data. Some of the most popular methods are described here.

Qualitative research is intended to gather a great deal of information on a very small number of individuals or groups with specific characteristics. Research questions best answered using qualitative research are based on previous observations and research on a particular phenomenon but require deeper exploration of the issue. Suppose that you have been assigned a research project to understand why international students decide to remain in Canada after they graduate from university. We know that many international students return home after they graduate, but others wish to stay in Canada. We already know how many stay in the country, since we can gather these figures from Citizenship and Immigration Canada, but we know very little about their decision-making processes. We do not have a hypothesis, since the existing research does not deal with the motives of international students for remaining in Canada. We do, however, have some hunches, based on our knowledge of the decision-making processes made by other immigrants coming to Canada. Many wish to stay because they feel they have better job prospects or may have a better standard of living in Canada. Others may marry a Canadian or have children enrolled in school here. Still others may have experienced changes in their family, or the political situation in their home country may have changed since they arrived in Canada. As researchers, we want to figure out why they stay, but we do not want to prejudice their ideas by asking them a series of directed questions. This is an example of a research project that would be amenable to a qualitative data collection strategy.

What are the characteristics of qualitative research? For one thing, the research question is larger, more complex, and more explanatory in nature than questions used in quantitative research (see below). It may have the word 'why' or 'how' in it. It is not intended to test relationships between a small number of independent variables. Instead, it is supposed to contextualize a situation or tell a story about the topic. The idea is to provide a holistic account of a phenomenon or social problem.

A classic example in sociology would be Elliot Liebow's *Tally's Corner*. Liebow was interested in understanding how poverty was experienced by African-American men during the 1960s. Remember, there was much discrimination against the African-American community at that time. In fact, Liebow conducted his research at the height of the American civil rights movement. At the time, little was known about the African-American community in the US. For this reason, Liebow had no preconceived ideas when he began his study. His research question was broad, intending to understand the lived experiences of homeless African-American men. In the course of his research, Liebow got to know the men living in a Washington DC ghetto. He even assisted in the court case of one of the men! There was no way that Liebow could predict in advance of conducting his research the kinds of questions he would ask the men, the kinds of data he would need to understand the situation faced by the men at Tally's corner, nor the kinds of situations he would need to observe to adequately understand the intersection of poverty and race in 1960s America. In the course of conducting his research, interviewing the men about their daily activities and observing their daily lives, he was able to produce an account that was full of detail, with the rich information needed to fully understand what it was like to live as an impoverished African-American man at that time. Even though it was conducted in the 1960s, this research remains relevant today. Students wishing to know more about poverty and racism can still learn a great deal about this phenomenon by reading Liebow's book.

In contrast to the rich detail provided by qualitative research, quantitative research is used to test relationships between two variables. This relationship is formulated by devising a hypothesis. A hypothesis states that a relationship exists between two or more concepts. In a research project, the hypothesis is the reference point on which researchers focus their activity. The role of a research objective is the same. Researchers should keep a statement of their hypothesis or research objective visible as a constant reminder of their specific task.

How does the hypothesis guide the research? The hypothesis claims that there is a relationship between concepts X and Y. Research is undertaken to determine whether there is evidence to support this claim. In order to carry out the research, two general tasks must be done. First, the concepts in the hypothesis must be defined in such a way that they can be measured. In Chapters 5 and 6, we learned how to select and measure variables that relate to concepts. However, research requires more than measuring the concepts in a hypothesis.

The second task is to find evidence that the relationship stated in the hypothesis actually exists. Measuring X and Y is one thing. Finding evidence that X and Y are related is another. While the issues concerning measurement of concepts are narrowed by the operational definitions, the existence of a relationship between X and Y is assessed by the research design.

Let us look at the diagram of a hypothesis again:

This hypothesis states that a change in X will produce a change in Y and that the nature of the relationship between X and Y is such that an increase in X will produce an increase in Y. One of the hypotheses we have been using as an example states:

More study leads to increased academic performance.

The conceptual form of this hypothesis was diagrammed:

A number of variables for each of the concepts were identified (if you cannot remember, turn back to Chapter 5). The selected variables were 'number of hours spent studying' for the concept 'study' and 'exam results' for the concept 'academic performance'. The hypothesis can be restated in its variable form as follows:

In Chapter 6, we devised measures for each variable. Students were asked to keep a record of the time they spent studying and to state their result for the history exam. The operational definition of the hypothesis—the statement of the hypothesis as a relationship between measures—would be as follows:

You may well be thinking, 'Surely that is enough!' But it is not. You do not have a measurement of the relationship between study and academic performance. How do you know that, generally speaking, it was the amount of study that produced the examination result? How do you know that a change in the independent variable produced a change in the dependent variable?

What kinds of relationships can there be among variables? There are three basic types:

1. The variables are causally related—that is, a change in one variable will produce a change in the other variable.
2. The variables are only associated—that is, they change together, but this happens through no perceived causal relationship and, in the absence of contrary evidence, could be a coincidence.
3. The variables are neither causally related nor associated.

It is relatively easy to determine whether two variables are associated. It is more difficult to determine that X (independent variable) causes Y (dependent variable). In order to establish that two variables are causally related, it is necessary to show that:

1. X and Y are associated.
2. Changes in the dependent variable, Y, always occur after changes in the independent variable, X.
3. All other variables that might produce changes in Y are 'controlled'—that is, their possible effects on Y are accounted for.

As we shall see, the experimental research design is the only design truly adequate for testing a causal hypothesis. Given that an experimental design is not always possible, practical, or permissible, other designs are used to approximate an experimental design or to provide some information relevant to the test of a causal hypothesis.

Choosing a research design is one of the most important and difficult parts of doing empirical research. For example, you may feel certain that an increase in study will produce an increase in academic performance. But how do you prove that these concepts are related in this way? How do you design your research to answer this question?

HOW DO YOU CHOOSE A RESEARCH DESIGN?

Research designs should be selected so that the collection strategies provide the data that would best answer the research question. Hence, one of the first considerations in selecting a research design is 'What kind of question is being asked?' Table 7.1 is a summary table of research designs and the questions each asks. Review it from time to time as we go on to describe the various methods.

TABLE 7.1   The five basic types of research design

TYPE OF DESIGN			QUESTION ASKED
1 Simple case study			
	(A)		What is happening?
2 Longitudinal study			
	(A)	(A)	Has there been a change in A?
	Time 1	Time 2	
3 Comparison study			
	(A)		Are A and B different?
	(B)		
4 Longitudinal comparison study			
	(A)	(A)	Are A and B different through time?
	(B)	(B)	
	Time 1	Time 2	
5 Experiment			
Experimental group	(A)	↓ (A)	Is the difference between A and B due to a change (↓) in the independent variable?
Control group	(B)	(B)	
	Time 1	Time 2	

If the hypothesis you are testing asks, 'Does a change in the independent variable produce a change in the dependent variable?', then an experimental design is required. However, an experiment is not always possible. What can be done then? Use one of the other research designs, and mention in the limitations section of your research report that it is not the ideal design. Make sure that you draw only such conclusions as your data and research design permit.

Once you have formulated your hypothesis or articulated the aspects of the problem you are researching, the next step is to decide how you will collect your data. As Table 7.1 indicates, there are five basic types of research design. Each type is appropriate for a different general kind of research question or problem, and the type you select depends on your hypothesis or research objective. In this chapter, we will examine the five types of research design by using each to examine the relationship between study and academic performance. Although one design may be more desirable than another, each can make a contribution to our knowledge about the relationship.

One way to become familiar with the logic of research design is to understand that each type of research design asks a different kind of question or confronts a different type of research problem. Thus, the five basic types of research design can be grouped according to five different sets of questions:

1. **The case study**
   What is going on?
   Is there a relationship between variables X and Y in entity A? (An 'entity' is a group, social situation, text, or other focus of research.)
2. **The longitudinal study**
   Has there been a change?
   Is the relationship between variables X and Y in entity A the same or different at time 1 and time 2?
3. **The comparison study**
   Is Group A different from Group B?
   Is the relationship between variables X and Y the same in entities A and B?
4. **The longitudinal comparison study**
   Has there been a difference between Group A and Group B over time?
   Has there been a change over time in the relationship between X and Y in entity A compared to entity B?
5. **The experiment**
   Why are Groups A and B different?
   Is the difference in Y (dependent variable) between Group A and Group B due to a change in X (the independent variable)?

We will develop each design in detail so that you can see the value and limitations of each.

1. THE CASE STUDY

The case study can answer the question 'What is going on?' The key element of the case study design is that it focuses on a single 'case' or 'entity', which might be one person, one group, one classroom, one town, or a single nation. The single case or entity is studied for a period of time and the results recorded. The aim of the case study is to find out whether there is a relationship between variables X and Y within the entity.

People who discuss research design have given the term 'case study' several meanings. Some limit the use of the term to an exploratory study in which no hypothesis is tested. For example, you might be interested in the factors a particular group of families considers when planning meals. You simply want to know what is 'going on' inside the entity (i.e., the group of families being studied). You are not testing a hypothesis. You are not comparing one group of families to another.

Researchers may also carry out exploratory case studies to ascertain relevant variables for further research. Such studies might also be done to formulate hypotheses for later study. An exploratory case study takes a very broad look at the phenomenon being investigated. The purpose is to gather information to build a description of what is 'going on'.

Other researchers use case studies to make initial tests of hypotheses. It is often useful to check whether two variables show an association before doing more rigorous testing. The sort of hypothesis that can be tested by a case study could take this form: 'There is an association between variables X and Y.' Case studies are not usually appropriate for testing causal relationships. This is because case studies usually bring the researcher into environments where several variables are operating and the case study design is not structured to isolate the influence of any individual variable.

Our example concerns the relationship between study and academic performance. What can a case study tell us? It can test for an association between the variables, 'hours of study' and 'exam marks', within the case being studied. Given the results, we can decide whether a more complicated test for a causal relationship between the variables is likely to show a causal relationship.

A case study designed to discover whether there is any relationship between study and academic performance might take this form. The questionnaire on time spent studying, developed in the last chapter, would be given to a specific history class who are the 'case' being studied. The measurement is carried out once. The results are assessed once for one class and one examination. The data would then be analyzed. While we will deal with data analysis in detail later, let's say that you discovered that the amount of study time was positively associated with the marks achieved. Your graph might have looked like Figure 7.1.

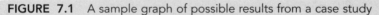

FIGURE 7.1   A sample graph of possible results from a case study

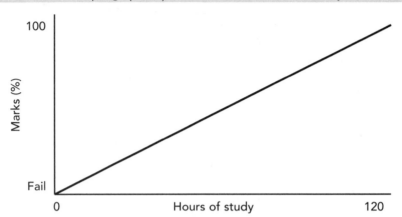

What would your graph have looked like if you had found that the amount of time spent studying related negatively to the marks achieved? What could you have concluded from this study if you had done it as described and obtained results like those in Figure 7.1? You could conclude that in the group of students examined, there was a positive relationship between amount of study and academic perform-ance as measured by the instrument devised. You could not conclude that greater amounts of study caused higher marks. All you know is that in one case (i.e., the class studied), at one point in time, the hypothesis was supported (by an observed association). This observation is very interesting, but it may well have occurred by chance. Also, you cannot rule out alternative explanations. For example, the stu-dents who studied longer might also have sat at the front of the room and paid bet-ter attention. What caused the differences in result—study or attention?

You might be prompted by your curiosity to test other factors or to compare test results from other groups of students. Knowing what happened in one case may prompt you to try other cases. Or it might persuade you to test whether it really was the amount of time spent studying that produced the results (by repeating your research with an experimental design).

Consider now the following example. You are an occupational health and safety (OH&S) officer at a large worksite. You are concerned that the nutritional status of the company's workers may affect the frequency of injuries on the job. You arrange for a guest speaker to talk to groups of workers during working hours about nutri-tion. You hope that this will motivate the workers to eat healthier food. You have also decided that you want to evaluate the effectiveness of the speech. How can you do so? What can a case study tell you? A case study can tell you 'what is going on'—whether the speech had the desired effect. You have the impression that the speech has not had the desired effect and that workers are continuing to choose less nutritious food. But you have no evidence to support that belief. You can check this impression by doing a case study.

Your research objective for a case study related to the issue of food selection might be:

To discover what snack food choices a particular group of workers makes at the company cafeteria.

To measure this concept, variables will have to be selected and a measuring instrument devised. You talk with the manager of the cafeteria. She agrees to let you observe the selections made at the cafeteria. You decide to devise a checklist with which to record your observation of the food selections made by a particular group of workers—for example, machine operators on A-shift. It might look like the chart in Table 7.2.

TABLE 7.2 A checklist for observing the snack choices of machine operators on A-shift

JUNK FOOD	FRUIT	OTHER

In this case study, you would be recording the total choices for the whole shift. The way you gather your data depends on whether you are asking about individual selections or the pattern for the group. Here our interest is the pattern of snack decisions for all machine operators on A-shift. Tables 7.3 and 7.4 present some hypothetical results. What would you conclude from each?

TABLE 7.3 A table of hypothetical results from a case study of the snacks selected by machine operators on A-shift

	JUNK FOOD	FRUIT	OTHER	TOTAL
Number of selections	24	3	3	30

Table 7.3 gives the numbers of selections made in each category. The workers appear to select less nutritious foods, such as junk foods, more often than nutritious items, such as fruit. Table 7.4 presents the same findings as percentages. The use of percentages helps in making comparisons among groups of different size. It is also a very common way of showing the pattern of a variable for a group within a case study.

TABLE 7.4 Percentage of snacks selected by a class of machine operators on A-shift

	JUNK FOOD	FRUIT	OTHER
Percentage of selections	80	10	10

In a case study, you could collect data showing the distribution of worker food selections at the cafeteria. What proportion of the selections were nutritious foods, such as fruit, or non-nutritious foods, such as junk food? There would be little point in pursuing a major study if in this simple case study you discovered that, contrary to your impression, most workers selected fruit for their snacks.

The case study is the basic building block of research design. In a case study, a variable or set of variables is measured for one entity at one point in time. The other research designs involve the study of more than one entity or compare studies of the same entity at different points in time. In a sense, all other research designs facilitate hypothesis-testing by comparing additional case studies designed to isolate the influences on the variables under study.

2. THE LONGITUDINAL STUDY

The longitudinal research design involves two or more case studies of the same entity with some time between the studies. The basic question posed by a longitudinal study is 'Has there been any change over a period of time?'

The longitudinal research design tests for an association between two variables in the same entity at different points in time. It asks, 'Has there been any change in the level of association between the variables over a period of time in entity A?' The answer is 'yes' or 'no'. If the answer is 'yes', the research design should also indicate the nature or size of the change. Given that longitudinal studies are really comparisons of case studies, they cannot identify and isolate the causes of changes in associations. The longitudinal design can be diagrammed as follows:

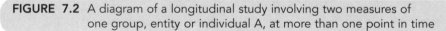

FIGURE 7.2 A diagram of a longitudinal study involving two measures of one group, entity or individual A, at more than one point in time

Time 1   Time 2

To do a longitudinal study you:

1. select variables relevant to the concepts under study;
2. devise a way of measuring those variables;

3. develop a data-recording device;
4. measure the same variables in the same way in one group (or for one person) at two or more times.

Longitudinal research designs are often employed in analyses of national data. You may hypothesize that increased female participation in the workforce leads to a general increase in the age of their youngest child. A possible way of investigating this would be to analyze national statistics as measures for the variables 'female workforce participation' and 'age of youngest child' at a number of points in time.

Table 7.5 compares the relationship at seven points in time from 1997 to 2003. As can be seen, the two variables are associated because measures (national statistics) for both variables have risen throughout the period under study. Therefore, the hypothesis is supported by the research.

You could also do a longitudinal study of the population growth rate of your neighbourhood and its relationship to the number of people actively participating in a religion in your neighbourhood for the past 10 years. Think of a longitudinal study you could do using the position of your favourite football team at the end of each of the past 10 seasons as a dependent variable.

Another common form of the longitudinal study is the 'before and after' study. Some professors give 'before and after' tests to see whether their lessons have had

TABLE 7.5 Employment of mothers by family status and age of youngest child, 1997–2003

	YOUNGEST CHILD UNDER AGE 3		WORKFORCE PARTICIPATION OF WOMEN BY YEAR (%)
	FEMALE LONE PARENTS (%)	WOMEN WITH PARTNERS (%)	
1997	35.5	62.1	57.8
1998	33.1	63.2	58.4
1999	37.6	63.1	58.9
2000	42.3	62.9	59.5
2001	46.0	63.6	59.7
2002	46.7	64.1	60.9
2003	46.9	64.9	61.9

Sources: Baker, M. 2005. *Families: Changing Trends in Canada.* Toronto: McGraw-Hill Ryerson. Statistics Canada. 2007. *Women in Non-standard Jobs: The Public Policy Challenge.* http://www.swc-cfc.gc.ca/pubs/pubspr/0662334809/200303_0662334809_13_e.html. Accessed on 27 June 2007. Statistics Canada. 2007. *Labour Force Participation Rates by Sex and Age Group.* http://www40.statcan.ca/l01/cst01/labor05.htm. Accessed on 27 June 2007.

any effect on their students' knowledge. Studies of the impact of diet on physical characteristics frequently use a 'before and after' longitudinal research design: 'He weighed 96 kg before following our strict diet and exercise regime, and three months later he weighed 80 kg.'

Taking our example of the relationship between study and academic perform-ance, we can ask, 'What additional information would a longitudinal study pro-vide?' In the section on the case study, we suggested that the result of the research was that amount of time spent studying and the mark on a history test were posi-tively related. The more time a student spent studying, the better that student's mark was. One possible longitudinal study would be to repeat the same case study for the next history test to see whether the relationship continued to hold. This would help to find out whether the result in the first study had been a fluke. If the result occurred again, our confidence in the finding and in the worth of the hypothesis would increase.

The study of workers' snack selections at the cafeteria lends itself to a 'before and after'-style longitudinal research design. Let us assume that when the OH&S officer conducted the case study, it was discovered that 70 per cent of the workers' choices were for junk food and only 10 per cent were for nutritious foods such as fruit. The OH&S officer decided to invite a guest speaker to speak to the machine operators on A-shift about nutrition. After this had taken place, the initial research would be repeated to see whether there were changes in workers' food selections.

What could the OH&S officer conclude if the results looked like those in Table 7.6? Would it be valid to conclude that the talk was a success? Could the OH&S offi-cer conclude that as a result of the talk there had been a shift in workers' snack selections towards more nutritious food?

TABLE 7.6 Hypothetical results of a longitudinal study of workers' snack selections

	BEFORE (%)	AFTER (%)
Junk food	70	50
Fruit	10	30
Other	20	20

The only valid conclusion is that workers were selecting more nutritious food—that is, more fruit. While it is likely that the speech had some impact, only an experi-mental design (see below) could test whether the speech produced the results.

There may have been other factors that caused the change in food selections, quite unrelated to the speech. For example, the stock at the cafeteria might have changed. The price of junk food might have gone up. Neither the simple case study nor the longitudinal study can control the influence of these other factors.

3. THE COMPARISON STUDY

In a comparison study, the research question is 'Is the relationship between variables X and Y the same in entities A and B?' A comparison study compares case studies of the relationships between the same variables done for different entities at the same point in time. The comparison study can be diagrammed as in Figure 7.3.

FIGURE 7.3 A diagram of a comparison study

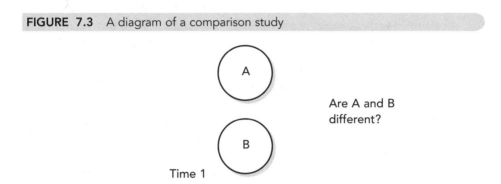

A great deal of research is of the comparative type. Basic examples are 'Is the relationship between "contraception availability" and "youth pregnancy" the same in Halifax and St. John's?'; 'Is the relationship between "ethnicity" and "sports achievement" the same in both the local girls' and boys' soccer teams?'; and 'Is the relationship between "family type" (one parent/two parents) and "academic achievement" the same for students at Vincent Massey Collegiate and Yorkton Senior High School?'

Comparison studies are undertaken for two main reasons:

1. To investigate a relationship further by testing it within different types of entities. This practice might be called 'doing the same test under different conditions'. Car tires are tested under different conditions, such as dry roads, wet roads, icy roads, snow-covered roads, paved roads, gravel roads, and so on. A social relationship hypothesis can be tested under the same principle, with tests conducted for the same point in time or time period for different social entities. If we hypothesize that there is a relationship between 'ethnicity' and 'sports achievement', we may wish to test this relationship under different 'sex conditions' to see whether the relationship is affected by the variable 'sex'. A possible way to do this would be to test the relationship in similar entities of different sex composition, such as the local girls' and boys' soccer teams.

2. To investigate a relationship further by testing it within similar types of entities. This practice might be called 'doing the same test under similar conditions' in which the tests are conducted for the same point in or period of time. Such studies are done to test the reliability of research and to examine the effects of outside variables. If we accept that Halifax and St John's are similar

cities, we could use them to study the relationship between 'contraception availability' and 'youth pregnancy'. If our research demonstrates a relationship between the variables in both places, then the reliability of the research is supported. However, if our research shows a relationship in St John's but not in Halifax, then our research method could be unreliable and in need of re-evaluation. There may also be an unconsidered but critical difference between the two cities that is affecting the relationship—that is, there could be a third variable in the relationship. If we strongly suspect this, then further research needs to be carried out to identify the mystery third variable.

Let's explore this last point with an example. Suppose you postulate a relationship between the variables 'English proficiency' and 'unemployment'—that is, groups with lower English proficiency experience higher levels of unemployment. You decide to compare this relationship in Richmond and Surrey, British Columbia.

Suppose your research yields different results for the cities. In Surrey, the results support your hypothesis because you find that adults with low English proficiency do experience high unemployment. On the other hand, the research carried out in Richmond does not support your hypothesis. In Richmond, adults with low English proficiency have a rate of unemployment that is unexpectedly low. Therefore, the hypothesis that English proficiency is related to employment would not be supported for both cities. Consequently, the simple theory would need to be refined or challenged. This refinement would usually begin with the question 'What are the differences between Richmond and Surrey that change the relationship between English proficiency and employment?'

Further research could confront this question by pursuing the research objective 'To observe patterns of employment acquisition' in Richmond. It might be observed that the language spoken most frequently by adults in Richmond is Mandarin. As a result, most local employers (given that they do business with local residents) tend to hire people proficient in Mandarin rather than English.

A more complete view of the relationship between English proficiency and unemployment begins to emerge. It has been shown that the significance of the relationship between English proficiency and unemployment is inconsistent between the two cities. Further research has found a possible factor in this inconsistency—that is, the prevalence of languages other than English among local residents. In fact, the independent variable can be modified to 'local language proficiency', developing our hypothesis for further testing.

To do a comparison study, you:

1. select variables relevant to the concepts under study;
2. devise a way of measuring those variables;
3. develop a data-recording device;
4. measure the same variables in the same way in two or more entities at the same time (or at 'practically' the same time).

Such a study will enable you to determine whether there is any difference between the two groups.

For example, the OH&S officer concerned about workers' snack selections in the cafeteria might have been interested in finding out whether there was any difference between machine operators on A-shift and those on other shifts. To make this comparison, the OH&S officer would have to observe and record the selections made by two groups of workers. It would be best if they could be observed at the same time (in this case, on their respective meal breaks on the same night). The data-recording form might look like that shown in Table 7.7.

TABLE 7.7 A data-recording form for a comparison study of snack selections made by two groups of machine operators

	GROUP A	GROUP B
Junk food		
Fruit		
Other		

Let us say that Group A are the workers on A-shift and Group B the workers on other shifts. What could the OH&S officer conclude if the results looked like those in Table 7.8? She could conclude that of the workers observed, workers on A-shift on average selected less junk food and more fruit than workers on other shifts did. The OH&S officer might think that this difference was due to the nutrition education talk given to the workers on A-shift. However, there is no way of telling that from the above study. The study simply asks the question 'Are these two groups of workers different?' From the results in Table 7.8, the answer would be 'yes'.

TABLE 7.8 Hypothetical results of a comparison study of workers' snack selections

	MACHINE OPERATORS ON A-SHIFT (%)	MACHINE OPERATORS ON OTHER SHIFTS (%)
Junk food	60	70
Fruit	30	20
Other	10	10

Information regarding the relationship between study and academic performance can be provided by a comparison study (see Table 7.9).

It may have occurred to you that the relationship between amount of study and mark on the history test held true for history but might not hold true for the math class. You might ask the question 'Is the relationship between study and academic

TABLE 7.9 A data-recording form for a comparison study of the relationship between amount of study and marks by each class member in the separate subjects of history and math

	HISTORY CLASS			MATH CLASS	
STUDENT	STUDY (HOURS)	1ST SEMESTER EXAM MARK (%)	STUDENT	STUDY (HOURS)	1ST SEMESTER EXAM MARK (%)
Craig	95	90	Elise	53	90
Casey	85	80	Ben	59	80
Emma	75	70	Kim	29	70
Kathy	65	60	Tina	64	60
Eva	55	50	Nadine	72	50
etc.	etc.	etc.	etc.	etc.	etc.

performance the same in the math and the history class?' One way to find out would be to compare the results of case studies of this relationship, conducted during the same period, for the math and the history class.

The results of the two classes could be plotted on one graph, as in Figure 7.4.

FIGURE 7.4 A sample graph of possible results from a comparison study

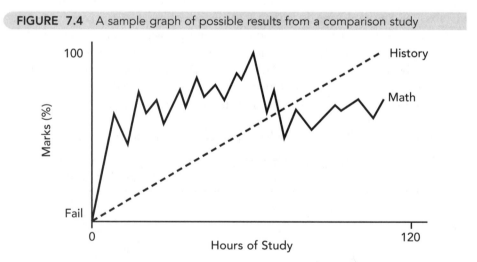

Figure 7.4 shows a clear and positive relationship between the number of hours spent studying and examination results in history. The same is not true for the math class, where there is no strictly linear association between the variables and more studying does not necessarily produce higher grades. You would conclude that the relationship between the amount of time spent studying and examination results differs between Groups A and B. Therefore, the relationship between study

and results is different for Groups A and B, and the hypothesis is supported in the history class but not in the math class. A and B are different.

What would be concluded if the results had been like those in Figure 7.5? Be careful in reading this graph.

FIGURE 7.5   A sample graph of possible results from a comparison study

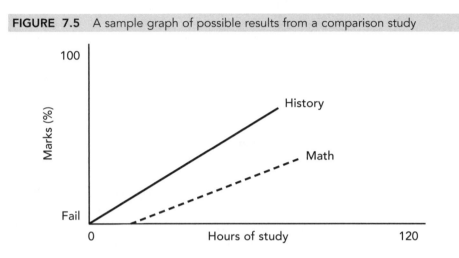

Given these results, you would conclude that in both the history and the math class, the amount of time spent studying was positively related to examination results. The conclusion would be that Groups A and B were not different in terms of the relationship between hours of study and marks in history and math.

4. THE LONGITUDINAL COMPARISON STUDY

We noted earlier that the case study was, in a sense, the basic building block of research design. We combined two case studies of the same group at two different times to produce a longitudinal study. Similarly, by combining two case studies, each one of a different group at the same time, we produced a comparison study. When the comparison and the longitudinal types are combined, the longitudinal comparison research design is produced. This type of research design asks the question 'Have the differences between X and Y in entities A and B changed over time?'

A good example of this type of research would be a study of two groups of babies: one group bottlefed and the other breastfed. Each group would be measured at the same interval—weekly for eight weeks beginning one week after birth. The observation-recording device developed earlier would be used. We will assume that Group A is bottlefed and Group B is breastfed.

This study is longitudinal in that it involves a series of measures of the same variables in the same groups over time. It is also a comparison because it compares two separate groups. How might the data look? You have weight and length measures for each infant at weekly intervals. For the purpose of comparison between the two groups, assume that you report the average weight gain each week. The following table might be used to present the results:

TABLE 7.10 A table of possible results from a longitudinal comparison study of two groups of babies

AVERAGE WEIGHT GAIN PER WEEK (GRAMS)

WEEK	1	2	3	4	5	6	7	8	TOTAL
Group A	13	14	14	15	16	16	15	15	118
Group B	14	15	15	16	16	17	16	16	125

The research into the relationship between amount of study and academic performance can be done using a longitudinal comparison type of research design. We will retain the comparison between a history class and a math class. We will also use the same data-recording form as before. In our last hypothetical research into this topic, we discovered that there was a difference between math and history in the relationship between time spent studying and examination result. The question that can be asked is 'Does this difference persist through time?' By having the two classes keep a record of the time spent studying each subject before two exams a few months apart, we produce a longitudinal comparison. We have two measures for each of the two groups at two different times. A diagram of this research design might look like Figure 7.6.

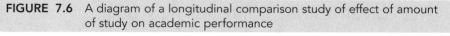

FIGURE 7.6 A diagram of a longitudinal comparison study of effect of amount of study on academic performance

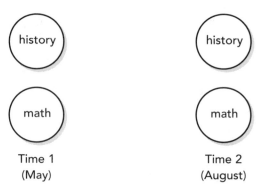

You may recall that our first comparison study of history and math results looked like Figure 7.7. A longitudinal comparison essentially involves doing a second comparison study using the same measures as the first one to see if there has been any change between the two groups.

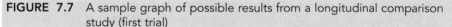

FIGURE 7.7 A sample graph of possible results from a longitudinal comparison study (first trial)

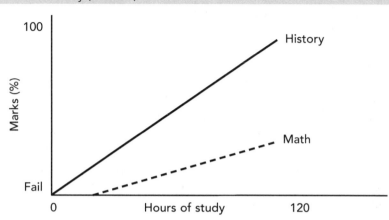

If the results of the second study are the same as the first, the conclusion would be that the difference between the two groups has persisted. On the other hand, the results of the second part of this longitudinal comparison study might look like Figure 7.8.

FIGURE 7.8 A sample graph of possible results from a longitudinal comparison study (second trial)

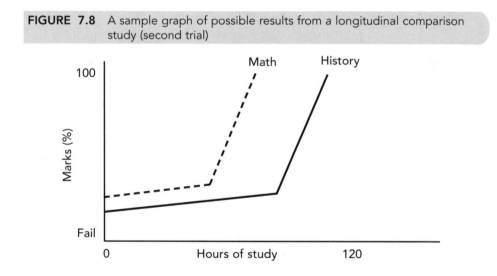

What conclusions could be drawn from these results? First, the differences between Groups A and B (history and math in this study) have lessened. Second, the pattern for both subjects has changed. Have the students changed their study patterns? Were the examinations different? What has produced the change? That is still unknown. The longitudinal comparison research design can demonstrate changes in differences between groups over time, but it does not provide the tools to test hypotheses about factors that cause changes in differences.

The same problem arises in the case of the OH&S officer who is concerned about workers' snack selections. Let us say that the OH&S officer, after conducting the first comparison study between machine operators on A-shift and other machine operators, decided to put up posters in the cafeteria that promoted fruit as a healthy snack. After a few weeks, she repeats the original comparison study. By being repeated, the original comparison study is transformed into a longitudinal comparison study.

What conclusions could the OH&S officer draw from the results shown in Table 7.11? Both groups have changed. Both groups shifted 20 percentage points in the direction of greater consumption of fruit. What is more significant, though, is that the difference between the two groups has persisted. The machine operators on A-shift are still more likely to select fruit than the machine operators on other shifts. However, it is impossible to conclude that the posters produced the change. It might have been something else, as suggested before. There might have been a change in the offerings at the cafeteria. There might have been a major television campaign at the same time. Other factors, not accounted for in this research, might have produced the result.

TABLE 7.11 Hypothetical results of a longitudinal comparison study of workers' snack selections

	MACHINE OPERATORS ON A-SHIFT (%)		MACHINE OPERATORS ON OTHER SHIFTS (%)	
	MAY	JULY	MAY	JULY
Junk food	60	40	70	50
Fruit	30	50	20	40
Other	10	10	10	10

To use a longitudinal comparison research design you must:

1. select variables relevant to the concepts under study;
2. devise a way of measuring those variables;
3. develop a data-recording device;
4. measure the same variables in the same way in two (or more) entities at two (or more) different times.

Such a research design is diagrammed in Figure 7.9. A research design like this can answer the question 'Are entities A and B different through time?' It cannot, however, explain differences between variables in time or test hypotheses about the causes of such differences.

FIGURE 7.9 A diagram of a longitudinal comparison study

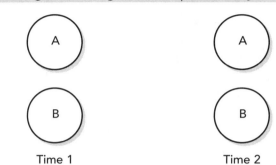

5. THE EXPERIMENT

If the aim of your research is to determine the effect that a change in one variable has on another, an experimental design is required. While the other research designs provide useful information, the experimental design provides the most rigorous test of a hypothesis that specifies that changes in variable X cause changes in variable Y. The fundamental requirement of an experimental design is that the researcher has some control over variation in the independent variable and can control the influence of other variables.

The ideal form of the experimental design can be set out as follows. Take the hypothesis that a talk on nutritious snacks will promote healthier snack selection by workers at the cafeteria. It can be diagrammed in this way:

In order to test this hypothesis using an experimental design, the researcher must follow this procedure:

1. Select two groups of workers. These two groups must be as alike as possible on any variable that might affect the dependent variable or the relation between the independent variable and the dependent variable (e.g., age, same proportion of males to females).
2. Devise measures for the variables. The dependent variable will be measured by the workers' snack selections observation checklist we developed earlier. The independent variable is whether the worker was present at the talk on nutritious snacks ('yes' or 'no').
3. Select one of the two groups of workers to be the control group. The control group will not be given the talk on nutritious snacks; the other group will.

4. The dependent variable will be measured before and after the talk is given to Group A.
5. The principle of experimental design is that since the groups are as alike as possible, except that one has been exposed to the talk on nutritious snacks while the other has not, any difference between the two groups' snack selection behaviour can be attributed to the talk. The diagram of the experimental design is shown in Figure 7.10.

FIGURE 7.10   A diagram of an experimental research design

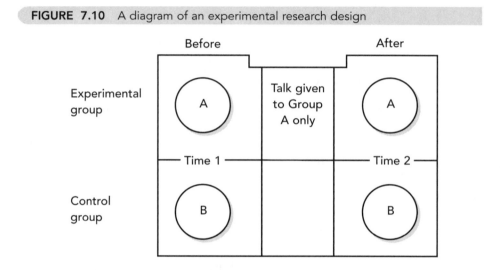

This research design asks the question 'Is there a change in the difference between the experimental group and the control group following the manipulation of the independent variable?' Here the manipulation of the independent variable is the talk on nutritious snacks. Tables 7.12 and 7.13 provide two sets of hypothetical results. What would each set of results lead you to conclude?

TABLE 7.12   Hypothetical results of an experimental study

| | BEFORE | | AFTER | |
	A (EXP)	B (CONTROL)	A (EXP)	B (CONTROL)
Junk food	70	70	50	70
Fruit	20	20	40	20
Other	10	10	10	10

WORKERS' SNACK SELECTIONS AT CAFETERIA 1 (%)

What do you conclude from this table of data? Did the talk have any impact on workers' snack selections?

Alternatively, what conclusion would you draw if the results were like those in Table 7.13? Both groups changed, but they changed by the same amount (A1 – A2 = B1 – B2). It would appear that the talk had no effect. Make additional tables of possible results, and interpret them. It is good practice. First make one in which the control group changes but the experimental group stays the same. What would you conclude?

TABLE 7.13 Hypothetical results of an experimental study

	BEFORE		AFTER	
WORKERS' SNACK SELECTIONS AT CAFETERIA 2 (%)				
	A (EXP)	B (CONTROL)	A (EXP)	B (CONTROL)
Junk food	70	70	60	60
Fruit	20	20	30	30
Other	10	10	10	10

How can an experimental research design test the hypothesis that changes in study cause changes in academic performance? Which is the independent variable? Which is the dependent variable? The operationalized form of this hypothesis has been diagrammed as follows:

In order to design an experiment, the researcher must be able to manipulate (change) the values of the independent variable. How can the researcher exercise control over the independent variable in this hypothesis? How can hours of study be manipulated?

The researcher selects two history classes that are the same in terms of variables considered critical to academic performance—age, past performance level, standard of teaching, and lack of personal problems. For each class, the researcher distributes a reading and allows students 45 minutes to study it. She then administers a test on the reading. Later in the year, the researcher repeats this exercise with a reading of similar difficulty. For one class (the experimental group), she changes the amount of study time to 75 minutes. For the other class (the control group), she does not change the amount of study time. This class receives the same amount of time that was allocated in the original exercise—45 minutes. The researcher collates the results of each test for both classes and compares the results. This research would be diagrammed as shown in Figure 7.11.

FIGURE 7.11 A diagram of an experimental research design testing a hypothesis on study time and academic performance

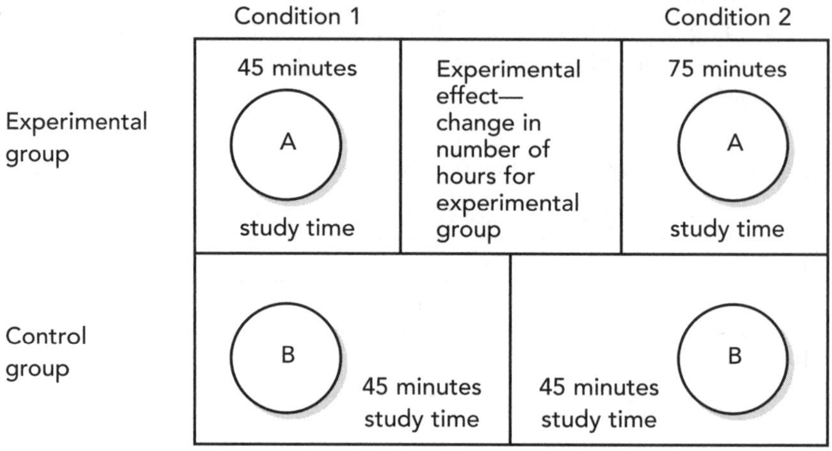

The independent variable 'time spent in study' is manipulated by the researcher in such a way that any time spent in study should be observable in the form of a change in the dependent variable 'test marks'. The groups have been selected to be as alike as possible in all other respects. The results will be reported as average scores for each group, since the researcher is interested in group performance rather than individual performance.

Tables 7.14, 7.15, and 7.16 depict possible results of such an experiment. Assume that the possible scores on the test ranged from 0 to 100. How would you interpret the results in Table 7.14? Clearly, the results for the experimental group have improved, and those of the control group have not. The results show that an increase in study has led to improved test results.

TABLE 7.14 Hypothetical results of an experiment

AVERAGE RESULTS ON COMPREHENSION TESTS FOR TWO CLASSES 1 (%)		
	CONDITION 1	CONDITION 2
Experimental group	60	80
Control group	60	60

The data in Table 7.15 are inconclusive because results for both groups changed in the same direction by the same amount. The experimental group did better than the control group under both conditions, but both groups improved from the first time to the second. It is not possible to conclude that an increase in study time contributed to the increase in results for the experimental group, because the control group increased by a similar amount.

TABLE 7.15 Hypothetical results of an experiment

AVERAGE RESULTS ON COMPREHENSION TESTS FOR TWO CLASSES 2 (%)

	CONDITION 1	CONDITION 2
Experimental group	65	70
Control group	60	65

Look at Table 7.16. What would you conclude from these results? They indicate that both groups improved but that the experimental group showed a much greater improvement. A likely conclusion would be that some of the improvement (that exhibited by both groups) was due to increased skill in doing this sort of examination because of the practice both groups received when writing the first test but that the rest of the improvement (that shown only by the experimental group) was due to the increase in study time. Produce other hypothetical results in tables similar to these ones, and practise interpreting them.

TABLE 7.16 Hypothetical results of an experiment

AVERAGE RESULTS ON COMPREHENSION TESTS FOR TWO CLASSES 3 (%)

	CONDITION 1	CONDITION 2
Experimental group	65	80
Control group	60	65

In summary, an experimental research design is used to determine whether changes in the independent variable actually produce changes in the dependent variable. Does a change in X cause a change in Y? If you are planning to design an experiment, consult the following checklist.

Checklist for designing an experiment

1. Are you able to manipulate the independent variable? Are you able to change the independent variable for the experimental group while holding it constant for the control group? Many independent variables cannot be manipulated satisfactorily. This may be due to our sense of what is ethical.

For example, we do not arbitrarily move babies from one caregiver to another in order to assess the impact of the change.

2. Are you able to select two (or more) groups that are alike in all essential ways, one of which will become the control group and the other the experimental group (the group that gets the treatment)? Are you able to isolate the two groups so that the experimental group does not communicate with or otherwise affect the control group?

3. Are you able to measure the dependent variable for each group both before and after the change in the independent variable? An experiment requires before and after measures of the dependent variable for both the experimental and the control group.

4. Have you recorded your data and presented your findings in such a way that you can draw conclusions about the effect (or lack of effect) on the independent variable?

If you can answer 'yes' to all of these questions, then you have designed an experimental study to test your hypothesis. You must be able to answer 'yes' to the first two questions in order to eliminate other possible explanations for the relationship between variables X and Y. By studying two groups as alike as possible, you eliminate the effects of outside variables. By manipulating the independent variable, you come as close as possible to demonstrating that changes in variable X cause changes in variable Y.

CONTROLLING THE INFLUENCE OF OTHER VARIABLES

At a number of points in this chapter, we have referred to the possibility that other variables, not included in the study, might have been responsible for observed changes in the dependent variable. This is one of the greatest fears of a researcher—their results may be due to something not accounted for in the research design. For example, the improvement in students' exam performance might be due to increased skill in taking such exams and not to the increase in study time. For such reasons, it is important to control the influence of all other variables that might affect the variables under study.

How does the researcher control the influence of other variables? First, be aware of the fact that other variables may be influencing the data. As you design a piece of research, it is important to keep a list of other potentially influential variables. You may or may not eventually do anything about them, but it is important to be aware of such variables. All scientific conclusions are tentative, partly because of the impossibility of controlling everything. Thus, the first step is to be aware of the possible influence of other variables.

The second step is to take some of these variables into account when you design your study. You may wish to select people for your study who have the same characteristics so that the effects of outside variables will be the same for all people observed. If you were studying the relationship between age and smoking, you would have to control the effects of variables outside your research hypothesis—for example, sex, social class, type of schooling. Controlling the effects of these variables is a matter of keeping their effects constant for all people being studied—that way, differences in results cannot be caused by differences in the outside variables. For the study on smoking, you would ideally locate a sample of people whose attributes, according to the outside variables, are the same. The people would be of the same sex and social class, and would have attended the same type of school. Then you could be confident that differences in the smoking behaviour of respondents of different ages are not caused by differences in the variables you have controlled or kept constant.

The most important point about controls is to be aware of the possible influence of variables outside your hypothesis. Select groups in such a way as to eliminate the influence of as many outside variables as you can. Note the absence of controls for other outside variables in the limitations section of your report.

QUESTIONS FOR REVIEW

1. What basic question is answered by research design?
2. List the five types of research design. Diagram each design.
3. What question does each ask?
4. Why is the case study said to be the basic building block of all research design?
5. What is required to be done a longitudinal study?
6. What is required to be done a comparison study?
7. What is required to be done a longitudinal comparison study?
8. What are the key features of an experiment?
9. On what bases does a researcher choose a research design?
10. Why is it important to control for other variables?
11. How does one control for other variables?
12. What is done about variables over which the researcher has no control?

Sources

Baker, M. 2005. *Families: Changing Trends in Canada*. Toronto: McGraw-Hill Ryerson.

Statistics Canada. 2007. *Women in Non-standard Jobs: Public Policy Challenges*. http://www.swc-cfc.gc.ca/pubs/pubspr/0662334809/200303_0662334809_13_e.html. Accessed 27 June 2007.

Statistics Canada. 2007. *Labour Force Participation Rates by Sex and Age Group*. http://www40.statcan.ca/l01/cst01/labor05.htm. Accessed 27 June 2007.

Suggestions for further reading

Blalock, H.M., Jr. 1961. *Causal Inferences in Non-experimental Research*. Chappel Hill: University of North Carolina Press (a classic).

Campbell, D.T., and J.C. Stanley. 1963. *Experimental and Quasi-experimental Designs for Research*. Chicago: Rand McNally (a classic treatment of research design).

de Vaus, D.A. 2002. *Surveys in Social Research*. 5th edn, chapter 4. St Leonards, NSW: Allen and Unwin.

Judd, C.M., E.R. Smith, and L.H. Kidder. 1991. *Research Methods in Social Relations*, chapter 3. Fort Worth, TX: Holt, Rinehart and Winston.

Kumar, Ranjit. 1999. *Research Methodology: A Step by Step Guide for Beginners*, chapters 7–8. London: Sage.

Liebow, Elliot. 2003. *Tally's Corner: A Study of Negro Streetcorner Men*. Lanham, MD: Rowman and Littlefield.

Newman, W.L. 2000. *Social Research Methods: Qualitative and Quantitative Approaches*. 4th edn. Toronto: Allyn and Bacon.

8

Selecting a Sample

CHAPTER OUTLINE

To whom are you going to administer your questionnaire? Which history class will be the subject of your experiments? Which babies will be weighed and measured? Since it is impossible to weigh all babies, administer questionnaires to everyone, or experiment on all history classes, researchers study a 'sample' of their subject populations. Indeed, it is often more desirable to study a sample than to try to study the whole population. A carefully drawn sample not only makes the task possible, it often produces more accurate results.

In everyday life, we commonly use sampling to make judgments about facts and issues. If we want to check the seasoning of soup, we stir it, take a sample, and judge the seasoning level of the broth by tasting that sample. If we are buying a new car, we decide how the car can usually be expected to perform by taking it on a sample test drive. We make many judgments based on samples.

Care is taken to make sure the sample is an accurate reflection of the whole from which it is taken. In the case of soup, we stir so as to make sure the ingredients are as evenly distributed as possible, then we take a sample, taste it, and draw a conclusion about—i.e., generalize the findings of our study to—the whole pot of soup. If we have heard that the car we are thinking of buying drives well on city roads but not on country roads, we would sample its performance on both types of road for an idea of how it handles in general.

Sampling is an important feature of all research. Part of the whole is studied, and the results are taken to be an accurate reflection of the whole.

The most important point to remember about sampling is this:

The manner in which the sample is drawn determines to what extent we can generalize from the findings.

Only if the sample studied can be shown to represent a larger population can the results of a study of the sample be assumed to give reliable information about the larger population. If the sample studied is not representative, the conclusions drawn from the research must be limited to the sample studied.

For example, you might have developed a short questionnaire on attitudes towards nuclear weapons. If you had 20 of your friends, fellow students, and relatives fill out your questionnaire, the results would be limited to that group of 20 people. On the other hand, if you had selected a sample of 20 people that accurately reflected the views of a larger group of 200 (for example, all the students enrolled in your course), you could draw conclusions about the 200 from the results of the sample of 20. In the first instance, your findings were limited to the 20 people studied. In the second, you could generalize the results to the larger population that your sample represented.

Although sampling soup is easy, sampling groups of people is rather more complicated. The basic problem is to select a sample that accurately reflects a specified larger group. Several techniques for drawing samples from groups of people have been devised by social scientists. The most basic and potentially useful of these techniques will be described in this chapter. The strengths and weaknesses of each will be discussed to help you select a technique appropriate to your research.

It should also be remembered that for some purposes, sampling is not required. If the researcher is not interested in drawing conclusions for a larger population than that actually studied, sampling is not needed. For example, a psychologist might decide to study her baby's cognitive development. Only one baby (hers) is needed for the study. Why would she not be able to draw conclusions about all babies, or even other babies in her family? It is usually dangerous to rely on the observation of a single case to provide an accurate picture of a larger group. It would be like an Australian forming an opinion about all Canadians after meeting one Canadian. Depending on which Canadian was the basis of this 'case study', the most amazing and misleading impressions could be formed. In studies of single cases, generalizations cannot be safely drawn. There is no way of knowing whether the case studied will give an accurate impression of the whole.

Another situation in which sampling is not an issue occurs when researchers can easily study all members of the group about whom they wish to draw conclusions. If their interest is in the performance of one history class, or the comparison of two groups of workers—for example, those who did and those who did not hear a speaker on nutrition—then sampling is not an issue. In these instances, the whole population is being studied. As long as the researchers are willing to limit the conclusions to the population they study, sampling is not an issue. If, however, the researchers want to generalize—to draw conclusions about a large group on the basis of studying a few—then a sampling procedure must be selected.

Why do researchers sample? Samples are used to reduce the cost in time, energy, and money of studying large populations. It is often simply not possible or desirable to study everyone. A sample is drawn from a large group in order to gain a reliable picture of that large group by studying a carefully selected smaller number of the population. The way in which the sample is selected determines whether reliable conclusions about the larger group can be drawn.

HOW TO SELECT A SAMPLE

What do you want to know? About whom do you want to know it? These are the questions to answer first. Given that it is impossible to know everything about everyone or all groups, selections must be made. First, decide what you want to know. You did this when you formed a hypothesis, focused it, and made it operational. You devised instruments and designed research. Once these things are done, turn your attention to the second question: about whom do you want to know?

The first step in sample selection is to identify the population about which you want to know something. Think back to your hypothesis. For example, the hypothesis about amount of study and academic performance relates to students. The largest possible population would be all students in the world at any time past, present, and future. That would be an impossible population to sample. You may decide to limit your sample to students in Canadian post-secondary institutions. That is still a very large and diverse population. You might decide to limit your focus to students in your own institution. Finally, you might decide that making generalizations about all students everywhere is not so important, and you are happy to settle for finding out what is happening in two history classes at your own institution.

Remember! It is perfectly legitimate to select any population as the object of your study.

The population about which you wish to generalize will affect your selection of a sampling procedure. Once you have decided whom you want to draw reliable conclusions about, you are ready to select a sampling procedure. What other practical factors might help you to decide which population you wish to be able to generalize about? Think about time and money.

TYPES OF SAMPLING PROCEDURE

There are two general types of sampling procedure: random and non-random. A random sampling procedure provides the greatest assurance that those selected are a representative sample of the larger group. If a non-random sampling procedure is used, the researcher can only hope that those selected for study bear some likeness to the larger group.

Non-random sampling procedures

Non-random sampling procedures include accidental sampling, accidental quota sampling, purposive sampling, and systematic matching sampling. While useful for many studies, non-random sampling procedures provide only a weak basis for generalization. They are more suited to qualitative research studies.

Accidental sampling

This sampling procedure, also known as haphazard sampling, involves using what is immediately available. A professor studies her own students; a psychologist studies his own children. A student studies the interaction patterns of the families of two friends and a cousin. These are all accidental samples. The persons, families, and classes studied were selected because they were available, not because they were known to be representative of some larger group.

Some people confuse accidental sampling with random sampling. Persons met at random—that is, accidentally—do not comprise a random sample. Another difference with accidental samples is that the researcher does not know in what ways the sample is biased. How is the sample a misleading representative of the larger population about which information is desired? There is no way of checking this without doing a study of everyone or a study of a properly drawn random sample.

The people on a given street at a given time will be a biased sample of residents of that suburb. Such an accidental sample will not give you reliable information about all residents of the suburb. A questionnaire on attitudes towards abortion given to every tenth person encountered at a suburban shopping centre will not provide a reliable indication of the opinions of residents of the suburb. It will only tell you the opinions of people who shop at that place at that hour on that day of the week. If you are interested in the opinions of the residents of the entire suburb, an accidental sample of Tuesday morning shoppers will not provide the information.

Similarly, the families you know will be a biased sample of families in your city. They may be members of the same clubs, churches, or political parties or be at similar stages in the family life cycle. In the same way, students enrolled in a particular course or institution will be a biased sample of students. Think of ways in which the students enrolled in your course would be a biased sample of students in your institution. This is why *the results of a study of an accidental sample apply only to the sample studied.*

An accidental sampling procedure is appropriate if you do not intend to draw conclusions about a larger group on the basis of the group you study. They are not appropriate when the researcher wishes to utilize statistical modelling techniques to identify trends. Accidental samples are handy, require little effort, and are useful for many studies. The major disadvantage is that the findings of a study of an accidental sample are strictly limited to those studied, because the researcher does not know in what ways the sample is biased. It is uncertain which aspects of the total population are included and which are not.

Accidental quota sampling

In an accidental quota sampling procedure, the researcher selects individuals or groups on the basis of set criteria. A researcher comparing the opinions of males and females might set a quota of 50 males and 50 females. This will ensure that the sample studied has both females and males. Another researcher, comparing the performance of history classes and English classes, might specify that the sample must contain the same number of students from each type of class. Someone interested in the difference between students of different universities, social classes, incomes, or ethnic groups might specify in advance the number or proportion of each desired in the sample.

Perhaps a more developed example will help. Assume you are interested in comparing the attitudes towards university held by secondary school students from different ethnic groups. To make sure that the sample you study has students from each of the ethnic groups, you might set a quota of 10 students from each of the ethnic groups you wish to compare. By selecting 10 students from each ethnic group—that is, by filling your quota—you make sure that your sample includes people or groups with certain specified characteristics, in this instance ethnic background.

Quota sampling is useful when a particular group or characteristic is relatively rare in the population. By setting a quota and selecting people until the quota is filled, you ensure that the group or characteristics you want in the sample are adequately represented in the sample for the analyses you want to do.

Quota sampling, however, suffers from most of the same defects as accidental sampling. Can you see why? Although the researcher is assured of the presence of certain categories in the sample—for example, males and females or Greek, Dutch, English, and Vietnamese students—the representativeness of the sample is still not ensured. This is because the individuals or groups are not selected randomly. The sample may have 50 males and 50 females, but of whom are these males and females representative? This is not known. The sample selected may have 10 Greek students, 10 Dutch students, 10 English students, and 10 Vietnamese students. But it is not known whether the 10 Dutch students are an unbiased sample of Dutch students. It is not known whether a study of the 10 Greek students will provide reliable information about other Greek students. In other words, it is risky to draw conclusions about a larger group from an accidental quota sample of that group. Nonetheless, this sampling procedure is often used because of time and budget pressures. Conclusions drawn are strictly limited to the population actually studied. Tentative implications for others may be suggested.

Purposive sampling

Some researchers believe that they can, using their own judgment or intuition, select the best people or groups to be studied. The 'typical' rural school is selected and studied, and the results are generalized to all rural schools. The 'typical' first-year sociology class is compared with the 'typical' first-year history class. How are these known to be typical? Unless objective criteria are set out beforehand and each group is shown to meet these criteria, there is no way of knowing. However, there are times when this is the only practical way to draw a sample. If a purposive sample is studied, only tentative generalizations can be made. The conclusions drawn from a comparison of a few 'typical' rural schools with a few 'typical' urban schools might be phrased in this way:

> The results of this study comparing three rural and three urban schools have revealed the following six major differences. While it is not strictly possible to generalize from this sample to all rural and urban schools, we think it is likely that these differences will be found in other instances.

This technique is very appropriate for case study and qualitative approaches in which the intent is not to generalize to a larger population but to examine a 'typical' case in order to understand it more fully. Also known as judgmental sampling, this procedure is most often used when the topic is new and has not yet been fully explored. According to Neuman (1997), purposive sampling is appropriate in three instances: for selecting cases that are illustrative of a phenomenon; for selecting 'difficult to reach' members of a unique population; or for identifying particular types for investigation in greater detail. In other words, purposive sampling is appropriate for studying extreme cases of a phenomenon.

Palys (2003) advises that researchers should not place too much emphasis on the opinions or information provided by any single respondent who has been selected using purposive sampling methods. This is because they have not been selected randomly and because purposive sampling is usually done with smaller sample sizes. However, the information they provide may lead you to investigate other aspects of the phenomenon that you had not previously considered.

The snowball technique

The snowball sampling technique is used when you need to gain access to certain types of people or to a particular group, but you know only a few people who fit the category and there is no publicly available listing. In this technique, you gather your sample by first approaching those who are available and then asking them to nominate others whom they know, who nominate still others. In this way, your sample grows like a snowball, the most recently formed layer providing the contact with those to be added next. For example, you may wish to interview practising Falun Gong members in order to understand some aspects of their religious practices. But you know only one practising Falun Gong member, and the local telephone book was not much help. You would ask the member you know to nominate others, whom you then ask to nominate still others until you have a sample large enough for your purposes. The snowball technique is used a great deal in qualitative research into less well-organized aspects of social life. It can be seen as a variation of purposive sampling. The conclusion of your study of Falun Gong might be phrased in this way:

> This study of a sample of practising Falun Gong members reveals that those interviewed practise a form of body and mind meditation exercise, come from certain backgrounds, and have been practising an average of X years. While these findings cannot be generalized to all practising Falun Gong members, those interviewed represent about 5 per cent of known practitioners in Toronto.

Systematic matching sampling

In this procedure, individual subjects or groups are systematically matched with others who are similar in all but one critical attribute. It can be effective in at least two situations.

First, it is useful for controlling the influence of variables outside the research hypothesis or research objective. Say you wish to sample Grade 3 students in a large elementary school to find out whether male and female students have reacted differently to a new method of teaching. The school has a great deal of ethnic diversity, and you suspect that the new system will have different effects on students from different ethnic backgrounds. To control the variable 'ethnicity', you construct your sample by systematically matching males and females of the same ethnic background. You might arrive at a sample of 10 students, containing a male and female from five different ethnic groups—British, Vietnamese, Italian, Greek, and Indian. You can now compare the differences between males and females for each ethnic 'pair' and summarize the general sex differences, noting any variations among the ethnic categories.

Second, a systematic matching sampling procedure is often appropriate when a researcher wants to compare two groups of very different sizes. A study might compare female and male politicians in terms of their goals for social reform. There are currently significantly fewer female politicians than male, so in sampling male politicians for comparison, the researcher needs to be careful. The population of males in Parliament is so much greater that they can be expected to be far more diverse than the females, and many would be inappropriate for a sex-based comparison study. Some would have been in Parliament much longer than any of the female politicians. Because of the greater diversity among male members of Parliament, they are more likely to represent most economic classes, rich and poor. Since there are fewer females, they are less likely to have incomes that are fully representative of the entire income structure. Also, given their greater numbers in Parliament, men are more likely to represent different marital statuses, such as single, common-law, separated, divorced, or widowed. Therefore, it is important to 'match' the subjects in the sample. If the researcher doesn't do this, then their sample of females will be compared to males who are too different for a reasonable comparison.

We could select 10 female politicians (randomly or non-randomly) and systematically match them to 10 male politicians. Each male would be selected because he matched a female politician in certain features deemed to be important to the consideration of social reform. Examples of such matching features might be age, length of service in cabinet or on the backbench, education, marital status, and sexuality. Though the claim to representativeness is weak, this sampling procedure is often a suitable compromise when comparing groups of extremely different size.

Summary of non-random sampling procedures

These examples of non-random sampling procedures are given because they are frequently used by researchers. If a non-random sampling procedure is used, the researcher must be aware of the limitations to the conclusions drawn. Technically, the conclusions drawn from a study of a non-random sample are limited to that sample and cannot be used for further generalizations. Read through some research literature in your library. Can you find an example of non-random sampling being used?

Random sampling procedures

Random sampling procedures provide the greatest assurance that the sample accurately represents the population. There are four basic random sampling procedures: simple random sampling, systematic sampling, stratified random sampling, and cluster sampling.

Simple random sampling

This is the ideal method of drawing a sample. It is, however, very difficult to do. A simple random sampling procedure guarantees that each element (person, group, university, and so on) in the population has an equal chance of being selected and that every possible combination of the specified number of elements has an equal chance of selection. The mathematics of such selection procedures is very complex and beyond the scope of this text.

In order to draw a simple random sample, the researcher must:

1. identify the population from which the sample is to be drawn;
2. enumerate and list each element (e.g., persons, households, car owners) in the population;
3. devise a method of selection that ensures that each element has the same probability of selection and that each combination of the total number of elements has the same probability of selection.

Given the virtual impossibility of meeting all these criteria, it is not surprising that a number of acceptable compromises have been devised. Essentially, the task is to devise some form of lottery in which each combination of numbers has an equal chance of coming up.

The first set of 'compromise' random sampling procedures involves studies in which it is possible to identify and enumerate the total population. For example, while possible, it is usually too much work to identify and enumerate the total population of university students in a particular year. It would be possible to identify and enumerate the students enrolled in your course. Other populations that are relatively easy to enumerate are the members of a particular club, the students in a history class, the teachers in a school, the children in a particular daycare centre, the people in a home for the elderly, the people whose names are in a telephone directory or on a voter registration roll, or the students attending any of the provincial high schools in New Brunswick. The telephone directory may pose particular problems. If the city is large, do you enumerate all the subscribers? What about non-representativeness, since it only includes subscribers and usually only one name for each household? In what ways would a voter registration roll be biased? Once identified and enumerated (that is, numbered from beginning to end), a sample may be selected.

Here is an example. You want to study a simple random sample of the 250 first-year sociology students at a particular university. The first step is done. You have identified the population. The second step is to identify and enumerate each element in the population. In this instance, the elements are the 250 students. The students will have to be listed and numbered from 1 to 250:

1. Marjorie Althouse
2. George Black
3. Frank Cardinal
4. Amirah Dube

...

250. Mildred Zylstra

You have identified and enumerated the whole population to which you want to generalize the findings of your study. It is now possible to move to the next step— selecting the sample. We will deal with issues of sample size later in the chapter. Let us assume that you decided to draw a sample of 50 students from the larger population of 250 students.

An acceptable way of selecting a sample from an enumerated population involves the use of a table of random numbers. Such a table appears in Appendix B of this book. A starting point in the table is picked (using a random technique), and those elements of the whole population whose numbers come up as you move down the column from the starting point are selected for the sample. Do this until a sample of the required size is achieved.

To draw the sample of 50 students from 250 sociology students by this procedure, you would do the following. Remember: each student has been given a number from 1 to 250. Table 8.1 is a section from a table of random numbers. Because the numbers you need to select have between one and three digits (or are comprised of three digits, 001–250), you will use the first three digits of each number in the table (or the middle three digits or the last three digits—your choice). The next step is to select a starting point. This can be done in several ways. An easy way is to close your eyes, point a pen at the table, and start there. Another way is to let a computer program generate a random starting number (most statistics packages have programs allowing users to generate random numbers). Let's say that we have selected the easiest way: closing our eyes and selecting a random number by pointing our pen (note that this is not the most precise method). It is permissible to move up or down the columns, since the numbers are random—that is, there is no pattern in the table. The numbers are in no particular order. Had your pen landed on a number for which the first three digits were outside the range 001–250, you would try again or move to the next number for which the first three digits were in this range.

TABLE 8.1   Using a table of random numbers

28071	03528	89714
48210	48761	▷ 02365
83417	20219	82900
20531	43657	45100
94654	97801	▷ 01153
52839	42986	28100
74591	▷ 16100	91478
38921	56913	32675
40759	84027	52831
45980	70523	47985
52182	68194	62783
12890	59208	▷ 00691
08523	74312	▷ 13542

Assume your random selection method resulted in number 161. If you decided to move down the columns, the next number to be selected would be the next number in the range 001–250 that was not 161 (since 161 has already been selected). In this table, it would be element (student) number 023. The next would be student 011, then 006, then 135. You would continue this procedure until you had selected a total of 50 students. You would then have a simple random sample of 50 students, which is more likely to be representative of the population of 250 than a sample chosen non-randomly.

To give yourself practice, start again at number 161, but move up the columns. Which numbers would then be selected? A different sample of 50 would be drawn, but because it was randomly selected, the results of studying it would also be more likely to give reliable information about the whole group than the results of a non-random sample. Indeed, we would expect only the smallest difference between a study of the first sample and a study of the second.

Another acceptable form of selection is to put all the names or numbers into a hat and draw out the number required. To ensure that each element and combination of elements has the same probability of selection, each time a selection is made the name or number should be returned to the hat. If a number is drawn more than once, it is again returned to the hat, but the number is not 'selected' twice.

The random selection of a sample of 50 students from 250 according to this method would require that all the students' names, or a set of numbers from 001 to 250, be put into a container. The container would be shaken before each draw. The first 50 students whose names (or numbers) were drawn would form the sample.

By far the most precise and most accurate method of obtaining a simple random sample is to use a computer program to select the sample. Many computer programs contain functions that can generate random numbers based on user-entered protocol. Users would enter the required number of participants and the range of numbers of available participants. The program would generate a random sample of respondent numbers. When available, this is the preferred method of selecting sample respondents. It is the most random method of selecting respondents (it does not rely on where your pen might fall on a random number table) and is easy to use.

Although these techniques are somewhat laborious and time-consuming (with the exception of computer-generated samples), they do provide the most reliable sampling procedures. The simple random sample is the ideal.

Systematic sampling

A systematic sampling procedure involves the selection of every nth case in a list. Again, the population must be identified, but it is not necessary to enumerate the list. For example, if you had a list of 400 students in Sociology 101 and you wanted a sample of 80, you might select every fifth name on the list. To draw a systematic sample, you need to know the total number in the group and the number you want in the sample. By dividing the total number by the sample number, you find the interval at which you will select people:

Total population	=	400
Sample desired	=	80
Interval	=	$400 \div 80 = 5$

If the interval is an uneven number, the nearest whole number is selected:

Total population	=	393
Sample desired	=	80
Interval	=	$393 \div 80 = 4.9$ (round up to 5)

The critical step in systematic sampling is to select the first case randomly. To do this, one of the first elements (names, groups, numbers, schools) in the long list must be selected. If the interval is 5, one of the first five must be selected as the starting point. If the interval is 10, then you must select one of the first 10, and so on. One way to make a random selection is to put all the numbers (1 to 5, or 1 to 10, or whatever) into a container, shake it, and draw out a number. That number will be your starting point. Or you could use a computer program to generate a random start number. Regardless of which method you use, the first element must be selected randomly. Once the first element is selected, then each *n*th element (*n* = interval) thereafter is selected. In the example of students in Sociology 101, the list had 400 names, and the interval was 5. Assume that the number 4 was drawn out of the container. Selection would start with the fourth student on the list (M. Belanti). You then count down to the fifth next student on the list, E. Chatterly, and add that name to your sample.

S. Aaron	D. Enticott
J. Adams	R. Farah
K. Adams	I. Grozdanovski
M. Belanti*	S. Harris*
A. Bordignon	T. Ho
P. Bourne	M. Todorovic
N. Bradley	E. Warnecke
L. Brookman	B. Wignell
E. Chatterly*	G. Yates
H. Donaldson	

If a selected student is unavailable, they are replaced by the preceding student on the list. If S. Harris is unavailable, then Grozdanovski will be selected. When a selected student has dropped out of the course, they are replaced by the next student on the list. If E. Chatterly has dropped out, H. Donaldson will be the replacement. Another replacement strategy is to flip a coin (heads = name before, tails = name after). Note that names are replaced only if the person is genuinely unavailable, not because the researcher might prefer someone else to be in the sample. As well, replacing names with the next on the list increases the probability that a particular student will be selected. For this reason, systematic sampling is not as precise as other methods of random sampling.

A systematic sampling procedure provides an acceptable approximation of the ideals of the simple random sampling procedure. It helps to overcome researcher bias in sample selection. Selection is done independently of the researcher's preferences and prejudices. As long as any biases in the ordering of the list do not occur at the same interval as the sampling interval, a reasonably reliable sample will be drawn by this procedure.

Stratified random sampling

This procedure is basically a type of quota sampling in which members of each 'quota group' within, or stratum of, the sample are selected randomly. You may wish to compare types of schools in terms of the overall performance of students. A simple random sample of schools might not provide enough cases in some of the categories of analysis you intend to use. You might classify the schools into urban, suburban, and rural schools. Having done that, you would identify and enumerate the schools in each group and identify a random sample of each group.

In another example, you might want to compare the attitudes towards the building of additional nuclear power plants held by university students studying math and science to those held by humanities students. Rather than doing a simple random sample of the students collectively enrolled in these faculties at a particular university, you would identify all students in each category, list them separately, and draw a sample from each list using one of the random selection processes outlined above—using a table of random numbers, drawing names from a hat, or using systematic sampling.

The criterion for identifying quota groups or strata will be suggested by your hypothesis. A hypothesis comparing males with females could be studied using a random sample with quotas of randomly selected males and females. Similarly, if the hypothesis compares high-income families with low-income families, it would be possible to use a random sample with quotas of randomly selected high-income and low-income families.

Cluster sampling

The fact that simple random sampling becomes tremendously complex and costly for large and scattered populations has led to the development of cluster sampling procedures. They usually involve several stages of random selections. Rather than enumerating the whole population, the population is divided into segments. Then several of the segments are chosen at random. Elements within each segment are then selected randomly following identification and enumeration. In this way, only the elements in the selected segment need to be identified and enumerated.

National samples are usually drawn on a multi-stage cluster sample procedure. So are samples of cities. For example, a sample of households in the Montreal metropolitan area might be drawn by first dividing Montreal into segments (these already exist for purposes of the census). A number of segments could be drawn at random. Within each segment, residential blocks would be identified and enumerated and a random selection of blocks drawn. Finally, the residences on each selected block would be identified and enumerated, and a random sample of residences would be selected on the basis of an unbiased rule of selection. In this way, a random sample of Montreal residences would be approximated. Cluster sampling procedures have been devised to provide a reliably random—

and hence representative—sample of a large population without having to identify and enumerate the entire population at the outset. In this procedure, only smaller randomly selected segments (clusters) have to be identified and enumerated. Please note that this explanation of cluster sampling is simplified. Students interested in learning more about cluster sampling should consult one of the suggested readings at the end of this chapter.

Choosing a sampling procedure

The essentials of the basic forms of sampling have been presented. How do you select a sampling procedure for your research? This depends largely on the population about which you wish to draw conclusions. If you are happy to limit your conclusion, for example, to the students in your tutorial group, that accidental sample will do perfectly well. If the demands of time and expense force you to examine a subgroup of a larger population, one of the random sampling procedures should be used. The extra effort pays great dividends in the value of your research conclusions. For a relatively small effort, you can dramatically increase the representativeness of your findings and reduce the influence of any known or unknown biases.

Random sampling procedures are particularly important in research that aims to assess the attitudes, values, or beliefs of a population. Public opinion polls usually use some form of random sampling. On the basis of their samples, such pollsters predict how people will vote, what brands of detergent they will buy, and in what direction popular tastes are shifting.

Finally, it is impossible to generalize from most case studies. If a case study is conducted for the residents of a street, it cannot be stated that the street is representative of the suburb, the city, or the province. Case studies only include observations of sections of larger populations and provide the researcher with no observations outside their boundaries.

DETERMINING SAMPLE SIZE

How large a sample do you need? What is the appropriate sample size for your project? These are very difficult questions to answer. Several basic issues need to be considered in determining sample size.

First, if statistics are going to be used in the analysis and interpretation of data, there are usually requirements for sample size. We will not elaborate on these requirements, since this text takes a non-statistical approach to the research process. Professional researchers must take these considerations into account.

Second, the more questions asked, the more variables controlled for, and the more detailed the analysis of the data, the larger the sample will have to be to provide sufficient data for the analysis. In professional research, samples of hundreds or thousands will be drawn to accommodate this demand.

While large samples may seem more conclusive, it is how the sample is drawn that determines how representative it is. In general, large samples are not necessarily better than smaller ones. We do not have to taste a large amount of soup to determine whether it needs more salt—a taste will do. In addition, practical considerations of time, money, and effort often combine to keep sample sizes relatively small.

Most of the research you will read about in journals or papers is based on large samples, but we have a few suggestions regarding sample size for student projects. Since the goal of such projects is to learn basic research skills rather than to produce results that are generalized to large populations, several basic compromises are possible. These suggestions for student projects take the form of two basic rules:

1. About 30 individual elements are required in order to provide a pool large enough for even simple kinds of analyses.
2. You need a sample large enough to ensure that it is theoretically possible for each cell in your analytical table to have five cases fall in it. A few examples will make this clear.

Remember the study of snack selection (in Chapter 7). Workers' snack selections were categorized according to the table in Table 8.2.

TABLE 8.2 A dummy table for the categorization of workers' snack selections

JUNK FOOD	FRUIT	OTHER
1	2	3

This is usually referred to as a 'dummy' table. It is a table prepared before the collection of data to help to focus the issues of the research, guide data collection, and help to determine sample size. In this case, the data-recording form, dummy table, and final table for presentation of data take the same form. This dummy table has three cells. The minimum sample size for this study would be 3 x 5 = 15 (but it would still be preferable to have 30 because of the first basic rule regarding minimum sample size).

This example was also turned into a comparative study between food purchases by machine operators on A-shift and other shifts. The dummy table for such a study would look like Table 8.3.

This dummy table has six cells; hence, the sample size required would be 6 x 5 = 30. Moreover, this study involves comparing two groups of machine operators. Since each group is accorded three cells in the table, each group requires a sample of 3 x 5 = 15. You might select an accidental quota, stratified random, or cluster sampling procedure to draw a sample of at least 15 of each group of machine operators.

TABLE 8.3 A dummy table comparing snack selections of machine operators on A-shift with machine operators on other shifts

SNACK SELECTION	MACHINE OPERATORS ON A-SHIFT	MACHINE OPERATORS ON OTHER SHIFTS
Junk food	1	2
Fruit	3	4
Other	5	6

It is at this stage that you can best see the impact of adding variables to the analysis. It is always a temptation to add a variable. Indeed, you may have good reason to want to assess the impact of a number of variables. Professional research often analyzes many variables. However, adding one variable will increase the sample size required and the complexity of analyzing the data. Again, the use of dummy tables is very helpful in clarifying this for the researcher. Adding one variable to the analysis of workers' snack selections doubles the sample size and doubles the size of the dummy table. If we add the variable 'sex', for example, we would require two tables like Table 8.3, one for males and one for females. The sample size would be 12 x 5 = 60. A combined dummy table for such a study would look like Table 8.4.

TABLE 8.4 A dummy table for a study of workers' snack selections comparing males with females and machine operators on A-shift with machine operators on other shifts

SNACK SELECTION	MACHINE OPERATORS ON A-SHIFT		MACHINE OPERATORS ON OTHER SHIFTS	
	MALE	FEMALE	MALE	FEMALE
Junk food	1	2	3	4
Fruit	5	6	7	8
Other	9	10	11	12

Adding another variable, such as 'marital status', would require yet another doubling of sample size and add further complexity to the data analysis.

What would a dummy table look like for a study of the impact of 'study time' on 'mark received in a history exam'? In our previous use of this example (in Chapter 7), we used a line graph to present possible results. A second use of dummy tables can now be seen. They help to specify categories of analysis and data collection. The data collection sheet suggested for this study (Chapter 6, Figure 6.5) asked the student to keep track of the amount of time spent studying and the mark received in a history examination. For each student, the data summarization form (Chapter 6, Table 6.4) recorded total study time and mark. The number of students required for your sample depends on how you are going to analyze your data. A minimum of about 30 is required regardless of the form of analysis.

However, if you were planning to analyze the data by placing it in a table, the number of cells in the table would also play a role in determining sample size. It would be possible to have a very large table with a row for every mark from 1 to 100. That would require a sample of 500 if only one category of 'time spent studying' were used (1,000 if two categories of 'time spent studying' were used, and so on). Needless to say, that is not suitable for our purposes. Hence, a smaller number of categories for reporting and analyzing both the dependent variable (marks) and the independent variable (time spent studying) must be found. The simplest categorization for marks would be pass/fail, but that might not be satisfactory. You might prefer fail, 50–64, 65–74, 75+. That would be four categories of marks (see Tables 8.5 and 8.6).

Then there is the problem of finding categories for 'time spent studying'. This poses a different kind of problem. Again, you could have a row in your table for each possible value reported from 0 to perhaps 120 hours. This suffers from the same fault as having a column for each possible mark does. Such a table would require 100 x 120 x 5 = 60,000 students in the sample. How are numbers of hours to be categorized? You will not know the range of values until the data are collected. But you might decide to have two categories—high and low. When the data have been gathered, you determine the average number of hours studied. All those above average are categorized 'high', and those below are categorized 'low'. Or you might decide to have three categories—high, moderate, and low. In this case, you divide the sample into three even groups, those with the highest number of hours, those with a moderate number, and those with the lowest number. It is best to work out these categories before you begin because of the indications for your sample size. Tables 8.5 and 8.6 demonstrate these categories.

In Table 8.5, two categories are used for the analysis of each variable. The sample required for such a study could be 4 x 5 = 20 (30 would be better). In Table 8.6, four categories are used for the dependent variable and three for the independent variable. The sample size required is 4 x 3 x 5 = 60.

The role of dummy tables can now be seen. They focus the research. They help to determine the categories of data analysis. They help to determine sample size. By devising dummy tables before collecting data, the researcher will not collect more data than are actually going to be used. There is no point in collecting data that will not go into the tables. The researcher is also guided in sample selection by decisions about data analysis. In this way, neither too much nor too little data are collected for analysis.

A few more examples may help to clarify this important procedure. What samples are required for longitudinal or comparative studies? Take the example of a 'before and after' longitudinal study. In such a study, the same group is studied at two points in time. Hence, the determination of sample size is made by only one of the tables.

TABLE 8.5 A dummy table for a study of the impact of number of hours spent studying on examination results using two categories for each variable

EXAMINATION RESULT	NUMBER OF HOURS SPENT STUDYING	
	HIGH	LOW
Pass		
Fail		

TABLE 8.6 A dummy table for a study of the impact of number of hours spent studying on examination results using four categories for the dependent variable and three for the independent variable

EXAMINATION RESULT	NUMBER OF HOURS SPENT STUDYING		
	LOW	MODERATE	HIGH
75+			
65–74			
50–64			
Fail			

Refer back to the example of a longitudinal study on nutrition in Chapter 7. Because the same group is measured twice, there must be a sufficient sample of that group in each measurement. The before and after measures each have three categories, so the minimum sample would be 3 x 5 = 15.

Take the example of the questionnaire developed to assess attitudes towards the building of nuclear power plants (Chapter 6). Data produced by questionnaires have to be categorized just like test results or numbers of hours spent studying. Like test results, scales on a questionnaire have a theoretical range. For the questionnaire on nuclear power plants, the range was from a low of five (indicating agreement with anti-nuclear statements) to a high of 20 (indicating disagreement with such statements). It is unlikely that you would want a table with 16 columns for this dependent variable. It will have to be categorized. High versus low agreement and high, medium, and low agreement are two possibilities. If you were comparing two groups—for example, a sample from Atomic Energy of Canada and a sample from the local Greenpeace Canada—your dummy table might look like that in Table 8.7. The sample for this study would comprise a minimum of 10 from each group. This might be achieved by a quota (accidental quota) or a stratified random (random quota) or cluster sampling procedure. Which would be best and why?

The example of a study of sexist attitudes among males provides another opportunity to examine the utility of dummy tables. The questionnaire suggested for such a study is found in Chapter 6. The hypothesis was this:

Males who have gone to single-sex schools are more sexist in their attitudes than males who have attended coeducational schools.

The independent variable is 'school social environment', single-sex versus co-educational. The dependent variable is 'sexist attitudes', as measured by responses to a five-item scale. The independent variable has two categories: single-sex and coeducational schooling (three if you include the 'mixed' category). Hence, the table for analyzing the data will have two columns, one for each category (or three if the 'mixed' category is included).

How is the dependent variable to be categorized? Again, it is unlikely that one row would be used for each of the 21 possible scores on the sexism scale. This would require a table with 21 rows. An alternative is to reduce the number of categories used to present and analyze the dependent variable. The way the scale was constructed, 'agreement' indicated a sexist orientation, and 'disagreement' indicated a lack of sexism. The midpoint on this scale was 15. A score below 15 could be taken to indicate low sexism. A score of 15 or higher could be taken to indicate high sexism. This would give two categories for the dependent variable. The break-point in the categories is determined here by the nature of the scale. Since there are two categories for the dependent variable, the table for analyzing data will have two rows.

Table 8.8 presents a dummy table for this study. The minimum sample for this study would be 20, 10 males from each educational context. If the researcher decided to use three categories for the sexism score, the minimum sample would be 30. If the researcher decided to include a category for mixed educational background as well, the sample size would have to increase to 45. Can you see

TABLE 8.7 A dummy table for a study comparing the views of two groups on the use of nuclear material

POSITION ON NUCLEAR POWER PLANTS	ATOMIC ENERGY OF CANADA	GREENPEACE CANADA
Agreement		
Disagreement		

TABLE 8.8 A dummy table for a study of the impact of educational background on sexist attitudes among males

	EDUCATIONAL BACKGROUND	
SEXISM SCORE	SINGLE-SEX SCHOOL	COEDUCATIONAL SCHOOL
High		
Low		

why? Adding a medium sexism category would add another row to the table, with the result that the table would have two columns and three rows and thus six cells. Applying our guide rule of an average of five per cell, we would need a sample of 6 x 5 = 30. If the 'mixed' category were added to the education context categories as well, the table would have three rows and three columns and thus nine cells: 9 x 5 = 45. Make up dummy tables for each of these proposed ways of analyzing the data.

For practical purposes, the sample size of student projects can be guided by two basic rules. First, 30 is the minimum sample size for most studies. Second, if analysis is to be carried out using tables, the sample size must be five times the number of cells in the table. Students should remember that in professional research, usually much larger samples are used. By limiting both the number of variables and the number of categories used to analyze each variable, smaller samples can be used. This will provide worthwhile experience in the research process.

SUMMARY

The way in which the research sample is drawn determines the degree to which you can generalize from the findings of your study. Only randomly drawn samples ensure that the sample is likely to be representative of a larger population. Although other forms of sampling are used, the findings of such studies are limited to the samples studied. Dummy tables are helpful in determining sample size, focusing the questions to be asked in the research, and preparing the way for the later analysis of the data.

QUESTIONS FOR REVIEW

1. Why do researchers use sampling procedures?
2. Why is it risky to rely on the observation of a single case in making generalizations about groups?
3. What are the two basic types of sampling procedure?
4. What are the advantages and disadvantages of each sampling procedure described?
5. What are the steps that must be taken in order to draw a truly random sample? Name two compromises with this ideal.
6. What are the critical issues in determining sample size?
7. While it is often necessary for researchers to study large samples in order to examine in detail the influence of many variables, what two basic rules can usefully guide student researchers in determining sample size?
8. Read several articles reporting research results that have been published in professional social and behavioural science journals. What sampling procedures were used?

9. Read an article, a report, or research published in a newspaper, then answer these questions. If you do not think the article contains enough information, say so. Then guess what might have been done.

a. How was the sample for this study drawn?

b. What type of sample would you say it was?

c. What dummy tables might have been used for this study?

d. What hypothesis might this study have been designed to test?

e. What were the basic concepts in this study?

f. What variables were selected to measure the concepts involved in this study?

g. How were the data collected?

h. What conclusions were reached?

Suggestions for further reading

Argyrous, George. 2000. *Statistics for Social and Health Research*. London: Sage.

Babbie, E.R. 2003. *The Practice of Social Research*. 10th edn, chapter 7. London: Wadsworth.

de Vaus, D.A. 2002. *Surveys in Social Research*. 5th edn, chapter 4. St Leonards, NSW: Allen and Unwin.

Foddy, W. 1988. *Elementary Applied Statistics for the Social Sciences*, pp. 104–5, 223. Sydney, Australia: Harper and Row.

Judd, C.M., E.R. Smith, and L.H. Kidder. 1991. *Research Methods in Social Relations*, chapters 6, 9. Fort Worth, TX: Holt, Rinehart and Winston.

Kumar, Ranjit. 1999. *Research Methodology: A Step by Step Guide for Beginners*, chapter 12. London: Sage.

Lawson, A.B. 2001. *Statistical Methods in Spatial Epidemiology*. New York: John Wiley.

Neuman, W. Lawrence. 1997. *Social Research Methods: Qualitative and Quantitative Approaches*. 3rd edn. Toronto: Allyn and Bacon.

Palys, Ted. 2003. *Research Decisions: Quantitative and Qualitative Perspectives*. 3rd edn. Toronto: Nelson.

Those interested might consult one of the following classic sources on sampling procedure:

Backstrom, C., and G. Hursh. 1963. *Survey Research*, pp. 23–66. Evanston, IL: Northwestern University Press.

Festinger, L., and D. Katz. 1953. *Research Methods in the Behavioural Sciences*, pp. 173–240. New York: Holt, Rinehart and Winston.

Goode, W., and P. Hatt. 1952. *Methods in Social Research*, pp. 209–31. New York: McGraw-Hill.

Kalton, G. 1983. *Introduction to Survey Sampling*. Thousand Oaks, CA: Sage.

Selltiz, E., M. Jahoda, M. Deutsch, and S. Cook. 1966. *Research Methods in Social Relations*, pp. 509–45. New York: Holt, Rinehart and Winston.

9

Ethics in
Human Research

The key to identifying ethical issues in research is to take the position of a participant. How would you feel if you were asked certain questions or observed doing
certain things, or if your records and papers were examined for research purposes?
How would you want researchers to handle and report on the information they
have about you? The ethical issues involved in doing research on humans are very
much the same for both quantitative and qualitative research.

Staff of Canadian universities, many research organizations, and members of
most professional organizations are now formally required to conduct their
research according to stated ethical principles and to demonstrate this to research
ethics boards (REBs). These ethical principles require that participants in the
research must be able to give informed consent to being part of the research, the
identity of informants must be protected unless they give written permission to be
identified in stored data and research reports, researchers must not coerce participants into participating or divulging information, and researchers must keep data
for up to seven years (depending on the province) to protect themselves against
charges of 'forging' data.

The purpose of this chapter is to outline major ethical considerations prior to
conducting the data collection. Typically, Canadian post-secondary institutions
and other research organizations must submit their research proposal or plans to

advisory bodies, who evaluate it based on ethical guidelines. This chapter provides information to students with regard to preparing their submissions to ethics review panels. It is a good idea to contact the board directly and obtain a copy of their guidelines and rules prior to submitting your proposal. This will help you to avoid unnecessary delays in launching your data collection, protect the integrity of the scientific research process, and likely strengthen your research results.

THE ETHICS OF RESEARCH

Research in the social sciences usually involves dealing with people, organizations, and groups. Unless you are only dealing with data that have already been collected, public records (such as census data), or public documents, you will be asking people questions, observing their behaviour, or collecting other information about them. All our dealings with other people raise ethical issues. We are familiar with the ethical issues relating to our personal lives—issues of loyalty, honesty, integrity, to name a few. Lately, businesses and corporations are beginning to ask questions about the ethics of economic life. So, too, are there ethical issues in research that need to be addressed.

As with many ethical issues in other areas of life, being thoughtful and considerate of the needs and feelings of others goes a long way towards guiding the researcher. How would you react if you were in the place of the person or group you intend to study? Would you respond well to the questions you intend to ask or the procedures you intend to employ?

Be considerate. You are asking people to do you a favour. You are appealing to their generosity to help you with your work. Not everyone will share your view of the importance of your research. This is true even if you are asking friends, family, or students you know. It is even more true if you are going into the community to do your research. You have a responsibility to the participants in your research to be considerate and not to waste their time. Moreover, you have a responsibility to researchers who will come after you not to irritate and alienate the community. If you are inconsiderate or poorly prepared, you let yourself down, waste the time and effort of others, and jeopardize future research.

Part of being considerate is being prepared. Another part is to take up only as much time as is essential. Not only does an unnecessarily long questionnaire waste your time, but it also wastes the time of those to whom it is administered. Ask yourself, 'Is this question necessary? Do I really need to know how many children the respondent has?' If the study is about sharing tasks between husband and wife, then yes, you probably do want to ask that question. But if you are inquiring about past achievement in math, you may decide to eliminate the question. Does each question really relate to the hypothesis? Or does it really reflect personal curiosity? Interviews and questionnaires with a clear focus not only produce better data but are also less disruptive and wasteful.

You should also be considerate of participants because you are, to some extent, invading their privacy. If respondents sense that you are being intrusive or asking inappropriate questions, they may refuse to cooperate or may sabotage the research by giving misleading information. Your manner and the nature of your research should be carefully designed so as not to offend, embarrass, or annoy those you are studying. They are doing you a favour.

Part of being a considerate researcher is being careful about the way you seek permission from those you wish to study. While it is appropriate to tell people why you are doing the research, it is usually not wise to tell them what you hope to find, since this may bias the information they provide. At the completion of their projects, many researchers offer to tell participants what they found and their conclusions. This often provides interesting feedback for the researcher and those studied.

A consent form signed by you and/or your professor or head of department is a requirement for conducting most research with human participants. It will help to identify you and to secure the cooperation of those you wish to be part of your study. The form should describe who you are (e.g., a student at a specified university), how you accessed the person's name, why you are doing your research (e.g., for a degree, a thesis, or a class project), and what the research will require from the person whose permission you are seeking (e.g., filling in a questionnaire that will take 10 minutes, an interview lasting an hour, a group interview lasting 15 minutes, participating in an experiment that will involve watching and assessing some videos for half an hour). Providing this information makes it possible for the potential participant to make an informed decision about whether to participate. The consent form, or 'plain language statement', about the research is essential to ensuring that 'informed consent' has been given.

A consent form usually concludes with information about what the participant should do if they have any questions or concerns about the research. This clause usually directs the participant to the REB of the university or another organization responsible for the research. Figure 9.1 gives an example of a consent form. Preparing the form is a good exercise to test whether you have thoroughly thought through your research plan. It will give your professor an opportunity to advise you about what you are doing. When students do research as part of their course, their professor is responsible for them and for the conduct of the research. Hence, it is in the interest of all for students and professors to confer carefully about each research project.

A personal card issued by your institution, stating your position (e.g., PhD student) and contact details is an effective introduction to participants (see Figure 9.2). When you give these cards to people, they see that you are being honest about your identity and purpose and that you are willing to allow others to verify who you are. This action, which shows prospective participants that you wish to act ethically and do the right thing by them, usually wins their attention and co-operation quickly. Further information, such as the contact information for the REB, can be placed on the reverse side of the card.

FIGURE 9.1 Sample consent form

Printed on university letterhead

Consent Form: Title of Project

Principal Investigator: Professor's name
Student Investigator: Student's name
Tel: XXX-XXXX
E-mail: researcher@umanitoba.ca

Date

A. PURPOSE AND BACKGROUND

This project has been funded by [*indicate funding organization if the research is sponsored*]. The research is being conducted by [*indicate professor's and student's names*] at the Department of Sociology, [*indicate university*].

In this research, we want to learn how people find work and whether they use their families and friends to find work. We are particularly interested in 1st, 1.5, and 2nd generation immigrant youth without post-secondary education. We want to talk to you about your job experiences to better understand your feelings about Canadian society. A study of youth employment will help us to understand how it may affect you and your well-being, along with its effect on the Canadian economy.

You are invited to participate in this focus group meeting. However, the participation is strictly voluntary. Only if you agree to be part of this study will you be invited to participate in the meeting and answer the questions presented to you.

B. PROCEDURES

You have been selected to participate in this research because you are a 1st, 1.5, or 2nd generation immigrant youth without post-secondary school experience. There are two ways that we obtain names for our research. First, we may have obtained your name from a list provided by [*name of organization*]. Second, someone affiliated with [*name of organization*] may have suggested your name.

If you agree to participate in this research study, you will attend a group interview, which will last no longer than two hours, to discuss your experiences looking for work. The group interview will take place at [*indicate location of focus group, date, and time*]. The group meeting will be audio-taped if you permit us.

C. RISKS

There is no anticipated physical or psychological risk related to participating in this study. Should you decline to participate, your access to employment, settlement, and/or counselling services will not be affected in any way now or in the future. You may choose not to answer any questions or may leave the

(continued)

focus group at any time. Please indicate to the researcher any sensitive question related to your personal information that you do not want to be disclosed. Confidentiality will be secured in a variety of ways. Your name and contact information will not be recorded in the interview or used in the publication of any results. All data will be kept in a secure filing cabinet in a locked office accessible only to the professor and the student.

D. COMPENSATION

You will receive $20 at the end of the group interview as compensation for participating in this research. We will also provide some light refreshments during the group meeting.

E. QUESTIONS

Please contact [*the professor, student*] if you have any questions about the project.

F. CONSENT[1]

Your signature on this form indicates that you have understood to your satisfaction the information regarding participation in the research project and agree to participate as a subject. In no way does this waive your legal rights or release the researchers, sponsors, or involved institutions from their legal and professional responsibilities. You are free to withdraw from the study at any time and/or refrain from answering any questions you prefer to omit, without prejudice or consequence. Your continued participation should be as informed as your initial consent, so you should feel free to ask for clarification or new information throughout your participation.

_____

Participant's signature   Date

_____

Researcher's signature   Date

I am interested in obtaining a summary of the findings from this research project:
No ( )
Yes ( ): If yes, how would you like to receive the results?
By e-mail ( ) Please provide e-mail address: _____
By surface mail ( ) Please provide mailing address:

_____

_____

_____

[1]This section is directly quoted from the University of Manitoba. 2007. *Human Subject Research Ethics Protocol Submissions (Ft. Garry Campus) Guidelines and Checklist for Submissions & Reviews.* http://umanitoba.ca/research/media/protocol_guidelines_checklist.doc. Retrieved 27 August 2007.

FIGURE 9.2   A sample card

<table>
<tr>
<td>

Canadian University

Reece Urcher
PhD student
Department of Sociology
Canadian University
111 Main Street
Toronto, ON A2K 2C7
Cellphone: ### ### ####
Fax: ### ### ####
E-mail: reeceurcher@canadianu.ca

</td>
<td>

If you have any questions about this study,
you may contact the Secretary of the
Research Ethics Board.

Telephone: ### ### ####
E-mail: HERB@canadianu.ca
Surface Mail:
Secretary, Research Ethics Board
Canadian University
111 Main Street
Toronto, ON A2K 2C7

</td>
</tr>
</table>

FORMAL ETHICAL REVIEW OF RESEARCH

Simply being considerate is not enough. The ethics of all research involving human participants has become a major area of discussion and policy review. Most professional associations, like the Canadian Sociological Association and the Canadian Association of Social Workers, have devised codes of ethics to guide their members. Read the code of ethics for the professional association related to your intended occupation. These ethical codes are usually available on-line.

Following a number of excesses perpetrated by some over-zealous or unscrupulous researchers in various fields, procedures have been instituted in all post-secondary institutions for the careful ethical scrutiny of research proposals by REBs prior to the commencement of the research and before funding is approved or passed on to the researchers. First instituted to guide medical research, ethical review is now required for all research involving human participants. The fundamental principles are stated in a document called the *Tri-Council Policy Statement: Ethical Conduct for Research Involving Humans* prepared by the Canadian Institutes of Health Research, the Natural Sciences and Engineering Research Council of Canada, and the Social Sciences and Humanities Research Council of Canada. This document states the current thinking on ethics for Canadian research involving humans. REBs use the principles in this statement to guide their consideration of research proposals. Most universities now require all research involving humans, including most sociological, psychological, business management, marketing, science, education, and oral history research, to be evaluated by an ethics committee.

Basic principles of research ethics

The following principles of research ethics summarize the concerns most REBs focus on in evaluating research proposals.

Principle 1: Researchers must treat with dignity and respect the persons, groups, and organizations who participate in their research.

People have feelings, orientations, cultures, rights to privacy, and rights to control their lives and information about themselves. The rights of people are greater than the researcher's 'need to know'. However important you think your research is, you must place participants' well-being first. Referring to participants as 'participants' rather than 'subjects' and remembering that you are dealing with people, not objects, helps to retain the levels of respect and concern appropriate to humans.

Sensitivity to others is very important but especially in social science research, where it is precisely that sensitivity that may open new insights into the nature of social situations. You are asking people, 'What is it like to be you? What is your perspective on this? How do you respond to this or that situation?' In order to 'hear' their responses, you need both to ask sensitive questions and to listen very sensitively to their responses.

Following current discussion of ethics in human research, we refer to people who consent to be researched as 'participants', rather than 'subjects', for several reasons. First, the term 'participant' implies a degree of cooperative activity on the part of those we study. Participants are not passive subjects but cooperate with us in our research. It is important to remember that without the cooperation of participants, we will not get our data. This helps to remind us of our dependence on them and to enhance our respect for them.

'Participants' is also a useful term because it encompasses groups, corporations, organizations, and neighbourhoods as well as persons. All participants have rights, needs for privacy, and a claim on our respect.

The respect accorded participants extends to treating the information they provide with great care and not violating their privacy. One way of protecting your informants is to mask their identity by never recording names, by changing the names on your files and using fictitious names in your reports, by assigning numerical codes, and by referring only to grouped data (that is, not to Tom Brown's score individually but to the average score of 'young males' in response to a particular question). You can mask the locality of your research by not naming the municipality or organization in which the research was done.

If you are promising participants that you will protect their identities, your REB will wish to know how you will accomplish this (e.g., de-identifying records and reports of information with codes, keeping records locked in a secure place).

After gaining permission, you must retain sufficient information, including letters of invitation, consent forms, and data, to prove that you actually did what you proposed to do and were given ethical clearance to do so. This is necessary to defend yourself against the possible charge of forging your data and to be prepared for an audit by your REB.

Personal information and privacy

In most social science research, there is no need to collect information that identifies individual participants. Researchers seldom need facts that can identify individual participants to others. However, if you plan to gather and publish such information, you must know the relevant law regarding privacy. Most provinces and territories have passed privacy legislation, which bind researchers to protect their participants' 'personal information'. It is a good idea to become familiar with the privacy legislation in your province. The *Tri-Council Policy Statement* contains general guidelines about protecting individual privacy. Personal information includes information given to the researcher by the participant. It may be answers provided to survey questions or in interviews. It may be health information from physicians' records or academic grades from school. Regardless of the source, 'personal information' identifies individuals and should be kept from public viewing.

Depending on the relevant privacy principles, there can be additional restrictions on the collection, use, and disclosure of a type of personal information—'sensitive information'. According to section 1(F) of the *Tri-Council Policy Statement*, this includes information or an opinion about an individual's race, ethnicity, sexual preference, criminal record, religious beliefs and affiliations, philosophical beliefs, health information, political opinions, and membership in political parties, trade unions, and professional associations. 'Health information' is information or an opinion about an individual's health or disabilities, their health service usage or intended use, personal information they give to health services, and personal information they give when arranging the donation of their body parts.

Before gathering personal information, always consult an expert in privacy regulations. If you research within a government department or private firm, talk to the privacy officer. If you research as a consultant or with a volunteer organization, seek advice from a lawyer. Most universities have units that will provide advice to researchers about privacy laws. Be familiar with the privacy legislation of your province. Otherwise, you may compromise participants' rights and break the law.

The following list contains some of the Tri-Council's guiding ethical principles. It is an introduction to the types of obligations that researchers face when the *Tri-Council Policy Statement* is relevant.

- **Respect for human dignity:** Researchers must maintain the physical, social, and cultural integrity of all participants.
- **Respect for free and informed consent:** Participants must be fully informed about the purpose and intended results of the research project. They must not be coerced into participating by any means.
- **Respect for vulnerable persons:** The Tri-Council (2005: i.5) defines vulnerable persons as 'children, institutionalized persons or others who are vulnerable'.

Researchers must take special care in studying these participants. This usually means obtaining consent from parents/guardians or primary caregivers.

- **Respect for privacy and confidentiality:** Care must be taken to protect 'access, control and dissemination of personal information' (Tri-Council, 2005: i.5). Participant information must be kept in secure locations and not shared for purposes outside the intended research. Published documents must remove any identifying information that may compromise the privacy and confidentiality of research participants.
- **Respect for justice and inclusiveness:** This clause is of primary concern to population subgroups subject to significant research. According to the Tri-Council (2005: i.6), 'no segment of the population should be unfairly burdened with the harms of research.' However, sub-populations should not be neglected in research, especially if they may benefit from the research results.
- **Balancing harms and benefits:** Participation in research should not result in harm to participants. At the very least, 'foreseeable harms should not outweigh anticipated benefits' (Tri-Council, 2005: i.6).
- **Minimizing harm:** It is the researcher's duty to avoid, prevent, or minimize harm to participants. To minimize harm, research projects should recruit the smallest number of participants and subject them to the smallest number of tests needed to achieve valid data.
- **Maximizing benefit**: In most research, the participant receives no direct benefit from participating in the study. The benefit is usually in the published research that helps to advance knowledge in a particular field or discipline.

Principle 2: Research must be based on knowledge of the work of others in the area and be conducted and/or supervised by persons qualified to do the work who have the necessary facilities to ensure the safety of participants.

It is unethical to rush into the field to collect data before doing a literature review to learn about what has been done before, what is known, and what questions remain in the field of study you propose. It is also usually a great help to see how others have tackled the problem you propose to study. It is unethical to carry out poorly designed research since, at the very least, people's time is wasted and, at worst, misleading results might be declared. It is likely that any research you do as a student will need to be cleared by an REB.

While many of the skills required for social science research are ordinary skills of human interaction, their use in research requires careful supervision, particularly when students are learning how to research. In one of the co-authors' experience on an REB, the most problematic research proposals have come from researchers who were just being introduced to the skills of social science research. New researchers require close assistance from their supervisors, who should not allow them to choose sensitive topics that are more appropriate for experienced researchers.

Supervision is also required because in the process of interviewing someone, you may uncover problems that are beyond your ability to resolve—a difficult domestic situation, a deeply troubled person, or some other such circumstance. You are probably not trained as a counsellor, as a family therapist, or in other helping skills, and hence you have no business trying to solve these problems. You should carry the name of a social worker, counsellor, or medical practitioner to whom you can refer people in need. You may have to report a particularly serious situation to the police or a social worker. However, you are only there to collect information relevant to your research project; you are not a helping agent. Your abilities and responsibilities are quite limited. Discuss these issues with the person responsible for your research, your professor or supervisor.

Principle 3: The potential benefits of a research project must substantially outweigh the potential harm to participants.

Again, discuss these issues with the person responsible for your research, your professor or supervisor. Your REB can also provide input on these issues. REBs are called on to weigh the promised benefits of a project against its potential to harm participants and also to ensure the collection of relevant data. While researchers have a responsibility to minimize harm, the role of the researcher is different from the role of the therapist or helper. Confusion of therapy and research often leads to serious ethical dilemmas.

Principle 4: Participants in research must be able to make a voluntary, informed decision to participate.

Informed consent

The decision to participate must be based on knowledge of what will be involved, what will be demanded in terms of time, activity, and topics covered, what risks are likely, and where to lodge a complaint should that become necessary. This information is usually provided by means of a consent form like the sample in Figure 9.1, otherwise referred to as a 'plain language statement'. Potential participants must understand such information. This may require translation, careful wording in everyday language, and avoiding the disciplinary jargon that researchers use for efficient communication with each other but that leaves the layperson bewildered.

Written consent from the participant is required in almost all instances of research where humans are participants. Increasingly, REBs are requiring researchers conducting on-line surveys and self-administered surveys to have all participants sign consent forms. The consent forms are usually stored in locked filing cabinets for a period of up to seven years (depending on the provincial legislation). These consent forms are stored separately from the data collected.

Usually, the risks and discomforts involved in social science research are minimal. However, there are risks that need to be carefully examined. The most important issue here is the risk of the disclosure of information, which might be damaging to a person. It is not possible for you to promise absolute confidentiality to the people you interview. There is always a chance that direct quotes may identify individuals. It is your duty to inform all participants of this, no matter how remote the chance. You could be subpoenaed for results if they have a bearing on a court case. Your files are open to searches under the freedom of information legislation current in your province. Before embarking on a project in which this might happen, ask yourself, 'How would I deal with it?'

Gaining informed consent poses particular problems for social research. Much of what is studied is public behaviour. This does not usually require consent. Some research is little more than having a conversation with someone. However, that conversation may have proceeded differently if the participant in the research had known the intent of the conversation. In such a case, it would be ethically correct to inform the participant, but such information might destroy the validity of the research. REBS now assist researchers to resolve some of these ethical issues.

Another issue related to discomfort and risk concerns asking questions about sensitive areas. Topics may be sensitive because they are public issues, politically sensitive, or personally painful. For example, interviewing parents a few months after the death of their child from sudden infant death syndrome might be important in understanding the grief process following such a death, but it might be too disruptive to the parents and in fact could affect (positively or negatively) the very process you intended to study. Students are usually encouraged to avoid such sensitive areas while they are learning to do research.

Voluntariness

While rarely an issue in social science research, it is important not to coerce compliance by offering overly enticing rewards for participation, such as large sums of money or holidays in the sun. At most, participants may receive reimbursement for expenses or some small compensation for the time they give.

In some cases of social science research, the investigator may be in a position of power over the participant (e.g., parent/child, professor/student, employer/ employee, supervisor/subordinate, parole officer/parolee). When this is the case, particular care must be taken in securing consent. In some cases, it may be impossible to get free consent, and the research may have to be abandoned. In other cases, a neutral third party may be able to secure the consent. Further, an interviewer wearing a lab coat or a clerical collar while conducting an interview may be playing on a symbol of authority to gain the participant's acquiescence. The style of clothing to wear while conducting an interview needs to be considered in terms of the power relations between interviewer and interviewee.

However, in most social science research, the most powerful figure is likely to be the participant, who can just walk away, refuse to answer, or give a 'safe' or misleading answer.

Freedom to withdraw

Participants in your research must not only be free to consent to participating at the outset, they must also be reminded that they are free to withdraw at any time without penalty. This can be very frustrating to researchers, but it is not ethical to pressure participants to complete interviews and questionnaires or to stay for the completion of the experiment. To do otherwise violates the rights and freedom of the participant. Arguing or pleading with a participant that their withdrawal will waste your time, threaten your grade in a subject, hold up your degree, necessitate another interview with someone else, or render invalid the questionnaire constitutes pressure and is therefore unethical. Students should bear this in mind when constructing questionnaires. Keep them short so that people will complete them.

Principle 5: Research is a public activity, conducted openly and accountable both to the researcher's community and to the participants in the research.

Research is a public activity conducted to increase our knowledge of some aspect of the universe. Its very public nature is one of the strengths of knowledge generated by research. Recall the definition of science in Chapter 1. This public nature of research also helps to keep researchers honest and affords a level of protection to participants.

This applies to research teams and covers the rights of co-researchers and assistants. It is important that all involved are as fully informed as possible so that they know what they are part of, what their role in the project is, what the overall goal is, and what procedures are involved. Keeping co-workers and subordinates in the dark is dangerous, inconsiderate, a waste of their input, and unethical. Imagine how you would feel if after working on some aspect of a project, you discovered that its overall goal or basic technique violated your sense of right and wrong.

The research ethics boards at most post-secondary institutions have representatives from a variety of disciplines—from medicine, law, and religion—and from the wider community to provide a public forum for assessing the ethical considerations in specific research projects. All research involving humans, organizations, and corporations requires the scrutiny and approval of an REB. Much of the research in social science does not raise life and death issues; however, many proposals require important advice, caution, or redesign to protect either the researcher or the participants.

ETHICAL ISSUES IN QUALITATIVE RESEARCH

Qualitative research often brings researchers and participants into close contact and creates a need for the interests of both to be balanced. Researchers can improve the lives of participants if they have access to such data, and they need support in their efforts. Since participants provide researchers with personal data, they need to be protected from infringements on their privacy. Research ethics boards consider a number of issues as they seek to support the interests of both participants and researchers.

First, the close and sometimes extended contact between researchers and participants can change researcher/participant relationships and compromise the original conditions under which studies receive ethics approval. REBs require formal relationships between researchers and participants based on clear explanations by researchers and the official consent of participants. During in-depth interviews and participant observation, you and your participants develop a rapport and personal trust, and the relationship can become less formal and more personal. Eventually, participants may reveal personal secrets, trusting you to remain silent. Such confidences are often of little consequence, but participants may confide personal information that will force you to make difficult choices. They may reveal facts that you as a researcher are obliged to report—that they are victims of abuse or perpetrators of crimes. In such situations, you would be faced with a conflict of trust. Either you betray the trust of your participant, or you betray your professional and ethical obligations.

Similarly, in-depth interviews about sensitive issues may stimulate memories that participants find upsetting. REBs often require that researchers make provisions for referring participants to counselling agencies should they have such problems. It is not ethical for you to conduct an interview or series of interviews that leaves respondents upset, with nothing in place to meet their need.

Given the personal nature of much qualitative data, REBs seek to protect participants' privacy. You must obtain permission from participants if you wish to quote them in reports. The general practice is to assign pseudonyms to all participants in publications and research reports. Researchers must also take steps to de-identify data—that is, they must remove all references to the identities of participants from tapes and transcripts, such as names and unique characteristics. Lastly, REBs oblige researchers to keep data in secure places, such as locked filing cabinets, that only they and their supervisors can access. You must have such places ready before collecting data and should officially notify participants in your explanatory statement that you have made such an arrangement to protect their data.

REBs also have concerns about observational studies. University and college students must obtain permission from their REB for all observational research. This includes observations of public events such as church services and concerts. In addition, when observation focuses on specific organizations, groups, or individuals, REBs require that researchers obtain permission from the intended participants. Therefore, if you wish to observe a local political group, an order of nuns, or a touring soccer team, your REB may not give approval until the potential participants supply their written permission. If researchers plan to conduct observation studies on premises that are privately owned or have restricted entry, researchers are obliged by their REBs to obtain permission to enter the premises from owners or caretakers. Hence, if you wish to enter factories to observe workers, convention centres to observe visitors, or nightclubs to observe patrons, your REB will require letters of permission from owners or managers. Most research done in shopping centres also requires permission from the manager of the complex.

Regarding covert or naturalistic observation, section 2.3 of the *Tri-Council Policy Statement* (2005: 2.4) contains a number of conditions that REBs use in considering research proposals. Generally, covertness in all research is unethical unless it is necessary for the research to have scientific validity, the researchers are able to accurately define the extent of the covertness, no alternatives exist, participants are not exposed to any increased harm by the covertness of the project, researchers make immediate disclosures to participants, participants are able to withdraw their data, and the research will not bring notoriety to the research community.

If you intend to audio- or video-record people in any situation, you must show your REB that you will take steps to obtain the consent of participants. Moreover, your REB will require that you tell potential participants about what you intend to do with their taped material and undertake not to use it in any other way.

Should you wish to consult archives, your REB will require that you obtain permission from the legal custodians. You would also be obliged to inform the custodians of how you intend to use the material and not to use it for any other purpose.

Research with Aboriginal peoples

The Canadian Institutes of Health Research (CIHR), the Natural Science and Engineering Research Council (NSERC), and the Social Sciences and Humanities Research Council (SSHRC) have developed ethics guidelines for research about Aboriginal peoples. Section 6 of the *Tri-Council Policy Statement* (2005) describes some of the guidelines for researching Aboriginal peoples. We summarize the arguments of a recent SSHRC document entitled *Opportunities in Aboriginal Research: Results of SSHRC's Dialogue on Research and Aboriginal Peoples* (McNaughton and Rock, 2003).

1. **Decolonizing research:** Current research on Aboriginal peoples should include 'indigenous knowledge, traditions, beliefs and values'; adhere 'to Aboriginal protocols at all stages'; involve Elders and Aboriginal researchers; involve partnership at all stages of research design; and use 'Aboriginal methodologies as appropriate to local traditions and the subject being addressed' (McNaughton and Rock, 2003: 15).
2. **Equity:** All participants should be treated fairly and equally by Aboriginal and non-Aboriginal researchers.
3. **Equitable treatment of Aboriginal researchers:** Aboriginal peoples should be represented on grant adjudication committees; the merit of non-academic contributions should be considered; Aboriginal researchers should be identified as such in projects.

4. **From obligation to opportunity:** This involves moving beyond the post-colonial critique that has defined much research on Aboriginal peoples in Canada. Recognition of the rights and self-worth of Aboriginal peoples can help our society move forward. Research on Aboriginal peoples that incorporates opportunity for Aboriginal researchers and common research goals may be a first step in social justice.

5. **Arm's length partnership with Aboriginal peoples:** SSHRC, NSERC, and CIHR have all created special advisory bodies that oversee research for and about Aboriginal peoples. The idea is to give 'Aboriginal scholars and other Aboriginal knowledge-keepers full responsibility for management of research' on Aboriginal issues (McNaughton and Rock, 2003: 17).

6. **Gus-wen-tah and joint exploration:** This refers to the Aboriginal way of knowing. Gus-wen-tah is also referred to as the Two Row Wampum, 'a treaty to express the rightful relationship between the Haudenosaunee (leadership of the nations) and European nations' (McNaughton and Rock, 2003: 18). The relationship between 'Western knowledge' and the 'Aboriginal way of knowing' should be equal. Today, the 'Aboriginal way of knowing' is not primary in Canadian society. Researchers should work to place the 'Aboriginal way of knowing' on an equal footing.

7. **Joint exploration of knowledge opportunities:** Using the Gus-wen-tah may be a way to promote equitable research in the social sciences and humanities.

Researchers must always exercise integrity in adhering to the above guidelines. These guidelines already have practical support in protocols developed by the Tri-Council with respect to research with Aboriginal communities. Researchers should engage with Aboriginal communities as 'collectivities'—that is, as entities representing their members. It is always necessary to negotiate formal participation and consent with Aboriginal communities through their representative bodies (usually band councils and chiefs). As when engaging with individual participants, researchers must obtain written consent. Research ethics boards usually require that negotiations occur in face-to-face situations. By doing so, researchers observe the guideline of equality. Researchers must also respect the power of Aboriginal communities to refuse their approaches, especially since Aboriginal peoples have been the subject of many dubious research projects over the past two centuries.

When consent is obtained, researchers must accept the role of 'guest' in their 'host' Aboriginal communities, thereby showing respect and observing reciprocity. Aboriginal communities must make the final decisions about the design and conduct of all stages of the research. Communities are then able to retain project ownership, ensure their receipt of benefits, protect themselves against exploitation, and preserve their voices and cultural viewpoints in the findings.

For example, communities and researchers must collaborate in the first stage— the formulation of research goals. Communities can then ensure that the goals are relevant to their needs and hence that projects will lead to benefits for them. In the past, researchers built careers studying Aboriginal peoples, who in return received little benefit. Such exploitation is no longer acceptable, and researchers must negotiate topics pertinent to communities' needs. Researchers must also present frequent progress reports in formats and language that host communities deem appropriate. This responsibility upholds partnership and ensures that projects remain true to agreements.

Communities should also participate in decisions about methodology, particularly with respect to issues of cultural sensitivity. For example, a community can stipulate that questionnaires be written in its first language or that the researcher should not interview members of their opposite sex.

Communities may also impose guidelines on the administration of research. A community may ask a researcher to only recruit assistants from among its members. It may also require a researcher to respect the secrecy of certain knowledge. A community may also stipulate that findings be presented in its own language and only in the context of its anticipated benefits.

Researchers should respect the knowledge of Aboriginal peoples—that is, their interpretations and viewpoints of the world. Aboriginal knowledge always takes precedence over that of other cultures, and researchers must acknowledge this in analysis and reporting. If a community attaches special meaning to certain wildlife on their land, researchers must respect this knowledge and, if the community consents, make it a context of their findings. This protocol supports the guideline of equality.

By entering into a formal contract with the Aboriginal community, the researcher formalizes their partnership. In doing so, the researcher observes the guidelines of responsibility and equality. Such contracts should contain clauses on administrative matters. These may include project timetables, principles for project evaluation, methods of obtaining consent from individual members, ways of negotiating changes to research, payments to communities, and procedures for resolving disputes between communities and researchers.

Contracts should also have clauses regarding cultural sensitivities. These clauses may formalize agreement on a researcher's access to culturally sensitive materials, information, and places; the production of images in reports; and appropriate forms of interaction between the researcher and individuals.

There should also be clauses on matters of cultural and intellectual property. The *United Nations Declaration on the Rights of Indigenous Peoples* recognizes that Aboriginal peoples have ownership of their cultural practices, artefacts, and knowledge. For research that incorporates these possessions, communities have legal claims to intellectual property such as final reports, books, cinema, and sound recordings.

This is only a general description of the ethics of researching among Aboriginal communities. You should look at the official documents on research ethics published by your university and from the major Aboriginal associations, including the Assembly of First Nations, the Congress of Aboriginal Peoples, the Métis National Council, and the Inuit Tapiriit Kanatami, for additional guidelines.

SUMMARY

For social scientists, the major ethical issues centre on gaining an appropriate form of informed consent, respecting individual privacy and confidentiality, being aware of the power dimension of the relationship between the researcher and the participants in research, and ensuring that the research procedures (variables selected, measurement used, sample selected, and design employed) are adequate to answer the questions being asked. Confidentiality is a particular problem, since it is necessary to keep original data in a readily retrievable form in order to prove that they really were collected, not faked. Further, your files can be subpoenaed if they are relevant to legal proceedings, and you would be liable to charges of withholding evidence if you refused to hand them over or to charges of destroying evidence if you obliterated your files. Therefore, it is not possible to guarantee absolute confidentiality to participants. You can promise to protect the privacy of participants and interviewees by assigning case numbers, changing names, and dealing with group-level data, but there are limits to all undertakings of confidentiality and anonymity.

You must remain aware that there are always ethical issues involved in doing research. Sometimes you need to discuss proposed research with others not as close to the research as you are so that you may become aware of these issues and can find a way to solve the problems. Some people think that only medical or biological research poses ethical issues. That would be true if social research were inconsequential, if it had no effect. But most social research *is* consequential and therefore does pose ethical issues regarding its consequences for those who participate.

The responsible researcher is considerate, does nothing to injure, harm, or disturb the participants, keeps data collected on individuals and groups secure, accurately records information, and reports the findings of the research in a public manner.

QUESTIONS FOR REVIEW

1. Why is the ethical review of research necessary? Why is this something for which researchers need outside help in the form of a research ethics board?

2. List some of the ethical issues involved in social research. Read research reported in journals or newspapers, and discuss with other students the issues you see. For example, would you like to have been a participant in the research? Is it ethical to waste other people's time? Is it ethical to conduct poorly designed research? Is it ethical to conduct research in such a way that those following you find it harder to gain access to people for research?

3. Find out the procedures in your university, college, or other institution for the ethical review of research. Try filling out the required form for a piece of research you are considering.
4. Does your professional association have a code of ethics? If so, read it, and compare it to the codes of two other professions.

Suggestions for further reading

Babbie, E.R. 2003. *The Practice of Social Research*. 10th edn, chapter 17. London: Wadsworth.

For research ethics regulation in Canada:
CIHR, NSERC, SSHRC. 2005. *Tri-Council Policy Statement: Ethical Conduct for Research Involving Humans*. Ottawa: Public Works and Government Services Canada.
The codes of ethics published by various professional bodies, such as the Canadian Sociological Association (http://www.csaa.ca/structure/Code.htm), the Canadian Association of Social Workers (http://www.casw-acts.ca), and the Canadian Psychological Association (*Canadian Code of Ethics for Psychologists*. 2000. 3rd edn).

For information and advice on the ethics of conducting research among Aboriginal communities:
McNaughton, C., and D. Rock. 2003. *Opportunities in Aboriginal Research: Results of SSHRC's Dialogue on Research and Aboriginal Peoples*. Ottawa: SSHRC.
United Nations High Commissioner for Human Rights (UNHCHR). 1997. *Fact Sheet No. 9: The Rights of Indigenous Peoples*. Geneva: UNHCHR. http://www.unhchr.ch/html/menu6/2/fs9.htm.
World Health Organization. 2003. *Indigenous Peoples and Participatory Health Research*. Geneva: World Health Organization.

PHASE 2

Data Collection

10

Making Notes, Organizing Data, and Constructing Bibliographies

By now you should be well aware that doing research involves far more than data collection. The research process does not begin, nor does it end, with data collection. Before worthwhile data collection can be done, the researcher must:

1. focus the problem;
2. identify and define the basic concepts involved;
3. select variables that relate to each of the concepts under study;
4. devise ways of measuring each of the variables;
5. select a research design that will provide the desired information about the relation between variables;
6. decide on a sampling procedure;
7. draw the sample.

Unless each of these essential first steps is completed, data collection will often be done in a wasteful, haphazard, and unproductive way.

If preparatory steps are completed, data collection can proceed smoothly, efficiently, and with little wasted time or effort on the part of either the researcher or the participants in the research. Time is a scarce resource for most researchers. Moreover, someone who is being interviewed has the right to expect the researcher to be organized, efficient, and professional.

You may think that with all the preparation done, all that is needed in this chapter are the words *Go to it!* While that is true in a sense, there are a few important issues to consider.

ATTENTION TO DETAIL

While you are collecting and recording your data, it is essential to pay careful attention to detail in observation. The loss of detail in data collection may make subsequent data analysis impossible.

The suggestions in this chapter largely assume that records will be kept in computer databases or computer files. Historically, notes, references, and data organization were collected on sheets of paper or written on cards. Today, however, most researchers record their bibliography in electronic format and keep their notes in a program that allows them to retrieve notes on similar topics and that records their data for analysis. The logic of these activities remains the same as in the past. Records must be kept, and they must be kept clearly and in such a way that they can be retrieved easily. If you rely on computer storage and retrieval for your information, make sure that you back it up frequently, and print out hard copies from time to time to protect yourself against loss as a result of computer failure or human error.

KEEP A RESEARCH JOURNAL

A research journal is a good idea. Keep a record of the ideas you have considered. Record the decisions you make and the reasons for the decisions. It is amazing how much you forget in a short time. What decisions did you make as you narrowed the focus of your research project? What forms of the hypothesis and research question did you consider? Why did you select the one you did? Why did you select the variables you did? How did you develop the measure for your variables? What issues did you consider as you chose a sampling procedure and actually selected your sample? A few notes on these issues kept in a research journal (or logbook) will be very helpful when you write your report. They are also helpful in answering questions that people may raise about the research.

MAINTAIN A BIBLIOGRAPHY

Another useful tip is to keep a record of the material you have read or consulted in the course of your research. If you note the bibliographic details when you consult the material, you save yourself the effort of tracking it down later. It is best to keep your bibliography and note cards separately. Then at the end, you will have a complete bibliography in one place and your notes where you need them to write the text of your report. Both notes and bibliography records can be kept on cards or as electronic files. Remember to back up files to prevent accidental loss. Some examples of bibliographic referencing follow.

FIGURE 10.1 A sample bibliography for a book

Schissel, B. 1997. *Blaming Children: Youth Crime, Moral Panics and the Politics of Hate*. Halifax: Fernwood.

The information required for a book is author(s), date, title, place of publication, and publisher.

FIGURE 10.2 A sample bibliography for an article

Helly, D. 2004. 'Are Muslims discriminated against in Canada since September 2001?'. *Canadian Ethnic Studies* 36, 1: 24–47.

The information required for an article is author(s), date, title, journal, volume number, issue number (if there is one), and page span.

FIGURE 10.3 A sample bibliography for a chapter (or an article reprinted) in an edited book

Campbell, Lori D., and Michael Carroll. 2007. 'Aging in Canadian Families today'. In David Cheal, ed., *Canadian Families Today*, 117–33. Don Mills, ON: Oxford University Press.

The information required for a chapter in an edited book is author(s), date, title of chapter, name of book editor, title of book, page span of chapter, place of publication, and publisher.

Rather than providing an example of every possible type of publication, the order of the information required is given below. In this way, if you encounter a type of publication you are not sure how to handle, you can work it out for yourself. If you are still confused, ask your professor. There is no single universally accepted format for referencing. Each discipline and every publisher have their own preferences. This one is common in the social sciences and is called APA (American Psychological Association) format. There are some very useful computer programs for storing useful bibliographic information. As well, writing and style guides will help you decide which referencing format best suits your discipline.

1. **The author(s).** The authors are listed as they appear, in the order they appear, with initials or full names as you wish. If the author is a group or organization—for example, the Canadian Institutes for Health Research—it is listed as the author. If the author is unknown, put 'anon.' for 'anonymous' in place of an author's name. If the author(s) is in fact the editor(s) of the book, place 'Ed.' or 'Eds' after the name of the author(s) as appropriate.

2. **The date of publication.** This should be the date of the edition to which you are referring. Some people put the date of original publication in brackets after the publication date if the two dates are different. If one author has more than one publication in a year, they are listed in alphabetical order by title in the following manner:

Author (date + a)
Author (date + b)

3. **The title of the work cited.** Book titles are underlined or put in italics. Journal articles or chapters in a book may be enclosed within single quotation marks.

   a. For journal articles, chapters in books, and articles in newspapers, the title is followed by a statement of the larger source of which it is a part and the pages on which it is found. The form for an article and a chapter in an edited book is given in Figure 10.3.

   b. For books, government publications, newspapers (unless it is absolutely obvious), and encyclopaedias, the title is followed by the place of publication and the publisher.

The general rule is that a bibliographic reference must include all the information someone else would need to find the reference quickly and easily. You should keep a separate computer file for each document you consult. Another handy tip is to create a bibliography at the beginning of your project. Add sources as you reference them. That way, your bibliography only requires double-checking (to ensure that all sources are cited or to remove unneeded references) before submitting your paper.

RECORDING NOTES

Note cards are useful for keeping track of ideas and information you read in the sources you consult. When it comes time to write your report, you need to merely consult your notes, and you will have all the information you need for a proper quotation and reference. Begin a new note record for each work from which you take notes. Head the record with the name of the author and the date of publication. A sample record is depicted in Figure 10.4. Keeping your bibliography cards and note records in alphabetical order will help you to find material when you need to consult your notes.

Most researchers today utilize various kinds of computer software designed for note-taking and retrieval. Most programs allow you to 'scan' your notes using key concepts to locate relevant material.

When taking notes, put quotation marks around direct quotations, and note the page on the note record. If you are summarizing the material in your own words, do not use quotation marks, but make a note of the page(s) on which the summarized material appeared in the source.

If you quote from a source when writing your report, you will have the information needed for a proper reference on the note card, from which you will draw the

FIGURE 10.4   A sample note card

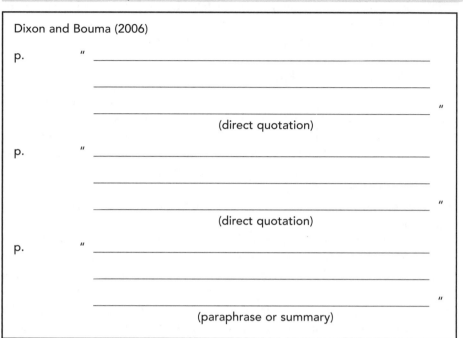

quotation. One convenient form of referencing, called the Harvard (or scientific) system, uses the following format. The author's name, the date of publication, and the page number(s) are given in the body of the text. In the bibliography at the end of the report, the full information is listed. Readers wishing to find out more about a reference need only consult the bibliography under the relevant name and date. This reduces the clutter of bibliographic detail.

Dixon and Bouma (2006, 42) report that:

_____

_____

_____

If a direct quotation is used, the quotation is placed in quotation marks. The following forms are also used:

According to Dixon and Bouma (2006, 86–8):

'_____

_____

_____'

or

'_____

_____' (Dixon and Bouma 2006, 92).

The decision about which form to use depends on the preference of the writer and the flow of the sentence, but it is also dictated by the format used by your publisher or the preferences of your professor. The reference is placed before the full stop, not after it. Long quotations are usually indented.

DATA COLLECTION SHEETS

Data collected for each 'unit of analysis' should be recorded separately. A unit of analysis can be any of the individual or collective elements of the entity being researched. You will need one data record for each unit of analysis—for example, each person, group, or hour of television in your study. This is required for later analysis of the results. Therefore, you must keep separate the data collected on each entity studied, each person or group. For example, do not ask for the responses of more than one person on a single questionnaire form. It will be impossible to disentangle the results later.

To do this properly, you must first ask what the unit of analysis in your research is. Is it the individual, the (university) class, or the group? It is possible for the same hypothesis to be researched at different levels of analysis. For example, in studying the impact of the amount of time spent studying on the result of a history examination, the unit of analysis was the student. Each student in each class filled out a questionnaire, so the researcher had a record of hours spent studying and exam result for each student. In contrast, the class was the unit of analysis in the experimental study of the relation between the amount of time a class had to read material and a test of the class's comprehension of that material. This study design was described in Chapter 7. Classes were given different amounts of time to study the material, and the average results for the classes were compared. In that case, a data sheet for each class was all that was required.

Similarly, in the study of workers' snack selections (in Chapter 7), machine operators on A-shift were used as the unit of analysis. The proportions of the selections made by all A-shift machine operators of junk food, fruit, and 'other' snacks was the datum collected. The machine operators on A-shift received the talk on nutritious snack selection, and the results for the shift were recorded. One data-recording sheet for each shift, not each worker, was necessary.

By keeping separate records of each unit of analysis, you effectively manage data for both analysis and review. When conducting analysis, you can easily recover data for each unit, allowing you to distinguish between cases that follow trends and those that do not. Further, if you suspect that some of your data is incorrect, you can review each unit individually.

In summary, be careful as you collect your data. Be careful and considerate with those you study. Be careful and meticulous in carrying out your research with precision and in recording your findings accurately.

QUESTIONS FOR REVIEW

1. What seven steps need to be taken before a researcher can collect data?
2. What information should researchers record in their journals?
3. What information should be kept on bibliography cards for:
   a. a book?
   b. an article?
   c. a chapter in a book?
4. What is a 'unit of analysis'? Why is it important to know this in preparing data collection sheets and data-recording sheets?

Suggestions for further reading

de Vaus, D.A. 2002. *Surveys in Social Research*. 5th edn, part II. St Leonards, NSW: Allen and Unwin.

Foddy, William. 1993. *Constructing Questions for Interviews and Questionnaires: Theory and Practice in Social Research*. Cambridge: Cambridge University Press.

Minichiello, Victor, Rosalie Aroni, Eric Timewell, and Loris Alexander. 1995. *In-depth Interviewing: Principles, Techniques, Analysis*. 2nd edn, chapters 10, 11. Melbourne: Longman Cheshire.

Northey, Margot, Lorne Tepperman, and James Russell. 2005. *Making Sense: A Student's Guide to Research and Writing, Social Sciences*. Updated 2nd edn. Don Mills, ON: Oxford University Press.

11

Summarizing and Presenting Data in Quantitative Research

You have collected your data. What are you going to do with the stacks of questionnaires, data sheets, or completed interviews? You will have made some tentative decisions about this when you prepared dummy tables earlier. Nonetheless, when you are confronted with a pile of data, new problems emerge, and further decisions will have to be made. Once data have been collected, it is necessary to decide how they are to be summarized and presented. This chapter provides an introduction to presenting data collected using quantitative research. Chapter 12 examines how qualitative data is analyzed and presented. Remember, there is no 'contest' between quantitative and qualitative data. The selection of data collection strategies depends on the theory used and the research question asked.

Since this text presupposes no knowledge of statistics on the part of students, some methods of data summarization and presentation will not be covered. It is strongly suggested that students wishing to make statistical inferences about correlation and causation consult the statistical readings presented at the end of this chapter. This book also assumes that the projects undertaken will be very limited in scale so that in-depth computer analysis of data is not required. Most of the techniques described in this chapter can be completed manually or by using standard computer software. Regardless of the method of data collection you choose, a standard 'common sense' approach to data summarization and presentation is necessary in projects that involve both very simple and very sophisticated analysis. It is worth covering the basic rules of this approach to illustrate the common sense involved.

Summarizing and organizing your data involves three steps:

1. Categories must be selected in which the raw data can be summarized.
2. Once the categories are selected, the data are coded—that is, they are sorted into the categories.
3. The data are presented in a form that helps you to draw conclusions.

CATEGORIES

Although data are collected in detail, they usually cannot be reported or presented at the same level of detail. In other words, it is unlikely that you will be able to report all of the data that you have collected. The first step in summarizing and presenting data is to construct tables, graphs, or charts; averages and percentages are calculated. To do this, you must first categorize the data. We saw this earlier in the case of research into the effect of the amount of study time on academic performance. Assume that the data presented in Table 11.1 were recorded on the data summary sheet suggested in Chapter 6 (Table 6.4).

As it stands, no conclusions can be readily or reliably drawn from this data summary form. No pattern emerges from a quick scan of the data. In this form, the data are too detailed. More inclusive categories are required for reporting both the amount of time spent studying and its result on the examination. A possible starting point for constructing categories is determining the extreme scores and the average scores.

What are the extremes:
- for amount of time spent studying?
  most ____ least ____
- for result on examination?
  highest ____ lowest ____

Scan the list and record the results.

What is the average:
- for amount of time spent studying?
- for result on examination?

The average, or the mean, is calculated by totalling the measures (number of hours or result on examination) and dividing by the number of measures (in this instance, students).

$$\text{Mean, or average, history result } = \frac{\text{Total number of history results}}{\text{Number of students}}$$

TABLE 11.1 A completed data summary form for a study of the relation between hours spent studying and result on a history examination

STUDENT NUMBER	NUMBER OF HOURS SPENT STUDYING		EXAMINATION RESULT	
	RAW SCORE	CODE	RAW SCORE	CODE
1	30		98	
2	25		99	
3	10		50	
4	12		44	
5	20		65	
6	22		68	
7	25		80	
8	30		75	
9	30		80	
10	20		60	
11	24		65	
12	19		55	
13	18		54	
14	21		58	
15	22		60	
16	24		62	
17	28		70	
18	26		70	
19	27		65	
20	24		60	
21	18		58	
22	19		57	
23	25		68	
24	20		65	
25	21		60	
26	14		45	
27	20		35	
28	22		50	
29	26		55	
30	10		40	

Several ways of categorizing these data are now possible. The students could be classified into those who studied more than the average and those who studied less than the average. Similarly, the students could be classified into those whose results were above or below the average. Other ways of classification might include separating those who passed from those who did not. The results could be separated into high pass (65–100), pass (50–64), and fail (49 or less).

Once the categories are selected, the data are coded. That is, the raw data are reclassified into the more inclusive categories. Let us say that you decided to use the categories of 'above average' and 'below average' for both number of hours spent studying and for examination result. Go back to Table 11.1, and codify the data—after each raw score indicate the category into which it fits. For example:

TABLE 11.2 A completed and codified data summary form

	HOURS STUDYING		RESULT IN EXAMINATION	
	RAW SCORE	CODE	RAW SCORE	CODE
Student 1	30	AH	98	AR
Student 2	25	AH	99	AR
Student 3	10	BH	50	BR

AH = above-average hours   AR = above-average result
BH = below-average hours   BR = below-average result

In this way, the raw data are codified and can be more readily analyzed.

If your calculations agree with mine, the average number of hours spent studying was 652 ÷ 30, or 21.7 hours. Hence, students who studied more than 21.7 hours were coded as 'AH' (above average), and those who studied less were coded as 'BH' (below average). How many students were there in each code?

Number coded AH = 16
Number coded BH = 14

How about the examination results? What was the average result? My calculations were 1871 ÷ 30, or 62.4. Students who scored over 62.4 were coded 'AR', and those who scored below 62.4 were coded 'BR'. How many students fell into each category?

Number coded AR = 13
Number coded BR = 17

You have codified your data and established the frequency of students appearing in each code. You are now ready to present your data in a form that will show the relationship between the two variables.

You can see that if you used different categories, the coding would look different. To give yourself practice, copy out Table 11.1 and codify the data results using high pass (65–100), pass (50–64), and fail (49 or less) as the categories. Whatever categories you choose, your aim is to reduce the raw data to a more manageable set of categories. Decide on the categories, and then code the raw data into those categories.

The first two steps have been done. Categories have been selected and the data codified. How are they to be presented? The hypothesis guiding this research asserts that there is a relationship between the amount of time spent studying and the result of an examination. This means that the way in which you present your data needs to show the strength of the relationship between the two variables. There are several ways to do this. They are presented in the following tables.

TABLES

The most basic form of data presentation is 'tabular presentation'.

TABLE 11.3 A table for presenting the data from a study of amount of time spent studying and result on an examination

RESULT ON HISTORY EXAMINATION	AMOUNT OF TIME SPENT STUDYING (NUMBER OF STUDENTS)	
	ABOVE AVERAGE	BELOW AVERAGE
Above average		
Below average		

To come up with the numbers to put in Table 11.3, it is necessary to cross-tabulate your data. That is, you have to locate each case of data collected (in this case, each student) in the appropriate box of the table. For this example, you would take each student listed on the data summary sheet in Table 11.1 and place a check mark in the appropriate cell (blank square) of a table like Table 11.3. Student 1 was categorized as 'above average' in both variables, so check the upper left-hand cell of the table. Student 2 was also categorized as 'above average' in both variables, so place another check mark in the upper left-hand cell. Student 3 was categorized as 'below average' for both variables, so place a check the lower right-hand cell of the table. When all the data have been cross-tabulated in this way, your preliminary table should look like Table 11.4.

TABLE 11.4 The relationship between time spent studying and result on a history examination (preliminary table)

RESULT ON HISTORY EXAMINATION	AMOUNT OF TIME SPENT STUDYING (NUMBER OF STUDENTS)	
	ABOVE AVERAGE	BELOW AVERAGE
Above average	✓✓✓✓✓✓✓✓✓✓	✓✓
Below average	✓✓✓✓✓	✓✓✓✓✓✓✓✓✓✓

Next, add up the check marks in each cell, and put that number in the cell. What do your results look like? They should look like those in Table 11.5. Eleven students were above average in both examination result and amount of time spent studying. Five were below average in result but above average in study time. Twelve were below average on both variables.

TABLE 11.5   The presentation of the results tabulated in Table 11.4

EXAMINATION RESULT	AMOUNT OF TIME SPENT STUDYING (NUMBER OF STUDENTS)		
	ABOVE AVERAGE	BELOW AVERAGE	TOTAL
Above average	11	2	13
Below average	5	12	17
Total	16	14	30

The numbers at the right side and the bottom of Table 11.5 are called marginal totals. They are the same as the totals you calculated earlier for the frequencies of each variable. They serve as useful checks to make sure that your coding and cross-tabulating were done accurately. It is amazing how many errors can creep in at this stage of the research process. The marginals must add up to the total used for the construction of the table. They must also add up correctly both across the rows and down the columns. It may seem tedious, but it provides a critical check on accuracy.

How would you interpret Table 11.5? It shows a very clear relationship between the two variables. It shows that the two variables are related in such a way that the more there is of one (study time), the more there is of the other (marks on an examination), with few exceptions. Note that these tabulations are not equivalent to stringent statistical measures that examine relationships. The strongest evidence is provided by statistics that indicate the direction and strength of the relationships between the independent and dependent variables. Students are strongly advised to consult texts listed at the end of this chapter for more advanced readings in statistical modelling.

While interpreting Table 11.5 is relatively straightforward, sometimes it is better to present the tabular results as percentages. There are two ways of doing this. Since each accurately reflects the data but does so in a slightly different way, the selection depends on which mode of presentation is easiest to interpret. Table 11.6 presents the findings in Table 11.5 as percentages of the total, 30. In all tables giving the results as percentages, it is very important to indicate the total number upon which the table is based. That is why 'n = 30' (which means the total number is 30) is placed where it is. It is nearly a universal convention to use the lower-case 'n' to refer to the number of cases in a table or graph. Thirty is usually considered the minimum number of cases for the use of percentages in a 2 x 2 table like the one in Table 11.6. The more cells a table has, the higher the number of cases should be.

TABLE 11.6 The relationship between amount of time spent studying and result on history examination

RESULT ON HISTORY EXAMINATION	AMOUNT OF TIME SPENT STUDYING	
	ABOVE AVERAGE	BELOW AVERAGE
Above average	36.6	6.7
Below average	16.7	40.0

$n = 30$
100%

Table 11.7 presents the findings in Table 11.5 in column percentages—each of the columns adds to 100 per cent. When you set up a table like Table 11.7, you show the impact of the column variable (in this instance, amount of time spent studying) on the row variable (result in history examination). This is exactly what you want to do, because amount of time spent studying was your independent variable and examination result the dependent variable. When you construct and interpret tables, it is crucial to keep in mind which is the independent and which is the dependent variable. Failing to do so can lead to nonsensical interpretations of data.

TABLE 11.7 The percentage of students spending above- or below-average amount of time studying who scored above or below average on their history examination

RESULT ON HISTORY EXAMINATION	AMOUNT OF TIME SPENT STUDYING	
	ABOVE AVERAGE	BELOW AVERAGE
Above average	68.7	14.3
Below average	31.3	85.7
	100% $n = 16$	100% $n = 14$

How you read a table partly depends on which variable is the independent and which variable is the dependent. In this example, 'time spent studying' was the independent variable, and 'examination result' was the dependent variable. Table 11.7 would be read in this way. Among those students who spent an above-average amount of time studying, 68.7 per cent received above-average examination results, and 31.3 per cent received below-average results. In contrast, among those students who spent a below-average amount of time studying, 14.3 per cent received an above-average result in the examination, and 85.7 per cent received a below-average result. We therefore conclude that the amount of time spent studying had a definite and positive effect on the examination results of this group of history students; our hypothesis is confirmed or accepted.

As a general rule, if you are presenting your data in tables using percentages, it is best to percentage the independent variable across the dependent variable (as in Table 11.7). In this way, you display the impact of the independent variable on the distribution of the dependent variable, which is of course what you are trying to show. A good rule to follow is to place the independent variable in the columns and the dependent variable in the rows. The percentages would be calculated where each column would total 100 per cent.

If you look back over Tables 11.4 to 11.7, it should become clear that the interpretation would be the same in each mode of tabular presentation of the data. Tabular presentation of data is very basic and very useful. To give yourself practice at tabular analysis, take the data in Table 11.1, and recode the exam result data into the three categories of high pass (65–100), pass (50–64), and fail (49 or less). Construct tables by cross-tabulating the data again. Present the tables numerically and as percentages of the whole, row percentages and column percentages.

There are other ways of presenting data as well. Remember, data are summarized and presented so as to clearly demonstrate the strength of the relationship between the variables under study. Other ways of summarizing and presenting data include several kinds of graphs, the scattergram, and the use of means (averages).

GRAPHS

Bar graphs

In order to prepare a graph, it is necessary to perform steps 1 (selecting categories) and 2 (coding the data) of data summarization and presentation. It is also necessary to cross-tabulate the data in some way. Take, for instance, the bar graph or histogram. In both methods, the amount of space given to each variable is proportional to that variable's portion of the sample. Figure 11.1 shows a bar graph presenting the data in Table 11.5.

Essentially, this graph presents the information in the top two cells of Table 11.5. It shows a bar graph based on the frequency distribution of the data (the numbers falling into each category of analysis in the test). Figure 11.2 is a bar graph that gives all the data in Table 11.5.

Bar graphs can also be used to present percentage data. Figure 11.3 presents the data in Table 11.7 in the form of a bar graph. In this instance, a table presented as column percentages is converted to a bar graph by making the space in the graph proportional to the percentage of each cell. The essential feature of a bar graph is that the size of the bar is proportional to the size of the variable. Again, it can be seen that different methods of presenting the same data, when used correctly, do not lead to different conclusions.

FIGURE 11.1 A bar graph showing the relationship between hours studied and history examination result

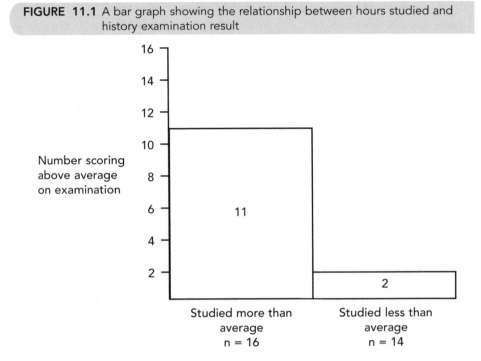

Number scoring above average on examination

Studied more than average
n = 16

Studied less than average
n = 14

FIGURE 11.2 A bar graph showing the relationship between amount of time spent studying and history examination result

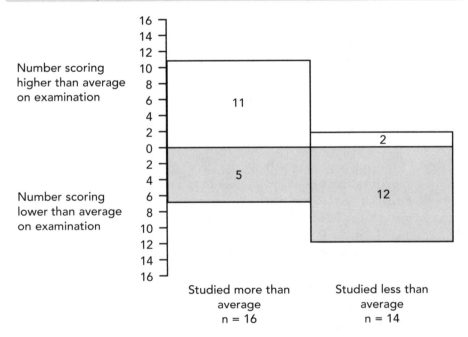

Number scoring higher than average on examination

Number scoring lower than average on examination

Studied more than average
n = 16

Studied less than average
n = 14

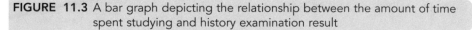

FIGURE 11.3 A bar graph depicting the relationship between the amount of time spent studying and history examination result

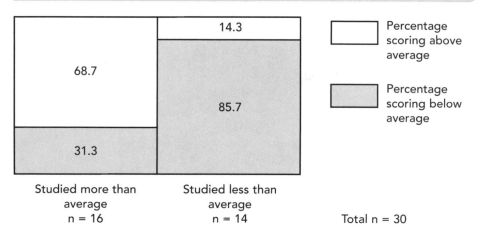

Studied more than average
n = 16

Studied less than average
n = 14

Total n = 30

Pie graphs

Pie graphs are appropriate when analysis examines the proportion of variable categories to all variable categories over the whole population. For example, we will construct a pie graph for the variable 'ethnicity' when it is measured for a class of students. The composition of each category of the variable might be as follows: Chinese 10 per cent, British 10 per cent, Canadian 60 per cent, Filipino/a 8 per cent, other 12 per cent. Accordingly, the pie graph would look like Figure 11.4.

Each group occupies a 'wedge' proportion of the total area of the pie graph equivalent to their proportion of the total class population. In Figure 11.4, the size of the wedge to represent the Chinese must be 10 per cent of the circle area. Pie graphs can be easily constructed by using commonly available computer programs. Alternatively, the pie graph can be drawn by hand. The pie can be measured by calculating 10 per cent of 360 degrees (there are 360 degrees in a circle). Ten per cent of 360 degrees is 36 degrees. Using a protractor, count 36 degrees, place a dot at 0 and at 36, then draw lines to the centre of the circle, and you have a wedge of the pie equal to 10 per cent of the circle. Repeat this for each group. The next group, the British, would also require 36 degrees. Starting where you left off (at 36 degrees), count off 36, place a dot at 72 degrees, and draw a line to the centre of the circle.

This procedure may seem tedious, but there are now computer programs designed to produce accurate pie, bar, and line graphs from data.

Figure 11.5 is a similar pie graph that could be constructed for the population of Canada. A comparison of the two graphs would show how the distribution of ethnic groups enrolled in your course compared with the distribution of such groups in Canada. The fact that the percentages are given as well as the visual impression of the different sizes of the various wedges helps us to interpret these graphs.

FIGURE 11.4   Ethnic makeup of class (fictitious data)

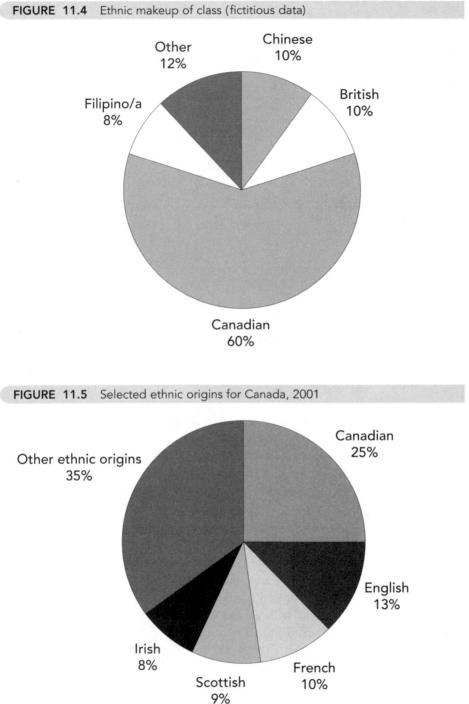

Other
12%

Chinese
10%

Filipino/a
8%

British
10%

Canadian
60%

FIGURE 11.5   Selected ethnic origins for Canada, 2001

Other ethnic origins
35%

Canadian
25%

English
13%

Irish
8%

Scottish
9%

French
10%

It should be noted that such differences are more precisely displayed in simple tables, such as Table 11.8.

TABLE 11.8 Selected ethnic origins[1], Canada, 2001

ETHNIC ORIGINS	TOTAL RESPONSES[2]	%
Canadian	11,682,680	24.6
English	5,978,875	12.6
French	4,668,410	9.8
Scottish	4,157,210	8.7
Irish	3,822,660	8.0
Other ethnic origins	17,244,930	36.3
Total	47,554,765	100.0

[1]Includes only ethnic origins with total response of 15,000 or more.
[2]Respondents who reported multiple ethnic origins are counted more than once in this table since they are included in the multiple responses for each origin they reported. For example, a respondent who reported English and Scottish would be included in the multiple responses for English and for Scottish.
Source: Statistics Canada. 2001. *Census Data.* http://www12.statcan.ca/english/census01/products/highlight/ETO/Table1.cfm?Lang=E&T=501&GV=1&GID=0.

The pie graph is not particularly suited to presenting the type of data with which we have been dealing. Pie graphs are difficult to compare. They are usually used in journalistic reporting and for presenting financial data, such as government funding allocations, rather than in scientific reporting. When presenting such data, the addition of labels that include the percentages is a good addition to the graph.

Scattergrams

The scattergram is another way in which data can be summarized and presented. A scattergram is produced by pinpointing each instance of measurement on a grid defined by the two axes of a graph. Figure 11.6 shows such a grid.

The two lines along which the units are marked are called axes, and the space between them is defined by the grid formed by the intersecting lines drawn from each unit point along the two axes. The first step in constructing a scattergram is to decide on the scale of units to be used on each axis.

Data are not usually categorized and coded before constructing a scattergram. Instead, the scale of each axis is adjusted to accommodate the range of the variable being analyzed. Remember, we suggested that you analyze the data from the study of the impact of amount of time spent studying on examination result. We asked you to identify the range of each variable by noting the extremes. This is a very

FIGURE 11.6 A scattergram grid showing horizontal and vertical axes

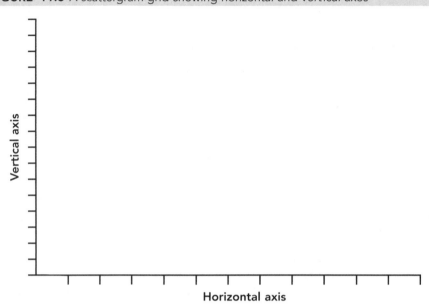

important step if you wish to construct a scattergram. Re-examine the data presented in Table 11.1:

- What is the range of the values recorded for the variable 'time spent studying'?
  Highest _____ ◄————► Lowest _____
- What is the range of the values recorded for the variable 'result on an examination'?
  Highest _____ ◄————► Lowest _____

The scale of units along each axis of the scattergram must be able to sensibly record the full range of collected data. In this instance, the scale of the horizontal axis, the one used to indicate hours spent studying, must range from 10 (the lowest reported) to 30 (the highest reported). The range for the vertical axis, the axis dealing with examination results, must go from 35 to 99. Figure 11.7 presents a grid upon which a scattergram for the data presented in Table 11.1 could be constructed. The scattergram is constructed by putting a dot on the grid in the place defined by the two pieces of data for each student. Using graph paper makes this task much easier. The axes are drawn and units marked along them. Now a dot is placed on the grid for each student. Student number 1 studied 30 hours and received a 98, so place a dot at the intersection of a line drawn up from the 30 position on the horizontal axis with a line across from the 98 position on the vertical axis. The positions of students 1 to 5 are given as examples.

Using a sheet of graph paper, make a scattergram of all the data in Table 11.1. Normally, the intersecting lines are not drawn on the table. Rather, two rulers are used to indicate where the lines intersect, and only the dot is placed on the grid. Place two dots close together where two data points are the same. The result is a pattern of dots. What does the pattern of 30 dots tell you?

Most conventional computer software can produce accurate scattergrams that can be used in published research papers and reports.

FIGURE 11.7 A grid for the construction of a scattergram for data on impact of amount of time spent studying on examination result

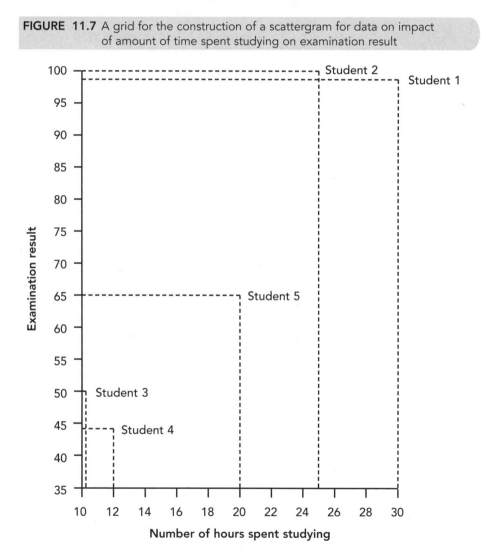

Line graphs

A line graph is almost the same as a scattergram except that consecutive points are joined by lines, making up one complete line joining all the data points.

The data tabled in Table 11.9 can be presented by a line graph (as in Figure 11.8). The independent variable 'age of child' is placed on the horizontal axis. The dependent variable 'number of additional hours' is placed along the vertical axis. The units are clearly marked along each axis. Then the data points are marked, as for a scattergram. The data points are joined by a line that begins at the first dot on the left and moves to the next dot to the right.

TABLE 11.9 Number of additional hours spent on household activities by non-employed persons due to presence of child

AGE OF CHILD	NUMBER OF ADDITIONAL HOURS
Less than 1 year	5.2
1 year	4.6
2–5 years	4.0
6–11 years	4.5
12–17 years	3.6

Source: Data from E. Walker and M.E. Woods. 1976. *Time Use: A Measure of Household Production of Family Goods and Services*, 50–1. Washington, DC: Centre for the Family of the American Home Economics Association.

As an exercise, convert your scattergram of the data on the relationship between 'number of hours spent studying' and 'examination result' (refer back to Table 11.1) to a line graph. To do so, start with the dot on the far left and move to the next dot on the right. You will encounter a problem. What do you do when there is more than one dot in a vertical line? Which is the 'next dot to the right'? In such a case, the average is calculated, and the data point is put at the average position. For example, you will begin with a problem in the data in your scattergram when you find that there are two data points in the vertical line above 10 hours of studying. One received a result of 50, the other a result of 40. The data point for a line graph would be placed at 45. In this way, a line graph 'smoothes out' some of the detail of a scattergram. The advantage is that it makes the pattern clearer, but the disadvantage is that it hides some of the variation.

There are several critical points to remember in constructing line graphs. First, the units of measure must be clearly specified, labelled, and marked on each axis of the graph. In Figure 11.8, the vertical axis is marked in hours (0–6) and labelled 'number of additional hours'.

Be aware that units of measure affect the appearance of line graphs and can make them misleading. Large units can underemphasize change in relative terms, and small units can overstate the magnitude of change. The following example will demonstrate this. There is a lot of talk these days about divorce statistics in Canada. The data on

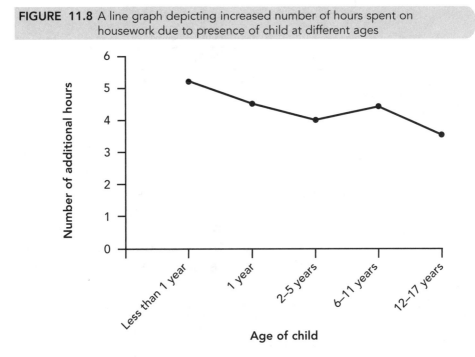

FIGURE 11.8 A line graph depicting increased number of hours spent on housework due to presence of child at different ages

the number of divorces in Canada for the years 1999 to 2003 are presented in tabular form in Table 11.10. The data given in this figure are from Statistics Canada.

Notice, however, that two ways of presenting those data in a line graph give very different impressions. Figures 11.9 and 11.10 show the same data recorded in line graphs using different scales of units. Do they look the same? They are both accurate, but they give different impressions.

They express the data differently because of the difference in measurement scale for the vertical axis. As an exercise, make line graphs for several provinces/territories from the data presented in Table 11.10. Use different scales to see what difference this makes.

This effect can be particularly confusing in graphs that have two vertical axes with different scales. Although there are legitimate reasons for using this device, it can be very misleading. Figure 11.11 gives an obvious example. It shows line graphs of annual environmental spending by City A and City B. Say that both cities commenced allocating funds for the environment in 1987. The graph seems to show that City A has been increasing its spending on the environment at a much faster rate than City B. But is that correct? Read the graph carefully, and keep in mind that the lines are drawn to axes of different scales, according to which spending for City A is expressed in smaller units ($100,000s) than data for City B ($millions). The same spending increases appear to be more dramatic for City A than for City B.

Thus, an examination of the graph will show that the dollar amounts spent by the cities were the same each year. Spending in both cities increased by the same

TABLE 11.10 Divorces by province and territory

| | NUMBER OF DIVORCES | | | | | |
	1999	2000	2001	2002	2003	TOTAL
Atlantic (Newfoundland and Labrador, Prince Edward Island, Nova Scotia, New Brunswick)	4,808	4,956	4,516	4,551	4,300	23,131
Yukon and Northwest Territories including Nunavut	195	169	182	164	153	863
Prairies (Manitoba and Saskatchewan)	4,809	4,624	4,435	4,355	4,344	22,567
Quebec	17,144	17,054	17,094	16,499	16,738	84,529
Ontario	26,088	26,148	26,516	26,170	27,513	132,435
Alberta	7,931	8,176	8,252	8,291	7,960	40,610
British Columbia	9,935	10,017	10,115	10,125	9,820	50,012
Total Canada	**70,910**	**71,144**	**71,110**	**70,155**	**70,828**	**354,147**

Source: Statistics Canada. 2006. *Divorces by Province and Territory.* http://www40.statscan. ca/l01/cst01/famil02.htm. Accessed on 28 June 2007.

FIGURE　11.9 Divorces in Canada from 1999 to 2003—rising and falling (small scale)

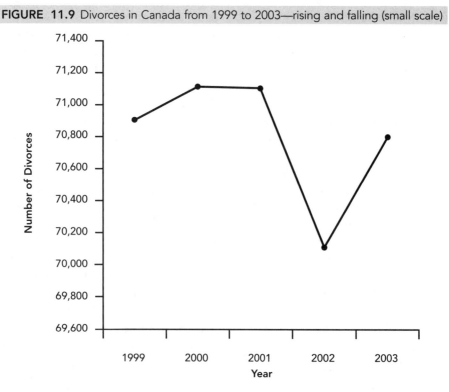

FIGURE 11.10 Divorces in Canada from 1999 to 2003—hardly changing (larger scale)

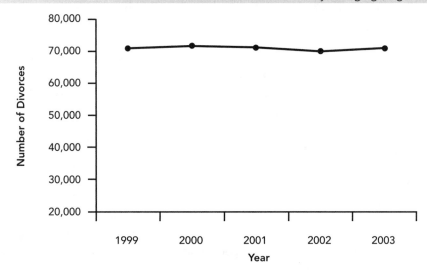

amount ($100,000 for City A, $0.1 million for City B) every year between 1987 and 1996. In 1996, both cities spent $900,000.

Spending on the environment was the same in both cities despite the different appearances of the lines plotted against the different scales.

FIGURE 11.11 A misleading line graph using different units on two vertical axes to compare growth in environmental spending

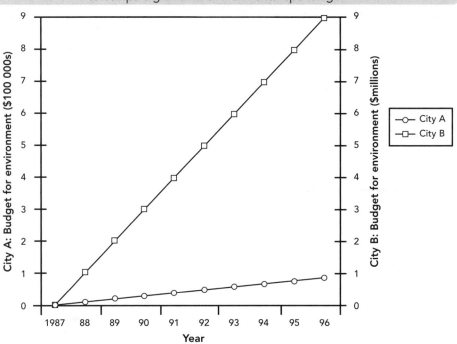

Finally, line graphs are very useful for comparing the trends or performance of several groups or persons. Figure 11.12 is a hypothetical line graph comparing the monthly phone calls received by three telephone counselling services in one year. The raw data are presented in Table 11.11.

These three services have different patterns of demand. The graph in Figure 11.12 shows these differences more clearly than the columns of numbers in Table 11.11.

Service A receives more calls in summer than in winter. It may serve a holiday region where social problems increase every summer and during a school holiday period when tourists arrive. Service B experiences a smooth pattern of demand, which begins at a relatively high level early in the year, bottoms out mid-year, and gradually increases as the end of the year approaches. The area covered by Service B might be a place where social problems change with the traditional holiday season. During the Christmas and New Year season, social problems increase, perhaps because of money shortages or increased alcohol consumption. The general 'mood' of the area calms after the New Year, and the demand for counselling services decreases, remaining stable until September, when spending and alcohol use begin to increase in anticipation of Christmas. Service C experiences increased demand in the winter months and a small upswing in the middle of the year. It may serve a northern area of the country where decreased daylight has been shown to increase bouts of depression, thereby increasing the number of calls to the counselling service.

The value of a line graph comparing the use of the three counselling services can be seen in Figure 11.12. Such presentation of data is very useful in policy analysis because it displays comparative information very clearly. What issues does Figure 11.12 suggest for a government administrator allocating funds among the three

TABLE 11.11 Phone calls received by three fictitious telephone counselling services

MONTH	SERVICE A	SERVICE B	SERVICE C
January	205	920	860
February	255	750	620
March	300	605	275
April	350	410	350
May	520	300	360
June	620	275	380
July	880	275	400
August	925	275	450
September	620	290	350
October	540	420	300
November	480	590	580
December	320	830	690

counselling services? Think about how you would allocate the funds, and justify your decision based on the graph.

As a further exercise, construct a line graph comparing the number of divorces in the Atlantic provinces, the territories, the Prairies, Quebec, Ontario, Alberta, and British Columbia, using the data in Table 11.10. By using a different style of line for each province, you can construct a graph that provides a good basis for drawing comparisons among the provinces on the number of divorces. Make sure you get the data points in the right place before you connect the lines.

Scattergrams and line graphs can be very useful ways of summarizing and interpreting data. They are frequently used in articles, books, and research reports.

To construct a line graph, you must:

1. select categories for your data;
2. code the data into the categories;
3. select a scale of units for each axis;
4. plot the data points;
5. link the data points with lines.

There are several computer programs available that will produce scattergrams.

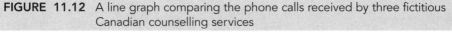

FIGURE 11.12 A line graph comparing the phone calls received by three fictitious Canadian counselling services

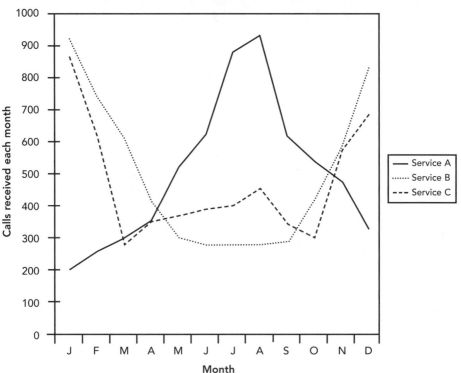

MEANS

Means, or averages, are often used to compare groups. Means are a useful way to summarize and present data. The average performance of groups, the average rates of consumption, or the average incidence of a particular event may be compared.

To calculate an average, you add up the individual data and divide by the number of individuals. For example, earlier in this chapter you calculated the average number of hours spent studying and the average examination result.

Means could be used to summarize and present the data from our study of the impact of the number of hours spent studying on examination results. The class could be divided into two groups, those who studied more than the average and those who studied less than the average. Once this is done, the average examination result for each group could be calculated. First, divide the students into two groups. Remember, the average time spent studying was 21.7 hours.

The data in Table 11.12 would simply be reported in this way. The group of students who studied more than the average received an average result of 70.3, and the group of students who studied less than the average received an average result of 53.3.

As an exercise, calculate the average number of hours spent studying for each of two groups of students. First, do it for those who received above-average results, and then do it for those who received below-average results.

We saw that the move from a scattergram to a line graph involved losing a certain level of detail in the presentation of the data. When groups are compared using means, all variation internal to each group is lost:

- scattergram: presents most information.
- line graph, bar graph, or pie graph: present less information.
- means: presents least information.

Using the data in Table 11.11, calculate the average number of calls received monthly by each counselling service. Service A's average monthly total was 501.25 calls, Service B's average was 495.0 calls, and Service C's was 467.92 calls. This example shows one potential problem with an average. It does not show the variation in the measures. Although Services A and B averaged almost the same number of calls per month, they experienced different trends of monthly increases and decreases in calls.

While averages are very useful, they must be used and interpreted with care. The average tells us nothing for certain about an individual in a group. It is not legitimate to infer that the average for a group applies to an individual. For example, the average household income of residents in a particular suburb might be $100,000 per year. There are many combinations of household income that would lead to that average. For example, one household earning $910,000 and nine each of $10,000 would result in an average income of $100,000. Some averages can be almost meaningless.

TABLE 11.12 The calculation of mean test scores for two groups of students

GROUP A STUDIED MORE THAN AVERAGE		GROUP B STUDIED LESS THAN AVERAGE	
STUDENT	MARK	STUDENT	MARK
1	98	3	50
2	99	4	44
6	68	5	65
7	80	10	60
8	75	12	55
9	80	13	54
11	65	14	58
15	60	21	58
16	62	22	57
17	70	24	65
18	70	25	60
19	65	26	45
20	60	27	35
23	68	30	40
28	50		
29	55		
16	1125	14	746
Group A average = 1125 ÷ 16 = 70.3		Group B average = 746 ÷ 14 = 53.3	

On the other hand, we are often interested in group performance and not so interested in the outstanding cases. The average is a useful indication of a characteristic of a group. Trends in averages, like trends in percentages, are particularly useful. The local electricity supplier, in predicting energy supply requirements for the month of July, will rely on the trends in average energy consumption for the previous 20 Julys. It will not be interested in the variations in individual household consumption.

SUMMARY

Once your data are collected, they are ready to be summarized and presented. To do this, you must select categories in which to summarize your data. Although you did some preliminary thinking about this when you constructed your dummy tables, the final selection is done when your data are in hand. Once you have selected categories, the data are coded into the categories. Then the data are cross-tabulated in some way to show the relationship between the variables in question. We have looked at tables, graphs, and means as the basic techniques for summarizing and presenting your data.

QUESTIONS FOR REVIEW

1. What are the three steps involved in summarizing and organizing your data?
2. Why is it necessary to categorize your data?
3. Why is it important to remember which variable is the independent and which is the dependent when constructing tables for the presentation and interpretation of your data?
4. What does it mean to cross-tabulate your data?
5. Describe the difficulties associated with your graphs.
6. What is a scattergram?
7. What are the advantages of using means (or averages) rather than line graphs or scattergrams in presenting data?

Suggestions for further reading

Babbie, E.R. 2003. *The Practice of Social Research*. 10th edn, chapter 15. London: Wadsworth.

de Vaus, D.A. 2002. *Surveys in Social Research*. 5th edn, parts III and IV. St Leonards, NSW: Allen and Unwin.

Judd, C.M., E.R. Smith, and L.H. Kidder. 1991. *Research Methods in Social Relations*, chapter 15. Fort Worth, TX: Holt, Rinehart and Winston.

Kumar, Ranjit. 1999. *Research Methodology: A Step by Step Guide for Beginners*, chapters 15–16. London: Sage.

Suggestions for further reading in advanced statistics

Healey, J. 2004. *Statistics: A Tool for Social Research*. 7th edn. London: Wadsworth.

Hazard Munro, B. 2004. *Statistical Methods for Health Care Research*. 5th edn. Philadelphia: Lippincott Williams and Wilkins.

Tabachnick, B., and L. Fidell. 2006. *Using Multivariate Statistics*. 5th edn. Boston: Allyn and Bacon.

Presenting Data Using Qualitative Research

THE QUALITATIVE RESEARCH PROCESS

Qualitative research has its own demands and integrity. Some of its similarities with quantitative research were discussed in Chapters 3–6 in the discussion of research guided by a research objective. While the qualitative approach shares some requirements with quantitative research, there are subtle and not-so-subtle differences in the way the research issue is conceived and the data collected, analyzed, and reported.

One of the major differences between quantitative and qualitative research is that once the basic decisions are made in quantitative research, there is little opportunity to alter them in the light of early findings. Once a questionnaire is designed and sent, it is out of the researcher's hands. Once an experiment has been carried out, it is over. However, qualitative research allows more continuous reflection on the research in progress and more interaction with the participants in the research, and there is usually more room for ongoing alteration as the research proceeds. For example, if early observations or interviews reveal that one approach is not working or that additional issues need to be considered, later interviews and observations can be adjusted accordingly. One way of expressing this is to say that in qualitative research, the researcher is more interactive with the data-generating process than in quantitative research in which, once set up, the research proceeds more according to a predetermined plan.

The general process model developed for the description of quantitative research will be used to describe qualitative research, because the underlying logic of the research process applies to both approaches.

PHASE 1: ESSENTIAL FIRST STEPS

Selecting a problem

As with the research procedures outlined in earlier chapters, selecting a research problem is the first stage. Each of the examples in Chapter 3 could have led to a qualitative research project, and the ways they were developed usually presumed that qualitative approaches to the issue had been taken to some extent. Take the first example of family decision-making. The prompting situation was this:

> **An important family decision**
> The Wright family has to decide whether to send their daughter to a public school or a private school.

There are many research focuses that this situation might stimulate. What is the nature of family decision-making? What kinds of issues arise? Whose arguments carry more weight—males' or females'? Young people's or older people's? Or you might focus on the differences associated with attending a public or a private school. You could select a more quantitative approach by asking questions such as 'What proportion of girls attending public schools, as opposed to private schools, go on to university?' Or you could ask a more qualitative question like 'What is it like to attend a public school or a private school?'

As with all research, it is necessary to focus when doing qualitative research. It is not possible to answer all the questions. If you focus on the nature of family decision-making, you might go to the library and look up information on various databases. In doing this, you will, in part, be checking to see whether much is known about family decision-making. You will also assess the nature of the research already done, which may lead you to do some basic qualitative research to find out the themes and issues in family decision-making. Or you may feel that previous research has focused on different groups from those you have had in mind—for example, Americans in 1980 rather than Canadians in the twenty-first century. The literature search will help focus the research.

On completing the background reading, you may be ready to state the goal, objective, or central question of the research. This will play the same guiding role as the hypothesis in quantitative research. It states your aim, goal, or focus. For example, you might express your goal as one of the following research objectives:

> **Objective**
> To ascertain the themes that emerge in family decision-making about a daughter's education.

Objective

To describe the way the Wright family decided where to send their daughter, Amy, to school.

Objective

To find out what it is like to be the subject of family decision-making about one's education.

There are other ways to state a research objective about family decision-making, but each of the above objectives provides a sharper focus and describes a qualitative approach to the general issue raised in the area of 'family decision-making'.

Sampling in qualitative research

Qualitative research is usually less concerned with generalization to large populations than with understanding what is going on in specific settings. However, you must not forget that the findings of any research project are limited by the nature of the sampling procedure. Sampling issues in qualitative research involve the selection of subjects, locations, groups, and situations to be observed or interviewed. Sampling issues therefore focus on how well the subjects and situations provide 'windows' on social processes. Qualitative research will not be able to tell what proportion of female managers feel a certain way about their work environments, but it will be able to present in detail what it is like for women to work in selected types of managerial environments.

Sampling will also be an issue in the selection of locations, timeframes, and points of orientation for observational research. Each of these selections will affect what is observed, so they must be made intentionally and described in the report so that readers will understand the nature of the observations upon which the research is based.

PHASE 2: COLLECTING, SUMMARIZING, AND ORGANIZING DATA

At this stage, some key differences between quantitative and qualitative research become apparent. One is the degree of focus on the topic and the degree of commitment to the given research method before gathering data. In quantitative research, much effort goes into preparing questionnaires, setting up experiments, or selecting groups for comparisons. This is done to ensure comparability of data and to make data summarization more efficient. Also, such preparation lowers the chance that collection will encounter problems after it starts. Quantitative researchers must know the research topic very well to foresee problems.

At the outset, qualitative research is usually less focused. One of the key aims of qualitative research is to provide the maximum opportunity for the researcher to learn from the participants. This requires flexibility in data collection. Quantitative research produces a relatively small amount of data focused on predetermined issues or variables. Qualitative research tends to produce large amounts of information that can only be focused after data collection. Generally, quantitative research progresses through a series of distinct stages—problem-focusing, choice of measurements, design of data collection instruments, and data collection. By comparison, in qualitative research these stages blend together and may be repeated or conducted at the same time at the researcher's discretion. Qualitative researchers progress back and forth through the stages, sensitizing themselves to the situation, so that they can eventually give a fuller description of 'what is going on'.

Data collection

Qualitative research usually involves one or more of the following data-gathering techniques: observation—including *participant* and *non-participant* observation— in-depth interviewing, focus groups, and the use of textual material.

Observation

Observation is a basic qualitative research technique that requires discipline, planning, and alertness. There are two basic forms of observation: *non-participant* and *participant*. Three general focuses of observation are relevant to both forms:

1. the whole situation—e.g., the 'whole situation' of a committee meeting can be aggressive, conciliatory, or defensive;
2. the participants in the situation—e.g., at a committee meeting, there will be people from different factions, expressing different points of view and expressing different interests;
3. what the researcher perceives given their own preconceptions and values— e.g., personal 'surprise' when a committee conducts itself in an unexpected way. It is important that you be aware of how you perceive and appreciate events. Later, when reviewing observations, you will be able to distinguish your opinions about events from the events themselves.

In *non-participant observation*, the researcher stands back from the situation and observes—for instance, when a researcher sits in a corner at a committee meeting to find out how the committee arrives at decisions.

As an example, say you were doing a project for which the research goal was to describe the job-search experiences of first- and second-generation youth in Canada. Part of this project could be an observational study of a section of Winnipeg's census tracts (neighbourhoods, as defined by Statistics Canada) in terms of the employment counselling services available and the types of individuals using these services. Your purpose is to observe the social situation when racialized youth utilize these services and compare their experiences with youth who are not racialized. You hope that this will give some indication of the social situation racialized first- and second-generation youth face every day. Using appropriate introduction procedures, you identify a suitable employment counselling agency in the census tract and obtain their permission to observe some of their job-search sessions, knowing that youth from various backgrounds will use their services at some point during your observation.

One of your tasks is to observe the 'whole situation'—that is, the whole social situation at the employment counselling centre, which includes every person: young or old, racialized or not. The whole situation might contain 'social tension' or 'social harmony'; it might be 'loud', 'quiet', 'energetic', or 'subdued'. The environment may seem very 'multicultural' because it contains people of a range of races and ethnic dress. You should be alert for changes, particularly if they occur when racialized youth participate in sessions.

Second, you must observe the participants, who in this case are racialized first- and second-generation youth and everybody else. There are two things to observe: how participants act and how these actions express intentions, group feelings, or states of social relations. When observing how participants act, the researcher may see that some groups of non-racialized participants stare at the racialized youth or pay them no special attention. Others might sit in sex, gender, or race groups. You should interpret these actions. If the group mixes (i.e., there is no pattern in how the participants sit), you may discern that race and gender are not as important in the employment counselling groups as you might have anticipated. If non-racialized youth sit apart from racialized youth or refuse to engage them in conversation, you might need to ask participants about the types of people they prefer to spend their time with.

Last, it is also important to observe and record how you personally react to the situation and the participants. Entries about 'how I felt', 'what I thought', and 'what I was reminded of' provide a vivid recording of the observation experience. Self-observation can also make you aware of biases or wrong preconceptions. If you felt surprised to see racialized groups sitting apart from one another, you should consider why this seemed unusual. It may signal that you have misconceptions about race and ethnicity, which, if not corrected, could lead to misinterpretations of other events and actions.

It is also necessary to find a suitable observation point. This would be a place from which you can observe things critical to the research objective without disturbing participants. If you are observing a job seminar at an employment counselling centre in a certain census tract in Winnipeg when youth are present, you would need a place from which you could discreetly observe facial expressions and body language. This will allow you to appreciate how racialized and non-racialized youth react to the presence of each other. A seat at the back of the room may be suitable. Then again, if people see you watching them and taking notes, they might feel self-conscious and not act or speak in their usual manner.

Even if you are observing in an unobtrusive manner, participants may notice you watching and taking notes and ask about your activity. Your research ethics board (REB) will probably ask you to prepare printed information for such inquiries. This might be a one-page summary of the project, including the title, project number, your student number, date of REB approval, project description, supervisor's contact details, and complaints instructions. Such a document can quickly inform others of the purpose of the project and demonstrate its legitimacy.

Participant observation is when the researcher becomes a participant. The distinction between researcher and participant blurs, since the researcher not only observes what is going on among the regular participants but also their own reactions as a participant. In effect, the researcher shares some aspects of the standpoint of regular participants.

If you are researching the first job experiences of racialized youth in Canada, you may become a participant by attending and participating in some of the job seminars held at the employment centre. You would not only observe other people—racialized and non-racialized youth—but also observe your own participant actions and reactions. You may feel physically uncomfortable, very self-conscious, or hardly different at all. Such data would directly inform you about one aspect of what it is like to be a youth looking for work in Canada.

Participant observation has three possible disadvantages. First, your presence may affect the situation and cause other participants to feel self-conscious or even 'trespassed' upon. People sometimes become upset if others pretend to be like them. Second, the researcher might be unable to observe much of the situation while participating. For example, if the researcher is significantly older than the participants, it may be difficult for you to 'blend in' with the youth. As well, it will probably be impossible to observe the youth in an actual job interview. Last, certain forms of participant observation are likely to be subject to scrutiny by an REB. These issues are considered further below.

What are some of the issues to consider when choosing between participant and non-participant observation? Some argue that participant observation is far superior and that the only way to get to know what something is like is to be 'part of the action'. However, as we have seen, researching 'what it is like to be an unemployed racialized youth in Winnipeg' raises several issues.

You have two choices. First, you could be a non-participant observer, watching and taking notes at job-search seminars and resumé-writing courses and observing job-counselling sessions. Alternatively, you could be a participant observer and take part in the job-search seminars, resumé-writing courses, and job-counselling sessions along with the other youth.

What level of participation is possible or desirable in observational data collection? The possibilities range from absolute non-participation (such as observation from a distance with a concealed video camera) to fully involved participant observation. The decision depends largely on the research question and the attitudes of participants involved in your study.

First, the research question can determine what level of participation is appropriate. If you wish to research how charity collectors obtain donations, you can make an informative range of observations by not participating and simply watching and listening as collectors solicit donations. If, however, your goal is to find out what it is like to be a charity collector, then participation would be appropriate, and you could expect to gather more relevant data by working as a collector.

Second, the research setting may lend itself more to either participation or non-participation. For example, if you are researching the society of a prison, there would be little advantage in doing participant observation. Unless you work undercover—which would be dangerous—other inmates and prison staff would never treat you as 'one of the regular prisoners', and you would never observe from the prisoners' viewpoint. However, through non-participant observation, you and the prisoners could interact without encroaching on each other's social space. You would also be free to interact with prison staff to appreciate how they affect the society of the prison.

Conversely, there are situations in which participation is the only option. If you wish to observe the crowd at a local dance bar, you are unlikely to gain entry without wearing appropriate clothing. You would have no choice but to participate.

The last issue is the policy on participation of your research ethics board. REBs are likely to delay projects involving unacceptable types of participation. For example, REBs are not likely to approve participation in dangerous activities. If you proposed to hang out with a violent street gang or take part in illegal drag-racing, your REB would almost certainly refuse the project because these activities are not safe. REBs will also oppose participation that may offend people because it seems culturally insensitive. For example, the wearing of a *hijab* or *qamis* by a non-Muslim may upset some Muslims, and most REBs would ask for reassurance that such a form of participation would cause Muslims no offence. Participation is also unacceptable to REBs when the researcher is likely to obstruct people in their regular roles and duties. Should you propose to participate in paramedic activities, your REB would certainly question the project because, without training, you would probably hinder the group's regular activity of saving lives.

Similarly, REBs are likely to be negative about non-participation that leads to possible identification or the recording of personal information without participants' consent. For example, for many REBs, the observation of people via hidden cameras is unacceptable because participants can be identified and they have no opportunity to consent or refuse.

Most professional organizations have a code of ethics that practitioners are expected to follow. The Canadian Sociology Association has a *Statement of Professional Ethics* by which all research sociologists are bound. Regardless of whether or not you are a sociologist, the code of ethics provides useful ethical guidelines for researchers in the social sciences.

Data recording

The most basic technique for gathering data in either type of observation is note-taking. There are three issues to consider in note-taking: first, the separation of observations and personal reactions; second, how to divide attention between observing and note-taking; and last, notation.

It is easy to get events and personal reactions to events confused and then take notes that do not separate the two types of observations. Therefore, you should note events and your reactions to them separately. For example, while observing a group of youth gangs in Winnipeg, you may see a white youth make unwanted contact with a racialized youth. Following is an inaccurate way to record the incident:

At this point, a white youth bumped into one of the Vietnamese youth. This deliberate act was the first example of unfriendliness today.

Such an observation is a mixture of objective fact and reaction. A collision took place, as someone else could verify, but you do not know for sure that it was the outcome of a deliberate and unfriendly act. Unless you separate your interpretations and observations, your notes will indicate that the collision was indisputably deliberate.

A simple way to keep observations and reactions separate is to divide pages as in Figure 12.1. On notepaper, draw a vertical line about one-third of the way from the right side. Use the 'two-thirds' column to record observations and the 'one-third' column to record personal reactions such as opinions and emotional reactions. In this way, records of events show observations and feelings separately but on the same page.

FIGURE 12.1 Data-recording sheet for recording observations

What you observe	Your reactions/thoughts

Second, you should not allow note-taking to distract you from the important task of observing. This can happen if you decide to take notes about everything you experience and feel. You may try to write too much and be distracted from the observation situation while frantically creating volumes of notes. Hence, it is better to spend most of your energy observing while taking notes on the things that seem most significant at the time. Your close observation will provide comprehensive memories of the situation, and you will be able to write up other details immediately afterwards.

Last, you should feel free to use any style of notation that is comfortable for you. You might use longhand, shorthand, abbreviations, diagrams or symbols, or foreign words. As long as the act of note-taking is not a distraction from the situation and your notes are legible, you should feel free to take notes however you wish.

During participant observation, it may not be practical to write down or record data, so a good memory is the most important data collection tool. It may be necessary to schedule a time, such as lunch break, to rapidly write notes from memory.

A popular set of tools for gathering observational data are audio and visual recording devices such as tape recorders and camcorders. They provide comprehensive records of situations, and the tapes can be reviewed many times. Tapes also allow you to re-observe a situation and refocus on events that had seemed unimportant.

While making recordings, you should also take notes to document the experience of observing the situation as it happened. It is also important to observe or listen to recordings with discipline. Recordings do not observe for you, they do not distinguish between significant and insignificant events, nor do they record your perceptions. Finally, be aware that under current principles of research ethics in Canada and for your discipline or profession, it is only appropriate to make recordings when participants give permission (see Chapter 9).

In-depth interviewing

In-depth interviews provide the best opportunity to find out what someone else thinks or feels. The idea of in-depth interviewing is to get a 'window' on reality from the point of view of a participant and to allow them to tell their story as they wish, identifying the issues that are important to them. The common approach is to ask only very general questions so as to encourage participants to 'open up' and lead the interview and give their perspectives with as little influence from the researcher as possible. Usually, researchers have a list of general topics but are ready to discuss others that the participant identifies as important.

Another feature of in-depth interviews is that they often take several hours and may extend over more than one session. This allows participants to talk as exhaustively as they wish. Hence, some people call them 'extended interviews'.

In-depth interviews are usually more productive if you gain some rapport or mutual sense of comfort with participants. You should conduct in-depth interviews in places that are safe and comfortable for you and the participants. It is important to be discerning in your style of language and careful not to use words that might cause participants to feel offended or patronized. Similarly, you should select your dress carefully, wearing clothes that do not cause offence. Ties or suits, for example, may cause factory workers to see you as a member of the same social class as their employers.

Also, it is important not to ignore participants' cultural practices. In some cultures, for example, women do not shake hands or remain alone with males who are not family members. Being aware of such practices not only prevents offence but also demonstrates respect, which participants are likely to return.

Two problems often occur during in-depth interviews. First, because participants have a lot of freedom in how they respond to general questions, they often drift to topics unrelated to the research. Listening to some idle talk is polite and can also be productive, particularly when it generates rapport. However, it is important to redirect discussion back to a research topic; otherwise, you will collect very little data.

One strategy is to show interest in the participant's discussion before redirecting them back to the research topic. For example, you might be interviewing racialized youth about their job-search experiences in Winnipeg. One male participant begins talking about a recent job interview but drifts into a discussion of a car he saw on a recent trip to the supermarket. You might get the discussion back on track with the following:

> That's interesting, it sounds like some car. I'd like to know more about that car when we finish. Just getting back to what we were discussing before, I'd like to hear you talk a bit more about what it's like to be a young Chinese man trying to find work in Winnipeg.

Communicate to the participant that you respect them enough to engage in friendly conversation and then gently restate the original question. Note that if you ever indicate that you will chat about other subjects later, it is respectful and considerate to do so. Participants usually ask for nothing in return for their time, and you can show appreciation by sharing some friendly talk.

A second common problem is the tendency of some participants to provide only brief answers. Some people just tend to answer 'yes', 'no', or 'maybe' without elaborating, thus rendering little data. Such responses often occur when questions do not invite participants to talk at length or reflect on personal experience. Take the following question that might be asked in an interview with a racialized young woman:

> What is it like to be young and looking for work in Winnipeg?

It would not be surprising for participants to give short replies like 'all right' or 'don't even think about it'. A short answer is sufficient, given the form of the question, and further, the question contains no explicit request for the participant to reflect on her experience. The question stands a better chance of eliciting an extended answer if it asks participants to tell a story about themselves. For example:

> Can you tell me about your personal experience of looking for work in Winnipeg?

> Could you describe what it's been like for you to look for work in Winnipeg since you first came here to live?

Before conducting interviews, researchers should consider whether their questions invite short or extended answers and make appropriate changes.

Sometimes you will have no success regardless of how you prompt a participant because they may be a person of few words or they may find the question sensitive. Once you realize that you will not get an elaboration, move to the next question. You must respect the right of participants to answer questions as they wish. Participants are not obliged to answer questions and may complain to your REB if they feel pressured. Also, it may be informative if participants generally tend to give only short answers to a particular question, indicating that the question touches on a sensitive subject.

One way of documenting an interview is to take notes of your dialogue with the participant and then do a 'write-up' immediately after the interview is over. However, any delay undermines the record's accuracy and reliability, so write-ups should be done immediately.

Another common method is to tape-record interviews and then do a transcription. This allows a thorough collection of the interview data, which you can review as many times as you wish. However, transcriptions do not record gestures and body language. So it is valuable to take notes while recording an interview and document a participant's physical reactions. Transcribing interviews is a time-consuming task. It may take four to five hours to transcribe an hour-long interview. While you may be able to hire a transcriber, this is very expensive, particularly if a project has a large number of interviews.

Rather than doing in-depth interviews, it is sometimes preferable to issue questionnaires containing 'open-ended' questions—that is, questions that request extended responses. If participants are literate and accustomed to expressing themselves in writing, it may be practical to ask for written answers. For example, a study of professors could ask, 'Please tell us about your thoughts and concerns about the ethical treatment of children during research interviews.' Such 'open-ended' questions (in this instance, without references to specific aspects of 'ethical practices') give respondents the freedom to discuss the things they perceived as important.

Life narratives

A modification of the in-depth interview is to ask people to write or record their life stories. In the field of oral history, a disciplined expertise has been developed in using this technique to gather material about what life was like in various places and times by asking people to narrate their life stories and recollections of significant events. Researchers can audio-record the narrations and produce written reports of life stories in the participant's narrative voice, like a piece of auto-biographical writing.

The main purpose of collecting life narratives is to give the participant the opportunity to tell their own story, their way. It is therefore critical not to impose your own viewpoints on the data—for example, by omitting events that are unimportant for you but important for the participant. It is also possible to misrepresent the participant by emphasizing events that are consistent with your own political, social, and moral concerns. It is important to be aware of these possibilities, particularly if you and the participants have different political, social class, cultural, ethnic, or educational backgrounds. Therefore, participants should view and appraise your edited versions of their life stories. They can comment, suggest changes, and verify that the report is representative of how they remember and feel about events.

Life narratives may include more than just biographical materials. They may include an examination of journal and newspaper articles written during the time period to contextualize the era. They may also involve interviewing those who are intimate with the subject matter. Minutes from meetings, personal notes, and other artefacts may augment the data collected in the life narrative. The process is different from content analysis, since 'the data are used to build the chronology and resultant life history' (Kirby et al., 2006: 158). With this in mind, Kirby and her colleagues (2006) suggest the following steps: (1) identify important milestones and personal events; (2) gather information about the person using a variety of different sources; (3) tell the history chronologically; (4) corroborate your version of events with others who were there or from other historical materials; and (5) repeat steps 1 through 4 until you are certain that the life history accurately reflects what actually happened.

Focus groups

Focus groups combine the strengths of in-depth interviewing and observation in a group context. In a focus group, a small number of people, such as between 6 and 12, agree to meet for collective discussion with the researcher, who acts as facilitator.

Focus groups are used increasingly as a way of learning about public opinion on a variety of issues. It would be possible to recruit a focus group of racialized youth to talk about their experiences looking for work and ask them to discuss issues they perceive as important. Other types of people may also attend, such as non-racialized youth or youth who have employment. This would generate data on a cross-section of views and provide observations of different parties reacting to each other's ideas. A drawback of focus groups is that they are more time-consuming for the participants. All participants must take time to listen to the responses of others. The advantage, however, is that by listening, all participants can create their own conversation, asking different questions and allowing the researcher to gather information on issues they might not have anticipated earlier in the study.

Note-taking can be very difficult when administering focus groups, simply because so much is usually going on. The best way to collect data is to make a video recording with a camera mounted in a non-intrusive place or audio-taping with a digital recorder. The recording should capture the dialogue of individual participants and their interactions. Video recordings also document body language and gestures, which can also be valuable data. Remember that use of any recording device must be approved by your REB.

Facilitators are the people who introduce the research topic to participants, ask questions, direct conversations, and record the results. Usually, the focus group facilitator is the primary researcher. However, it is increasingly common for researchers to hire focus group facilitators. Regardless of who directs the focus group, it is a very good idea to provide a questionnaire agenda to the facilitator. This consists of a list of discussion questions that must be covered during the focus group activity. The facilitator must be prepared to probe and ask additional questions when the focus group delves into topics that are tangential to the original research question. Usually, this additional information is interesting and helps to provide a fuller depiction of a research topic. Occasionally, however, the line of questioning may be unnecessary and unhelpful in understanding a problem. For this reason, the focus group facilitator should be intimately familiar with the research project, the researcher's intentions, and the primary research questions.

It is usually best that the focus group facilitator act as transcriber. The transcriber takes the audio or video information and records it word-for-word into a computer program. This becomes the primary textual material from which the researcher draws the analysis. The transcriber, having conducted the focus group, can more accurately record the conversation, especially when the recording is of poor quality. If this is not possible, a professional secretary should be hired to record the notes. Each hour of interview can take at least four hours to be transcribed. Professional secretarial staff with superior typing abilities may be able to transcribe at a faster rate, saving the researcher money from the research grant.

It is a good idea to provide refreshments for participants, since discussions tend to be long, especially on topics that are important to the participants. It is not uncommon for focus groups to last more than two hours. In focus groups on less sensitive or personally important topics, such as discussions among high school youth on ethnic identity, the focus group may last only half an hour. Length of time is dependent on the number of questions asked, the number of participants, and the centrality of the research question to the individuals who attend the focus group.

Focus groups have also been used for non-research purposes, such as television networks developing new programming. These 'misuses' of the method have had a negative effect on research. Increasingly, participants are reluctant to participate in such endeavours without the assurance that their data will be used for research purposes. It is a good idea for researchers to clearly identify themselves as such. Materials given to the participant should clearly indicate the university or institution the researcher is affiliated with. This may increase the chances that the individual will participate in the research. It is also required as an ethical practice.

Textual material

The use of textual material, including records, is described at length in Chapter 6 with respect to a quantitative form of research, content analysis. Here the researcher counts frequencies of themes, phrases, or ideas. However, texts can also be a source of data in qualitative research. Rather than just counting the number of times themes occur, researchers use the themes to construct a picture of what it is like to experience a given situation.

For example, documents can be used to answer the question 'What was happening in this time and place to these people?' Letters, diaries, and minutes of meetings are useful sources of data about what it is like to experience particular situations. When using documents, it is important to keep in mind the identities of the people who wrote them, who was to receive them, and for what purpose they were written. Such information specifies the perspectives of those who participated in the creation of the text.

In conducting a content analysis, the researcher must first identify the kinds of text that are appropriate for answering the research question. Are newspapers the best source of information? If so, which newspapers? What year? How many weeks? Are editorials included or excluded? These are important questions to consider prior to embarking on the assembly of textual materials.

Once these questions are addressed, the researcher needs to develop an analytical framework to make sense of the mass of materials collected. One way to go about this is to look for words or phrases that appear in the material. Count how many times a word or phrase appears. Count how many times the phenomenon is described positively and negatively. Another way of organizing the material is by the author or the newspaper. Perhaps the materials could be organized chronologically. Recall the literature review you conducted prior to collecting the textual materials. What themes are identified by this literature? This will give researchers a good beginning from which to identify their own themes. Be warned, however. The literature review should serve as a guide only. You are likely to discover many other themes not previously considered in the course of your research.

In short, textual material may be the main data collected for a qualitative research project or may supplement data collected in other ways. There are many cases in which content analysis can be used as the central data collection strategy. For example, a research project conducted by one undergraduate student involved examining the materials produced as part of the Bouchard/Taylor Commission on Reasonable Accommodation in Quebec. It was not practical or possible for her to travel to Quebec to interview all those who participated in the commission's hearings, given the time and cost constraints she faced as an impoverished student trying to complete her honours thesis.

Content analysis is an especially important form of data collection when the original participants are no longer alive to participate in interviews. In other cases, the content analysis supplements data collected in other forms. The project on high school youth described in Appendix A has a content analysis component. In addition to the data collection strategies discussed in the appendix, the researchers examined the school curriculum in social studies and geography in order to discover whether or not these programs included or ignored issues of identity formation. This information assisted the researchers in preparing a fuller view of identity formation among high school-aged youth in three provinces.

Organizing and summarizing qualitative data

Once you have made your observations, recorded or written up your interviews or focus group interactions, or collected your open-ended questionnaires, what do you do with the data? Qualitative research tends to produce vast amounts of information, which you must first organize and summarize.

Organizing data

As in content research, qualitative researchers look through interviews, textual data, and observational data for recurring 'themes' or issues. They identify themes and organize them into systems of categories, a practice called 'coding'. Following is a simple example of coding. When asked a question on the topic of employment, 'Why don't you work?', a young woman might answer:

My family prefers that girls study instead of working while going to school.

There are two dimensions to the thematic content of the sentence—the topic and the issue. The topic is 'looking for work', as given by the question. In response, the participant raised the issue of her family's preference that females do not work while they are studying for school.

The next task is to 'code' the theme—that is, apply a label designating the topic and the issues. A simple way to code the above statement is therefore:

1.1 Looking for work: Family preferences

The word or phrase before the colon identifies the topic; the following words or phrases identify the issues. The code is also given a number for easy indexing, in this case 1.1. In this example, 'Looking for work' is Topic 1 and 'Family preference' is Issue 1 for the topic; hence the full code is '1.1'. There are many ways to code themes, and you should devise or adapt ways that make the greatest sense for you.

As you read interviews and create new codes, write the code numbers on the pages of the interview transcripts where they occur. While doing this, also write a 'codebook'—that is, a list of codes, indexed to the interviews in which you identified them (see Figure 12.2). When finished, the codebook will be a useful tool for analysis. As a list of codes, it will give a structural overview of how you have perceived the data. The codebook will also indicate how often codes occur, thereby showing their relative importance according to your own reading of the data. Lastly, the index of interviews and page numbers will allow you to quickly review and extract coded text.

It is valuable to review a coding scheme at least once. This leads to a refinement of the coding and greater familiarity with the data. If possible, another researcher should review the coding to assess its coherence and depth of understanding of the data.

You can create a codebook on a computer with a simple spreadsheet or word processing program. There are a number of software packages designed specially for coding and analyzing textual data. Students should gain some skills with these programs if they intend to pursue research as a career.

FIGURE 12.2 Codebook: Muslim settlement

Topics: Issues	Interviews: Page numbers					Total
1. Looking for employment						
1.1 Racial discrimination	Int. 1: page 4	Int. 8: page 5	Int. 17: page 2	Int. 6: page 3	Int. 10: page 1	5
1.2 Language barriers	Int. 1: page 2	Int. 9: page 3				2
1.3 Age discrimination	Int. 14: page 1	Int. 1: page 2	Int. 13: page 1	Int. 6: page 3	Int. 5: page 2	5
1.4 Prior work experience	Int. 1: page 1	Int. 2: page 1	Int. 23: page 5	Int. 3: page 2		4
2. Social networks						
2.1 Family connections in Winnipeg	Int. 6: page 1	Int. 8: page 1	Int. 19: page 2	Int. 23: page 2	Int. 25: page 1	5
2.2 Cultural connections in Winnipeg	Int. 7: page 1					1
2.3 Friendship networks in Winnipeg	Int. 9: page 6	Int. 8: page 5	Int. 17: page 4	Int. 22: page 4		4
etc.						

PHASE 3: ANALYZING DATA

Having organized your data, how do you analyze or 'make sense of it' so that you can write about 'what is going on' with the benefit of an informed understanding? Most importantly, you have to develop your sense of having 'been there' or having 'been close' to the situation so that you can look at the data with the sensitivity of someone who knows the situation personally. When a person has visited a remote place, they can describe it with reference to personal experience—the sights, sounds, smells, social values, and customs. The visitor is 'sensitized' to the place and can analyze its social situation by referring to their first-hand knowledge of 'what it was like' to be there. Similarly, you have to develop the same type of sensitivity to the situations you research.

If you have done participant research for an extended period, your sensitivity may be adequate. Then again, if you have used less intimate methodologies like non-participant observation or interviews, you may need to develop extra sensitivity through immersion in the data. Read and re-read interview transcripts and notes, review and re-review sound or visual recordings and photographs, and continue to revise the coding.

As your sensitivity increases, take notes of your changing impressions. The notes will eventually expose 'forms' in the data. Patterns and relationships between actions and social structures will become perceptible, allowing you to explain 'what is going on' or 'what it is like' in the situation. For example, after a thorough reading of interviews with racialized youth in Winnipeg, you may 'see' systems of support within the racialized communities that participants never describe explicitly but take for granted. Their dialogues could contain assumptions of reciprocal duties of support to certain people—family, clergy, friends, school teachers—but participants may never make direct references to these duties. You may also perceive social problems to which most participants refer only in their jokes. Participants may make jokes because they cannot get work in Canada or because they believe their jobs are inferior to those of non-racialized youth. These jokes, however, may indicate a general problem for racialized youth in the labour market.

Fundamentally, you should approach all qualitative analysis with a view to developing sensitivity to the data. This way, you can discuss 'what is going on' or 'what it is like' to be in a situation just as though you had been inside it—or as close to it as possible. In addition to developing sensitivity, you can employ a number of frameworks to make sense of data from particular analytical perspectives. Descriptions of two appear below, the 'action/cultural' framework and the 'typical actions' framework.

Action/cultural framework

The action/cultural framework makes reference to cultural or social facts in understanding social actions. It often requires extra data about the culture of the people within the research situation. Therefore, it may be necessary to consult history books, religious texts, or company mission statements.

For example, if you are a non-racialized person researching racialized youth in Canada, you may want to understand the social context of discrimination in Canada. The immediate answer, as you would be told in interviews, is that racial and ethnic discrimination is rampant in Canadian society. This answer only provides a superficial understanding and raises the further question 'Why do racialized youth believe that racism is prevalent in Canadian society?' If you look more closely at the culture, social norms, and history of Canada, you will find that racism and discrimination do exist in Canada and are affected by events of both the past and the present. An examination of Canadian history reveals extensive racial discrimination in the job experiences of racialized and immigrant peoples. For example, the Chinese were prohibited from working in industries other than the railway, construction, manufacturing, and service sectors (Li, 1998). Ukrainians, Poles, Hungarians, Russians, and others faced significant ethnic discrimination when applying for jobs in Canada (Satzewich, 2002). More recent evidence reveals that racism still exists in the Canadian labour market today. For instance, Frances Henry and her colleagues have done extensive research revealing that racialized youth, particularly young men from Caribbean countries, are less likely to get job interviews and job offers (Henry and Tator, 2006; Henry, 1994; Henry and Ginzberg, 1984). Therefore, another way to understand youth's experience of racism is to contextualize their comments within historical and current events and the results of research conducted in Canada.

Typical actions framework

This analytic approach considers how people construct their social lives. It examines what actions are generally understood as 'typical actions', which make social life possible. For example, typical actions by which Muslims recognize other Muslims are attendance at Friday prayers, abstinence from pork, wearing the *qamis* or *hijab*, and the standard greeting of '*Asalam alykum*'. These are typical actions that for Muslims signify qualities of Islamic identity. Muslims recognize each other through these actions and have socially defined interpretations of meaning behind each.

In a study of Canadian Muslims, a significant issue among participants could be their relations with non-Muslims. In analyzing any friction between the communities, the researcher might search interviews for Muslims' negative interpretations of the 'typical' actions of non-Muslims. The participants may note that many non-Muslims stare at their *hijabs* and *qamis*, assume that all Islamic marriages are 'arranged', and express a lack of understanding of abstinence from alcohol and that some non-Muslims attempt to stop the building of mosques in their suburbs. Likewise, the interviews may indicate typical actions that Muslims interpret as friendly. Interviews may contain several references to participants' feelings of solidarity with non-Muslims at work or to the prayer facilities for their children in public schools. Repeated references to such types of social actions indicate what it is like to be a Muslim in Canada and how Muslims construct the social actions of others. The recognition of both negative and positive interpretations of typical actions by non-Muslims would be the basis for a rich description and set of explanations of 'what it is like' to be a Muslim living in Canada.

Reporting on qualitative research

Qualitative research does not always lead to clear conclusions. As with quantitative research, it is important that when writing up results, you remind yourself of the question or research objective that guided the research. It is that question that you must now answer, that research objective about which you must now draw conclusions. If you asked, 'What is it like to be a racialized youth in Canada?', your conclusion, based on your data, will express a response to this question. If the research objective was 'to describe how the Wright family made an important decision', then you will summarize the findings and observations in terms of themes, interaction patterns, sequence of argumentation, patterns of power and submission, or whatever you found. This will allow you to describe what is involved in the situation and to interpret it for readers.

Reporting on qualitative research involves careful description of what was observed and heard, 'what it was like', and how people felt, reacted, and behaved. This may involve data summarization and categorization into themes or patterns, or it may involve description and interpretation of observations. Generally, qualitative research 'tells a story'. It is more difficult to report, since the communication of such research means trying to make sense of the experiences of a number of different research participants. How do you write a coherent research report on the varied experiences of 30 participants or 175 participants? Appendix A provides an example of how this is done in practice. Here are some guidelines.

The report always begins with a statement on the research question and a description of the theory or theories used to inform your research. Remember that literature review you conducted prior to collecting the data and formulating your research question? This is another point at which it is helpful in the research process. The literature review serves different purposes in qualitative research depending on the topic. If the topic is new and not much has been written about the phenomenon, then the literature review will be short. When embedding your findings within the literature in that case, this part of the process may be short. If research on your topic has been widely published in the literature already, then the literature review will include a discussion of how your findings either support the existing literature or how your findings contribute to our understanding of the topic.

In qualitative research, the literature review and production of the research report are symbiotic. The researcher must constantly return to the literature review when analyzing the results to better situate the results of the project within the existing literature. Kirby and her colleagues (2006) tell us that this takes a significant amount of time to accomplish and that the writing occurs in stages. It may require the researcher to do a little work at one time, then put it aside for a while. Writing in stages can help to ensure that 'the analysis is solid, steady, and unlikely to change' (Kirby et al., 2006: 236).

In contrast to quantitative research, data in a qualitative project can take many forms. Typically, there is a research report. This informs funders and readers of the results of the study. However, it may contain material very different from that in a quantitative report. Reports for projects involving unstructured interviews, for instance, typically include long quotations embedded within deep theoretical analysis. Other data may include 'photojournals'—examples of photos taken by respondents, followed up by detailed interviews. As in the study examined in Appendix A, the project may include maps showing where individuals spend time. It may include examples of the participants' work. The researcher should contact the publishers and funders well in advance to ensure that they are able to provide the technical or financial assistance necessary to reproduce photos and other pictorial materials in the report. Further, it will likely take the researcher a bit more time to analyze such data in order to make connections between the visual material and the interview material.

Kirby and her colleagues (2006) provide some tips on reporting on qualitative research. While your analysis must address the research question, it is not possible to give equal attention to all themes that come out of the data. Some themes may be more poignant or more illustrative or occur more often than other themes. Do try to provide as much attention to these themes as your respondents do. Do not overemphasize points that the participants do not spend as much time discussing.

Data reduction is another tricky issue. Many researchers are tempted to report on every single detail raised by every participant. This approach is inadvisable and often leads to a lengthy report filled with tangential information. Instead, select only the most illustrative examples. Tied to this concern is the issue of 'forcing the data analysis'. Kirby and her associates suggest that all materials included in the research report should directly relate to the research question. Ensure that all data contribute to answering the research question in some way. If you are tempted to add parallel material, keep your description short and perhaps use this material towards the end of the report as illustrative of possible trends but not definitely linked to the research topic.

Finally, be careful in the way you convey the voices of the participants in your report. It is important for the 'voices' of participants to figure prominently in the report, but do not use their words as your own. The point of most qualitative research is to project the voices, opinions, and ideas of the participants. If their voices are not part of the research report, you are not doing a good job of explaining their reality. But remember not to confuse the voices in the report. Ensure that your voice and opinion as researcher are reported separately from those of your participants. As well, ensure that you clearly attribute quotes and research materials to the correct participants.

It has been our experience that preparing the results of a qualitative research report is more time-consuming and less intuitive than it is for quantitative projects. For this reason, you should allow more time to prepare the report. Consult Tuhiwai Smith (1999) and Kirby et al. (2006) for assistance with the process.

QUESTIONS FOR REVIEW

1. What are the basic data-gathering techniques in qualitative research? What are the advantages and disadvantages of each?
2. What is involved in the summarization of qualitative data?
3. In qualitative research, the subject of the research participates more in the project than in quantitative research. Discuss.

Suggestions for further reading

Babbie, E.R. 2003. *The Practice of Social Research*. 10th edn, chapters 10, 11, 13. London: Wadsworth.

Berger, Peter L., and Thomas Luckmann. 1966. *The Social Construction of Reality: A Treatise on the Sociology of Knowledge*. Garden City, NY: Doubleday.

Denzin, Norman, and Yvonna Lincoln, eds. 2000. *Handbook of Qualitative Research*. 2nd edn. London: Sage.

Eldridge, J.E.T., ed. 1971. *Max Weber: The Interpretation of Social Reality*, pp. 92–102. London: Thomas Nelson and Sons.

Eliaeson, Sven. 2002. *Max Weber's Methodologies*, pp. 41–4. Cambridge: Polity Press.

Gilcun, Jane F., ed. 1992. *Qualitative Methods in Family Research*. New York: Sage.

Henry, F. 1994. *The Caribbean Diaspora in Toronto: Learning to Live with Racism*. Don Mills, ON: Longmans.

Henry, F., and E. Ginzberg. 1984. *Who Gets the Work? A Test of Racial Discrimination in Employment*. Toronto: Urban Alliance on Race Relations and the Social Planning Council of Toronto.

Henry, F., and C. Tator. 2006. *The Colour of Democracy: Racism in Canadian Society*. 3rd edn. Toronto: Thomson Nelson.

Judd, C.M., E.R. Smith, and L.H. Kidder. 1991. *Research Methods in Social Relations*, chapters 11–13. Fort Worth, TX: Holt, Rinehart and Winston.

Kellehear, Allan. 1993. *The Unobtrusive Researcher: A Guide to Methods*. Sydney, Australia: Allen and Unwin.

Kirby, Sandra L., Lorraine Greaves, and Colleen Reid. 2006. *Experience Research Social Change: Methods beyond the Mainstream*. Peterborough, ON: Broadview.

Kreuger, Richard A. 1994. *Focus Groups: A Practical Guide for Applied Research*. New York: Sage.

Larson, Colleen L. 1997. 'Representing the subject: Problems in personal narrative enquiry'. *Qualitative Studies in Education* 10, 4: 455–70.

Li, P.S. 1998. *The Chinese in Canada*. 2nd edn. Don Mills, ON: Oxford University Press.

May, T. 1997. *Social Research: Issues, Methods and Process*. 2nd edn, Philadelphia: Open University Press.

Minichiello, Victor, Rosalie Aroni, Eric Timewell, and Loris Alexander. 1995. *In-depth Interviewing: Principles, Techniques, Analysis.* 2nd edn. Melbourne: Longman.

Satzewich, V. 2002. *The Ukrainian Diaspora.* London: Routledge.

Silverman, David. 1999. *Doing Quantitative Research: A Practical Handbook.* London: Sage.

Taylor, Steven J., and Robert Bogdan. 1998. *Introduction to Qualitative Research Methods: A Guidebook and Resource.* 3rd edn. New York: John Wiley and Sons.

Tuhiwai Smith, Linda. 1999. *Decolonizing Methodologies: Research and Indigenous Peoples.* New York: Zed Books.

Additional resources

Canadian Sociology Association. 2007. *Professional Code of Ethics.* http://www.csaa.ca/structure/Code.html. Accessed 27 July 2007.

PHASE 3

Analysis and Interpretation

Drawing Conclusions

You have now reached the point where you analyze and interpret the findings of your research. You have clarified your thinking, formed a hypothesis, and gathered data. Now what? Essentially, it is time to draw conclusions about your hypothesis on the basis of the evidence you have collected.

A proper conclusion is grounded on careful analysis and interpretation of data gathered in the light of the basic question being researched. Data have been collected and presented, but they still require evaluation and analysis. Four basic questions guide the activities of data analysis and interpretation:

1. What did you ask?
2. What did you find?
3. What do you conclude?
4. To whom do your conclusions apply?

WHAT DID YOU ASK?

The first step in drawing conclusions is to remember what it was you asked. It is surprising how easy it is to lose sight of the purpose of a piece of research. Before leaping to conclusions, it is useful to remind yourself about the questions that originally motivated you to do the research. You may have made many interesting discoveries as you gathered data or prepared your data for presentation. But what was the central issue?

Do you remember the questions that you first asked? If you kept a research journal, you should look back to remind yourself of your original questions. Some will seem very broad and unfocused now. You may be able to see how, in the process of clarifying your thinking and narrowing the focus of the research, you tackled a manageable part of a much larger issue. Try to clarify now how you see both the larger issue and the role your research plays in that larger issue.

The clearest statement of what you are asking is your hypothesis or your research objective. Recall the process by which you narrowed the focus of your project and formed the hypothesis or objective. Now look at your hypothesis again. How does your hypothesis relate to the larger issues? Take as examples the hypotheses we have used in this book.

We have spent a lot of time on research involving hours spent in study and exam results. The hypothesis stated:

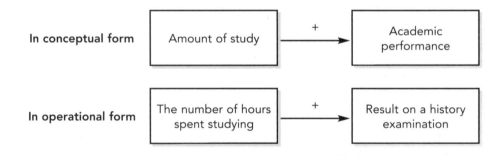

What was the background of this hypothesis? In Chapter 3, it was observed that some students get better marks than others. This prompted a series of clarifying questions. Refer back to Chapter 3 to remind yourself of the other possible explanations that were put forward. It should become clear that your hypothesis and hence your research will tell you something, but not everything, about the general issue. There were other factors, which were not explored. Hence, any conclusions you draw will be limited to the factor you examined. Your research pertains to the general area but deals specifically with one isolated factor. When asked, 'Why do some students get better marks than others?', you cannot conclude, 'because some study more than others do'. You know that there are many possible factors. Your research deals with only one. You could conclude that 'amount of time spent studying seems to be a factor in examination results'. Your research deals with one aspect of the overall issue. Be careful to ensure that in drawing a conclusion, you draw attention to the general issue and the way your research relates to it.

The first step in drawing a conclusion is to restate the general issue and the hypothesis, showing how the hypothesis relates to the general issue.

Another hypothesis used as an example throughout this book concerns the relationship between a talk on 'healthy snack selection' and the selections that workers actually make in the cafeteria. Reread the sections of Chapter 7 in which this example is first developed. Then answer these questions:

1. What is the general area of concern?
2. What is the conceptual hypothesis?
3. What is the operational form of the hypothesis?
4. How does the hypothesis relate to the general area of concern?

Here again you see the importance of stating conclusions in a way that clearly relates to both the specific hypothesis and to the general issue. There are many ways that the nutritional status of workers could be studied. In this case, snack selection in the cafeteria was chosen as the focus. First, a general observation study was done to discover the patterns of selection. Then an experiment was conducted to ascertain whether a talk on healthy snack selection would change workers' snack selection patterns. The conclusions of such research would relate to the general areas of worker nutrition, cafeteria operation, and nutrition education. How does the specific hypothesis tested relate to each of these areas? In this way, the conclusions of a small study are related to larger issues.

The first step in drawing conclusions is to clarify the way your research relates both to the hypothesis and to the larger issue. You did not start collecting data on the number of motorists who had run red lights for no reason. What were the reasons? How does your research relate to these reasons? If you did research comparing the degree of sexism among different groups of males, why did you do so? To simply conclude that levels of sexism among males who had attended coeducational schools were higher or lower or the same as those among males who had attended single-sex schools may be correct, but it is too limited. Relate the findings of your small study to the larger context of which it is a part.

WHAT DID YOU FIND?

Once you have reminded yourself of what it was you were asking and how your hypothesis or research objective related to that general area of interest, you can ask, 'What did I find?' Yes, the data your study produced are by now displayed in tables or graphs or expressed as averages. But what do you think they say? They do not analyze or interpret themselves.

There are several basic aspects to answering the question 'What did you find?' First, the data need to be interpreted. Second, the data must be related to the hypothesis or research objective. Third, you need to evaluate the data. We will discuss each of these aspects.

First, what do your data, as presented, say? This involves expressing in words what the tables, graphs, or averages say. We spent some time on this in Chapter 11.

Look again at Table 11.7. It is followed by a simple statement expressing in words the relationships between the data in the table. That is an example of interpretation.

Now turn to Figure 11.1. What does it 'say'? The interpretation of this figure might be written in this way:

Among those 16 students who studied more than the average amount of time, 11 (or 68.7 per cent) received an above-average result on the history examination, while among those 14 students who studied less than the average amount of time, two (or 14.3 per cent) received an above-average result.

Interpreting your data means restating the relationships depicted in your tables, graphs, or calculations of averages as clearly as possible in words.

How would you interpret the data presented in Figures 11.4 and 11.5 and make a comparison between the ethnic composition of one course and the ethnic composition of the Canadian population? The interpretation of these data depends on the question being asked. Let us assume that the question was this:

How does the ethnic composition of Course X compare with that of the Canadian population?

An interpretation of the data in the two figures might be as follows:

The data shows that the ethnic composition of the class enrolled in Course X is different from that of the general Canadian population. The ethnic composition of Course X shows a greater proportion of people of 'other' ethnic origins (including Chinese and Filipino/a) and a lower proportion of people of Canadian origin than is the case for the population of Canada as a whole.

When you interpret the data, you simply restate in words what is presented and summarized in the table, graph, or averages. You do not try to explain the data, nor do you draw conclusions from them. If the results are unclear, you report that the data are unclear.

As an exercise, try to interpret the data presented in Table 11.9. Remember, interpreting the data means restating in words the relationship between the variables presented in the table, graph, or average. Finally, interpret the data presented in Table 11.10.

Once you have interpreted the data, you are ready to relate your findings to the hypothesis or research objective. That is, what do these data tell you about your hypothesis? Is the evidence 'for' or 'against' the hypothesis? What are the implications of the findings for the narrowly defined research question?

This is usually straightforward. Problems emerge if the data are unclear and there is no strong trend one way or the other. If this is the case, your analysis should state that the implications of the data for the question, or the hypothesis, are unclear.

At this stage, it is best to report the implications of the data without discussion or comment. Either the hypothesis is supported or it is not. Ambiguous findings cannot be taken as support. It is important to remember that a hypothesis is never proved to be absolutely correct. Rather, a hypothesis is tentatively accepted or likely to be correct given the evidence, or it is not accepted given the lack of evidence. If you would like to investigate correlations and causation further, this would be an appropriate time to consult more advanced statistical methods to answer your question or to prove your hypothesis.

Once the findings are stated and related to the hypothesis or research objective, it is time to evaluate the data and to acknowledge the limitations of your study. General issues are critical here. First, the operationalization of the variables would doubtless have not entirely satisfied you. Again, if you kept a research journal, you would have noted limitations in it. These limitations can be noted at this point in the report or earlier in the discussion of variable selection, decisions regarding research design, sample selection, and data collection. You may have questions about the instrument (questionnaire) or the interviewers. The limitations of your sample are to be noted.

The most important limitations involve the possible influence of the variables that you are unable to control or measure. Possible alternative explanations for the relationship between the independent and dependent variables need to be noted. You may have suggestions for future research. It may be that your findings were not clear and you suspect the interference of some variable. It is useful to note this.

Your findings may have come out in an unexpected fashion. It is here that you can comment on this and suggest explanations. Your findings may conflict with the findings of others. This can be discussed.

Whatever they are, acknowledge the limitations of the study. This shows that you know what you might have done if you had more time, money, or other resources. It also shows that you know your conclusions are made tentatively in the light of the limitations of your research.

WHAT EXACTLY DO YOU CONCLUDE?

A good conclusion has two levels. First, it clearly states in simple terms what the data reveal. Second, it relates this simple statement to the larger issues. This can be seen as the reverse of the process by which you narrowed your attention in the first stage of the research process.

Here is a sample conclusion for the research on study time and marks:

Conclusion

A study of 30 students in a history class in a university in X revealed that those who spent more than the average time studying tended to receive above-average results in a history exam. While there were some exceptions, the data as presented in Table 11.7 show a clear trend in this direction. It is safe to conclude that these data provide evidence that support the hypothesis.

Thus, it is likely that amount of time spent studying is one among other factors that affect academic performance. Other factors such as IQ, social life, nutritional status, and specific study habits may account for some of the exceptions in this study. Further research is required to establish how widely this finding applies. Further research should compare students at other universities, the effect of time spent in studying on the examination results in other subjects, and the results of other methods of examination.

This conclusion clearly states the relationship demonstrated by the data. It supports this statement with references to the data summaries and graphs. Next, it states the implications of the data for the larger issue and future research. The first part of the conclusion restates what the data reveal about the operational form of the hypothesis. Data do not interpret themselves; you have to interpret them. Do the data support the hypothesis? Do they reject the hypothesis? Or is the situation unclear? Then the implications of the findings are drawn for the conceptual form of the hypothesis and, finally, the larger issue. The role of a conclusion is to restate the findings of the study and then to state the implications of the findings for both the hypothesis and the larger issue.

Take the example of the study comparing sexist attitudes among males. The hypothesis (see Chapter 6) was as follows:

Males who have gone to single-sex schools are more sexist in their attitudes than males who have attended coeducational schools.

The dummy table suggested for this study is found in Table 8.8. Let us assume that Table 13.1 presents the data from a study of 60 males, of which 30 had attended single-sex schools and 30 had attended coeducational schools.

TABLE 13.1   Findings from a hypothetical study of sexism among males

SEXISM SCORE	EDUCATIONAL BACKGROUND	
	SINGLE-SEX SCHOOL	COEDUCATIONAL SCHOOL
High	24 (80%)	20 (67%)
Low	6 (20%)	10 (33%)
Total	30 (100%)	30 (100%)

Given the data in Table 13.1, what would you conclude about your hypothesis? Is it supported or rejected, or are the results unclear? The data in Table 13.1 do not immediately present a clear picture. They are not compelling. There is too little difference. A conclusion drawn from a study based on these data might read as follows.

Conclusion

In an attempt to determine whether educational background played a role in the development of sexist attitudes among males, a questionnaire was administered to two groups of males. One group had attended single-sex schools for all of their schooling, the other group had attended coeducational schools. Does an educational context in which males have to interact with females regularly produce lower levels of sexist attitudes?

The results of our research indicate that males from both educational contexts show high levels of sexist attitudes as measured by the sexist-attitude scale used in the study. Males from single-sex schools are slightly more likely to have highly sexist attitudes. The differences between these two groups of males are not sufficiently large to conclude that the hypothesis is clearly supported. While the data are in the hypothesized direction, the relationship is too weak to draw any firm conclusions.

While educational context may well have an effect on the development of sexist attitudes among males, it cannot be concluded that this is so on the basis of this research. Additional research is required to ascertain whether the relationship is stronger or weaker in other schools. It may well be that the general level of sexism in our society is such that educational context has little effect on the development of sexist attitudes among males. Again, the role of the conclusion can be seen. It relates the specific findings back to the hypothesis and then to the general issue.

As an exercise, write a conclusion for this research given the findings in Table 13.2. In writing your conclusion, be sure to:

1. restate the general aim of the research;
2. restate the finding of the research;
3. indicate whether the hypothesis is supported or rejected, or whether the result is unclear;
4. explain the implications for the larger issue;
5. make suggestions for future research.

TABLE 13.2 Findings from another hypothetical study of sexist attitudes among males in two educational contexts

	EDUCATIONAL BACKGROUND	
SEXISM SCORE	SINGLE-SEX SCHOOL	COEDUCATIONAL SCHOOL
High	14	5
Moderate	10	10
Low	6	15
Total	30	30

In the conclusion, you state what the data as summarized and presented in your tables, graphs, or averages tell you about the hypothesis you formulated. The implications are then drawn for the larger issue. This is also true for a research objective. However, research objectives are not accepted or rejected. The data are simply summarized in words and a conclusion drawn.

Take the example of the simple observation study of one baby's growth. Once the data have been collected and recorded, the simplest conclusion would be that the baby had grown by the addition of X cm and Y g. But there is a background to this study. You could look up the average growth rates for infants and compare this baby's growth record with that standard. Then a conclusion about one baby's growth in comparison with the average could be made.

Since no specific comparisons are being made and no data on other factors are kept, no other conclusions can be drawn. If the purpose of the study had been to compare the growth rates of different infants—for example, one group that had been breastfed with another that had been bottlefed—then the study would have had a hypothesis about which conclusions could be drawn.

An appropriate conclusion for a study of infant growth guided by a research objective might take the following form:

Conclusion

The purpose of this study was to observe the growth of one infant over a period of eight weeks in order to see, in a specific infant, the general patterns of growth as described in the textbooks. The specific measures were of growth in length and weight. Other aspects of growth and development were observed but not systematically recorded.

The baby I observed grew by X cm and Y g during the eight-week period of observation. The baby was eight weeks old at the beginning and 16 weeks old at the end. A growth of X cm and Y g is well within the bounds of normal growth for infants of this age.

This observation has also made me aware of the complexity of observing infant growth and development. I would suggest that in future observations of this type, the following be considered . . .

Although a conclusion about a hypothesis is not drawn, the conclusion of a study guided by a research objective may well make suggestions for future research. For example, take an observation study guided by the following research objective:

To discover what factors are considered by the person(s) in charge of meal planning in the selection and preparation of food.

The researcher might conclude at the end of the research as follows:

Conclusion

An observation study conducted in a single household revealed that the following factors were taken into consideration in the selection and preparation of food:

- cost
- preferences of family members
- availability
- preparation time required
- preparation skills required
- nutritional quality
- balance and diversity in foods
- kilojoule content of foods

While in the single case study household, cost was the predominant factor, closely followed by preference of family members, this may well vary from household to household. Future research into the factors shaping household decision-making about food should ascertain how the importance of these factors varies among households.

While we interviewed each member of the household, we discovered that in this household, one person is responsible for meal planning and preparation. Given our experience in this household, we suspect that this person is not always 'the mother' in all households. This means that future research can focus on one member of each household but that care is required in selecting which member to interview. We also suspect that a questionnaire could be devised to measure the relative importance of various factors . . .

The researcher here used the observations of a single case study as the basis for many suggestions for the next stage of research on this issue. She could well have made other comments. Further observations regarding the amount of time spent in meal preparation, meal planning, and shopping might also have been made. The researcher might have commented on the accuracy of the information available to the participant and the suitability of the meals planned to the purposes outlined by the participant.

Thus, although research guided by a research objective does not lead to conclusions about hypotheses, the results are summarized and related to the general issues behind the research. Suggestions for future research may also be made.

This introduction to the research process has deliberately avoided covering more mathematical forms of analysis so that you can become familiar with the essential logic and flow of doing research without the burden of learning complex statistical modelling at the same time. There is not enough space here to discuss the application of statistical analysis to data. However, conclusions that are drawn using non-statistical techniques and are reliant solely on the reporting of percentages are very limited. There are a number of computer programs available that allow students to make quite complex statistical analyses, even students who consider themselves weak in mathematics. Consult your professor to determine whether your data are suitable for statistical analysis, and for advice on what programs and statistics courses are available.

TO WHOM DO YOUR CONCLUSIONS APPLY?

The question 'To whom do your conclusions apply?' can be answered in a narrow sense and in a broader sense. On the one hand, your conclusions are limited to the sample studied and to the population it represents. This is the narrow interpretation of a conclusion.

If you studied a representative sample of history students in your university, your conclusions are limited to history students in your university. If you observed one family, your conclusions are limited to that family.

The narrow interpretation of the applicability of conclusions is based on the limitations imposed by the sampling procedure selected. This narrow interpretation refers to the data—to the 'facts' produced by the research. Take the example of the study of sexist attitudes among males. The data in Table 13.1 relate to two groups of 30 males. The groups had different educational backgrounds. The specific findings are limited to those males. That is, the finding that two-thirds (67 per cent) of males from coeducational schools scored high on sexist attitude, while four-fifths (80 per cent) of males from single-sex schools did, is limited to those males. If those males were a representative sample of a larger population, then that finding would apply to that larger population. It is not permissible to conclude that in general, 67 per cent of males from coeducational backgrounds and 80 per cent of males from single-sex schools will score high.

The conclusions regarding the data apply to those from whom the data were collected or to the larger population of which they are a representative sample.

On the other hand, research is done to gain some understanding about larger issues. Some of the conclusions refer to the implications of the research findings for those larger issues. This is the broader sense of the applicability of the conclusion. In drawing conclusions, the researcher moves from the narrow conclusions about the findings of the study to the implications of those findings for the larger issues. It is in this sense that conclusions have a broader applicability.

Again, take the example of the study of sexist attitudes among males. The data in Table 13.1 were too close to conclude that educational context made much difference between those two groups. Then the conclusion discussed the implications of the findings for the larger issue. When drawing the implications, a much more tentative style of expression is adopted: 'It may well be that . . . ', 'Additional research is required . . . '.

The sample conclusion for the study of 30 history students demonstrates the shift between the narrow conclusion and the drawing of implications. First, it summarizes the empirical findings (the data), then it continues, 'Thus it is likely that amount of time spent studying is one, among others, of the factors . . . '.

Thus, in drawing conclusions, the first step is to restate the empirical findings. This part of the conclusion applies narrowly and strictly to those studied or the population of which they are a representative sample. Then the implications of the empirical findings for the more general issues are discussed. In this part of the conclusion, the findings are related to a broader context and made more generally relevant. However, the discussion of implications is done tentatively. In this way, the conclusion can be seen to have a narrow aspect (the summary statement of the empirical findings) and a broader aspect (the discussion of the implications of those findings).

QUESTIONS FOR REVIEW

1. What four basic questions guide the activities of data analysis and inter-pretation?
2. Interpret in words the data on the effect of age on school attendance, highest level of education, and income in Canada presented in Figures 13.2 to 13.4. Note that your task is simply to restate in words what is presented in the graph. Do not try to explain, moralize, or draw conclusions. Simply state what each graph 'says'.
3. Why is it important to acknowledge the limitations of a study?
4. How does the sampling procedure you choose influence the conclusion you draw?

FIGURE 13.2 Effect of age on school attendance, Canada, 2001

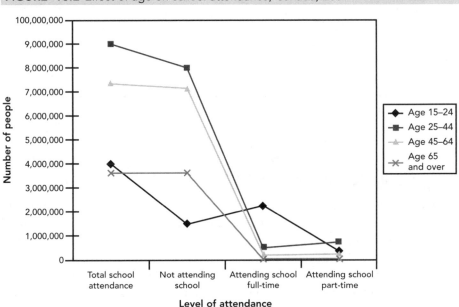

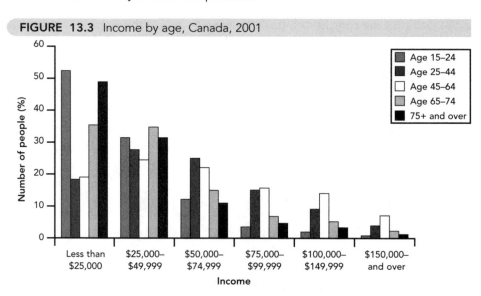

FIGURE 13.3 Income by age, Canada, 2001

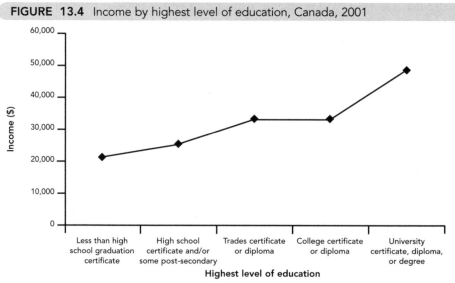

FIGURE 13.4 Income by highest level of education, Canada, 2001

Suggestions for further reading

Babbie, E.R. 2003. *The Practice of Social Research*. 10th edn. London: Wadsworth.

Betts, K., and A. Seitz. 1994. *Writing Essays and Research Reports in the Social Sciences*. Melbourne: Thomas Nelson.

Judd, C.M., E.R. Smith, and L.H. Kidder. 1991. *Research Methods in Social Relations*, chapter 19. Fort Worth, TX: Holt, Rinehart and Winston.

Minichiello, Victor, Rosalie Aroni, Eric Timewell, and Loris Alexander. 1995. *In-depth Interviewing: Principles, Techniques, Analysis*. 2nd edn, chapter 11. Melbourne: Longman Cheshire.

Reporting Your Research

By now you have focused on a research issue, identified and measured variables, drawn samples, selected research designs, collected data, summarized and presented data, drawn conclusions, and discussed implications. You are now ready to write the research report. If you have kept a research journal, you will probably have a mountain of notes and records. These will be valuable to you in writing the report.

We have not said anything about the research report until this time because it is the last activity in one cycle of the research process. The research process does not begin with a report. The research process consists of a series of activities that are completed and then reported. Although your assignment might be to write a research report, that task occurs once the research is complete. Not everything that is done during the research is reported in the research report. The research report summarizes the activities so that they are clear to the reader and so that the reader could repeat the research.

WHAT IS WORTH REPORTING?

What should go into your report? How much is worth telling? The research report communicates your research to others. This is as true of your report as it is of articles published in research journals and books that report research. In order to communicate your research, it is necessary to make clear what you did, why you did it, what you found, and what you concluded from your findings. Readers must be able to tell what you did and understand why you did it the way you did. Readers can then decide whether they would draw the same conclusions given the data you present. They could also conduct the research again to see if the same results were found.

A GENERAL OUTLINE

The research report should take the following general outline:

1. statement of problem
2. review of relevant literature
3. statement of hypothesis or research objective
4. selection and operationalization of variables
5. description of research design
6. description of sample selection procedure
7. description of how data were collected
8. data presented and summarized in words
9. conclusion, limitations, and implications
10. bibliography or references
11. appendices

A research report need not be very long. One paragraph should be adequate to introduce the problem. A brief statement of what the literature review revealed about the problem is all that is required. References to the material reviewed should be included.

Below is an outline of a possible research report. The important thing to remember is the form and what is covered. The length and degree of detail in the report depend on the size of the research project and the requirements of the assignment.

The problem

State succinctly the question or problem your research deals with. Some call this 'the human problem'—that is, the ordinary daily, policy, or intellectual issue that inspired you. Youth homelessness, marital breakdown, how to care for the elderly, the impact of legislation to prevent sexual harassment, and how people who live in Toronto are different from people who live in St John's are examples of such issues. They are unformed, large, wide-ranging issues, the sort of concerns that awareness of everyday life brings to the minds of social scientists.

The review of relevant literature

The literature review section of a research report takes the ordinary human issue and locates it in a body of theory and previous research. This helps to transform the human issue into a researchable question or hypothesis. For example, reviewing past work on youth homelessness will tell you what is already known, what questions are current in the field, and what research approaches have been tried and with what results. Your readers deserve to know that you have consulted the literature in the field, what your conclusions about the field on the basis of your reading are, and how you see your research contributing to the field and the understanding of or knowledge about the issue.

Statement of hypothesis or research question

At the end of the literature review section, it is possible to state your hypothesis or research question. In doing so, you transform the human issue into a limited, researchable issue. The human issue concerning youth homelessness becomes 'What is the incidence of youth homelessness in Vancouver during February?', 'How many housing enquiries are made each night at a youth drop-in centre?', or 'Has there been an increase in the incidence of youth homelessness as a result of the deepening of the recession?' The human issue concerning marital breakdown could be transformed into such hypotheses as 'Similarity of religious background and commitment is negatively related to marital breakdown', 'Strength of religious commitment is negatively related to marital breakdown', or 'Degree of financial stress is positively related to marital breakdown'.

The hypothesis or research question is a restatement of the human issue in the form of a researchable issue.

Methodology

In this section, you describe and give reasons for your choices in the selection and operationalization of variables, research design, and sampling. The discussion of methodology must appear at this stage. It cannot appear earlier because it will only make sense if the research problem and the hypothesis have already been explained. It cannot appear later because the next section, 'Description and presentation of data', will not make sense unless it is preceded by an explanation of the methodology.

Description and presentation of data

Here you briefly describe how the data were collected and present your findings. It is important to stick very closely to a simple description of the data, leaving speculation and discussion for the next section. This section, like the last, is guided by your hypothesis or research question. Here you present the data that are relevant to the issues you raised and clarified before. It is important to present the findings that are relevant to the hypothesis or question guiding your research in a consistent and clear manner. This section presents the results of your research into the researchable question.

Conclusion and discussion

In the conclusion, you return to the 'human issue' with which you began and relate the findings of your research to this issue. You state your conclusions clearly, then discuss the implications for the issue. The conclusion may include speculation on possible future research, plus discussion of some of the limitations of your research and its possible policy implications.

Bibliography

In this section, you list all the references you consulted while doing your research. Use a bibliographic format that is currently used in one of the major journals in your field. Pay careful attention to the information required for books, chapters in books, and articles. Some forms of material, such as documents, may have to be codified and listed separately. Consult your professor about the format required.

Appendices

Appendices are convenient places to put material that is relevant to your report but that would interrupt the flow or take too much space in the body of the report. This may include copies of questionnaires or other research instruments, letters written seeking permission to conduct the research, more detailed reports of data collected, or supporting documents.

Your research report should tell a story, or have a logical flow, so that the reader progresses from issue to issue and is always aware of how each section of the material relates to the rest. This 'storyline', or logical flow, is not always clear until the end of the project. If your report does not read well, think it through again, reminding yourself of the issues raised at each stage and how these issues are related to the overall flow of your argument.

The length of a research report depends on various factors. Your professor may set a word limit. You may wish to publish your report in a journal that has expectations about the size and style of articles it publishes. MA and PhD theses have book-length word limits. Your funding organization may have a template to follow for submitting the report. Your stakeholders may require different information. For some projects, you may be required to produce several research reports for different audiences. Appendix A presents a full article-length research report containing a mix of qualitative and quantitative data. It is a good example of a report that does not require advanced statistical analysis yet makes significant academic and policy conclusions about an area of social life. It contains all the elements needed for a research report.

CONCLUSION

Congratulations! You now have the tools to start and complete a small research project. Your next step is to conduct your own research project. Start small. Large projects are complex and time-consuming and can be difficult to manage for a first-time researcher. Once you have gained experience in small research projects, you are ready to tackle larger projects with more research questions.

We strongly advise students who are interested in gaining further knowledge to take as many courses in social science, research methods, and statistics as possible. These courses will provide you with the skills necessary to analyze results from qualitative projects and large datasets and to examine questions of correlation and causation related to your research questions. This skill set will not only make you a stronger researcher but will allow you to provide more definitive answers to your questions. As well, the job market for students knowledgeable in research methods is growing as more and more businesses, universities, and research centres acquire new recruits with these types of skills.

QUESTIONS FOR REVIEW

1. Why do professional researchers publish their findings? When they do, what information must the report include? Why?
2. What information must your research reports include? Why?

Suggestions for further reading

Babbie, E.R. 2003. *The Practice of Social Research*. 10th edn, London: Wadsworth.

Betts, K., and A. Seitz. 1994. *Writing Essays and Research Reports in the Social Sciences*. Melbourne: Thomas Nelson.

Judd, C.M., E.R. Smith, and L.H. Kidder. 1991. *Research Methods in Social Relations*, chapter 19. Fort Worth, TX: Holt, Rinehart and Winston.

Kumar, Ranjit. 1999. *Research Methodology: A Step by Step Guide for Beginners*, chapter 17. London: Sage.

Minichiello, Victor, Rosalie Aroni, Eric Timewell, and Loris Alexander. 1995. *In-depth Interviewing: Principles, Techniques, Analysis*. 2nd edn. Melbourne: Longman Cheshire.

Appendix A

Negotiating Difference and Democracy: Identifying the Landscapes of Familiarity and Risk among Youth in Canada

Lori Wilkinson
University of Manitoba

Yvonne Hébert
University of Calgary

Mehrunissa Ali
Ryerson University

ABSTRACT

Focus on youth in Canadian society has become increasingly interesting to academics and government policy-makers. In situating youth, there is merit in understanding how their identities are constructed and how the places and spaces they use in everyday life reflect their role as future citizens. In this report, we address the following questions: (1) Where do Canadian youth spend their time? (2) How does their use of space and neighbourhood contribute to the construction of identity? The answers to these questions help to uncover the life experiences of young people in Canada and can help us learn more about civic engagement. The paper analyzes data on youth's preferential use of urban spaces by 164 youth aged 14 to 19 in Toronto, Calgary, and Winnipeg using a qualitative urban mapping exercise, a short demographic survey, and follow-up individual interviews. The discussion contextualizes the findings with existing research on youth in other countries and makes several recommendations for governments and policy-makers with regard to planning city spaces for youth recreation and safety.

STATEMENT OF PROBLEM

A large body of psychological, criminological, historical, and sociological research has problematized the lives of young people in Canada. Stereotypes of the youth drug user, car thief, bully, school shooter, and binge drinker fuel the moral panic surrounding much of the public, media, and government beliefs about youth in our society (Schissel, 1997; Tanner, 2001; Wooden and Blazak, 2001). These stereotypes have led to a distorted picture of youth, as the media and researchers tend focus their projects mainly on the problems created by youth. While this information is useful for academics, policy-makers, social workers, and others working with youth at risk, this kind of research does not elaborate on the positive experiences of the 'average' youth, nor does it contextualize their experiences by the cities in which they live.

This report analyzes the data collected in one part of our Social Sciences and Humanities Research Council (SSHRC)–funded research project entitled 'Negotiating differences and democracy: The effects of social capital on identity formation among Canadian youth'. While there are many research questions asked in our project, for the purposes of this research report we examine only two questions: (1) Where do Canadian youth spend their time? (2) How does their perception of place contribute to identity formation?

REVIEW OF LITERATURE

A central concept in sociology is the term *gemeinschaft*, a German word referring to a community of people having long-term relationships with one another. *Gemeinschaft* communities are generally very small and members know one another personally. Because of their personal connections, there is a strong sense of duty towards the community because members depend on one another to provide services and support for one another (Byrne, 2001). These communities are tightly knit because members share in the successes and failures of other members. The *gemienschaft* was the predominant arrangement of human communities until the industrial revolution.

These communities have given way to looser associations of people known by another German term, *gessellschaft*. In *gessellschaft* settings, individuals have partial and largely impersonal relationships with one another. People no longer have obligations towards their community, since most of their commitments are to their families, jobs, and personal networks. This type of community best describes life in large urban centres of the twenty-first century (Byrne, 2001). The problem for politicians, policy-makers, and service providers is to instil a sense of unity, duty, and commitment among a large group of people so that members feel accepted and willing to give back to their communities. The challenge for educators, parents, and other professionals is to encourage these values among young people. The conundrum is that these are the values best expressed in *gemeinschaft* communities, not in *gessellschaft* communities. As a result, twenty-first-century youth face uncertainty about who they are, who they will be, and their place in society. Uncertainty about identity peaks in adolescence (Verkuyten, 1995), so not only is it more of a challenge for them to negotiate society, but living in a *gessellschaft* community does not promote social ties and makes it difficult for youth to feel integrated in their society.

Understanding one's place in the *gessellschaft* is affected by other forces, including individual characteristics. These characteristics, primarily sex, gender, social class, ethnicity, and immigrant status, are among the many forces shaping identity. A large body of social science research reveals that the expectations of males and females differ based on their social roles and the norms of the society they live in. For example, girls are taught from a young age to fear strangers. For this reason, girls are more likely than boys to report that they are afraid to walk alone at night. Social class plays a role as well. Youth from affluent families have more opportunities than those from poor families. This affects their ability to travel, their access to education, and their participation in leisure activities. Ethnic origin and immigrant status also play important roles in identity formation. In a multicultural society, although the ideal is acceptance of diversity, it is well known that racism and discrimination exist in Canadian society. For example, racist attacks against minority groups, particularly those of Middle Eastern decent, increased dramatically after the terrorist attacks of 11 September (Helley, 2004; Biles and Ibrahim, 2002). For these reasons, integrating into the *gessellschaft* has different meanings and consequences for racialized youth. Finally, the immigration process has profound implications for identity formation. Those experiencing more positive migration processes are more likely to have more success at situating themselves within their new society, culture, and language.

Differences in individual characteristics and uncertainty in identity of young people combine to influence how youth perceive the cities and neighbourhoods in which they live. Characteristics of the city also play a role in defining a sense of place among youth. All three cities, especially the neighbourhoods where the majority of the youth in our study live, have been characterized by media, police, and governments as having high rates of crime. As a result, the differing landscapes of crime in each city will affect how youth identify the places they feel are safe or unsafe and will partially affect their decisions on the places they prefer to spend their time. Furthermore, how others view their neighbourhoods also plays a role in how youth situate themselves in society.

It is our belief that youth have varying understandings of their place in society and that these understandings partially influence the development of identity. As Cresswell (1996), Massey (1998), and others have argued, individuals categorize and define the places where they spend time.

An examination of the places youth prefer to spend their time helps us to understand the factors influencing identity development. To evaluate the places where youth prefer to spend their time, we utilize a typology developed by Wyn and White (2004) to understand how youth view their neighbourhoods and cities. Youth categorize their spaces as being youth-specific, friendly, neutral, or unfriendly. A youth-specific place is one designed primarily for use by youth. They are places that young people themselves feel are most interesting, accessible, and suitable for them and reflect their particular needs and desires for entertainment and recreation. Examples of youth-specific places include swimming pools, movie theatres, libraries, arcades, parks, sports fields, and recreation complexes.

Youth-friendly areas are places where the general atmosphere is one in which young people are treated with respect and dignity, where they feel safe, secure, and welcome. They are not spaces created solely for youth—they are frequented by a wide variety of individuals with varying characteristics. This category includes places where youth can freely create culture, decorate, adorn, claim space, and mark their territory. Family homes, friends' homes, bedrooms, playgrounds, school lockers, certain parks and nature preserves, cinemas, sports-related settings, fast-food outlets, some retail shops, arcades, snooker halls, and places to skate, skateboard, and roller blade, are all examples of youth-friendly places.

Youth-neutral places are general community places, available and open to everyone and often of passing and transient nature. They are places where youth may feel less comfortable and welcome. Examples of youth-neutral places include commercial centres where the buy–sell functions predominate and public transportation, including buses and subways.

Youth-unfriendly places are those where youth rarely gain a sense of ownership. These are places where they experience a lack of control and independence and where individual identity-meaning and/or culture-meaning activities (such as graffiti) are considered transgressions. This category also includes places where youth may experience harassment (including sexual harassment), intolerance of difference, disrespect, or lack of safety (such as an unlit dark place, especially at night). It includes places where youth may experience physical violence and aggression and may be intimidated by others. Examples of such places include areas outside or behind schools and other public/community places, downtown city streets, places where homeless congregate, dark parks, and bushy areas. These places may also be intimidating to adults but are perceived as far more dangerous by youth.

According to research conducted in Australia, youth spend most of their time at home and at a friend's place in youth-friendly places. When they venture out, it is to hang out with friends in semi-public spaces, such as malls, or in areas defined as youth-specific. Security personnel and restrictions may transform commercial settings into youth-unfriendly spaces if the youth interfere with the powerful buyer–seller relationship (White and Wyn, 2004). In studies conducted in the United Kingdom, researchers reveal that social class and ethnicity play a role in how youth view their place in society and the places they identify as safe and unsafe (Watt and Stenson, 1998; Webster, 1996). Our study aims to test these observations among a similar group of youth in Canada.

GOAL OF RESEARCH

The goal of this research is to identify the places where youth spend time. Do youth spend most of their time close to home and school in youth-specific and youth-friendly places? What parts of their neighbourhood do they utilize? Do they feel safe or unsafe in the places they frequent? This information is useful to academics. It allows us to better understand how youth situate themselves within their city. We can look at differences related to sex, gender, ethnic origin, socio-economic class, and age to determine use patterns and preferences. The information can be used to compare Canadian youth with those living in other countries where similar research has been conducted. City planners would find this information useful as well. They would be interested in identifying patterns of use and in locating places where youth feel safe and unsafe. Perhaps the findings of this study could be used to design recreational facilities for youth living in neighbourhoods that lack adequate infrastructure. Planners could also use the findings to identify areas of risk for youth and make them safer, more inclusive places for everyone.

RESEARCH DESIGN

This research is part of a national longitudinal study of the factors influencing inclusion among youth in three Canadian cities. For privacy reasons, the names and neighbourhood locations of the schools are not revealed. Schools are denoted as Calgary School 1, Calgary School 2, Toronto School 1, Toronto School 2, and Winnipeg School 1 to protect the identities of the students, teachers, and principals who participated in this research project. Approval from the Research Ethics Boards of participating universities was obtained prior to the involvement of schools and school boards. Permission from the four participating school boards was obtained prior to contacting the schools. Principals and participating teachers were also required to sign consent forms.

After the ethical permission was obtained from the universities, school boards, and principals, students in Grade 10 at the five participating schools were approached to participate in the project. The project was described by the researcher, and information, along with a consent form, was sent home to parents. Students could not participate unless they and their parents had agreed and signed the consent form. Students who agreed to participate in Year 1 were approached in Grade 11 and Grade 12 for permission to continue with data collection related to other aspects of the project. The results of Years 2 and 3 of the project are not discussed here. For the purposes of this research report, only the data for 164 students in Grade 10 are discussed. To protect their identity, students were instructed to use pseudonyms instead of their real names. We use these in the discussion.

Sample selection procedure

Students were selected from five high schools in Toronto, Calgary, and Winnipeg. Since education is provincially controlled, each of the research sites had to gain permission to approach schools to participate from their respective boards of education. The school boards in Toronto, Calgary, and Winnipeg gave permission to the researchers to approach schools to participate in the study. Once permission was obtained from the research ethics boards of each school division, researchers then selected schools and approached principals for permission to conduct research. Principals and teachers were given copies of the research protocols and made a decision about participating.

Once the principal and teachers agreed, students in Grade 10 social studies classes were selected to participate. We selected Grade 10 students because uncertainty about identity is very high at this age. In the Toronto and Winnipeg schools, all the students in participating classes took part in the study [recall that parents and students were required to sign consent forms, similar to those discussed in Chapter 9]. In Calgary, students volunteered to participate in the study outside class time. They and their parents signed consent forms and completed the study activities as extracurricular activities.

A total of 164 students in Toronto, Calgary, and Winnipeg participated in Year 1 of the project. The sample size declined in Years 2 and 3 as students moved, dropped out of school, or lost interest in the project. This is a procedure best suited to study identity formation as it is unique to individuals.

Since the researchers were unable to randomly select the school and the students who participated in the study, our sample is known as a convenience sample. This type of sample is appropriate for qualitative research projects, since our goal is to understand a particular phenomenon. We are not interested in generalizing the results to students across Canada but in better understanding a particular aspect of youth life.

Data collection

Over a three year period, the students participated in the project using a range of data collection strategies. Making use of techniques developed by Cohen, Keith, and Back (1999), Räthzel and Hoerder (2001), and ourselves, we devised various activities to help us to better understand how youth envision inclusion and their place in Canadian society. It was hoped that the variety of techniques, including visual elements and self-expression, would provide us with perspectives not otherwise available to us, reduce the input and influence of researchers on the students' answers, and give the participants a chance to record their landscapes of familiarity and risk.

In total, students participated in eight activities. For the purposes of this research project, we explain the data derived from only three activities. In Year 1, students completed a short demographic survey intended to provide basic socio-demographic data about themselves. This data would be used to classify students and to contextualize individual characteristics such as sex and socio-economic status. The information would be used in interpreting the results of the qualitative data collection. Students in the three cities were then asked to complete an urban mapping exercise. Participants were given maps of their city and asked to identify their preferred places. Preferred places are defined as areas and buildings where youth feel 'at home' and included. They were then asked several questions about their preferred places such as 'what do you do there?', 'whom do you meet?', and 'why do you go there?' Students were also asked to identify places where they felt unsafe, unwelcome, or unwanted. Again, students were asked about their activities in these places and why they frequented them even if they were unsafe. The urban mapping exercise was followed by a short interview to ensure that the researchers would have the information necessary to correctly interpret the exercise.

A number of other activities were undertaken by the students during this three-year project. These activities included focus groups, photoscapes, sociograms, autobiographies, cultural collages, and written responses. The purpose of these activities was to answer other questions related to the larger research project. Interested readers may refer to Hébert, Wilkinson, and Ali (2008) for additional information about the analysis of other aspects of this project.

FINDINGS

Describing the sample

- Forty-seven students in Calgary, 39 students in Toronto, and 88 students in Winnipeg participated in the project.
- The sample contains 99 (57 per cent) female and 75 (43 per cent) male students. The age range was between 14 and 18 at Year 1.
- Of the total sample, 24 per cent are students who were not born in Canada. Another 36 per cent of students were born in Canada to immigrant parents. The remaining 40 per cent are youth with families who have been in the country three generations or more.
- Notice the great ethnic diversity of the sample. Just over one in five respondents declared their primary ethnicity as Filipino/a. This was followed by other European (10 per cent), British (9 per cent), Caribbean (8 per cent), Vietnamese (6 per cent), and other Asian (6 per cent). Note that 20 per cent of the youth did not know their ethnic affiliation.

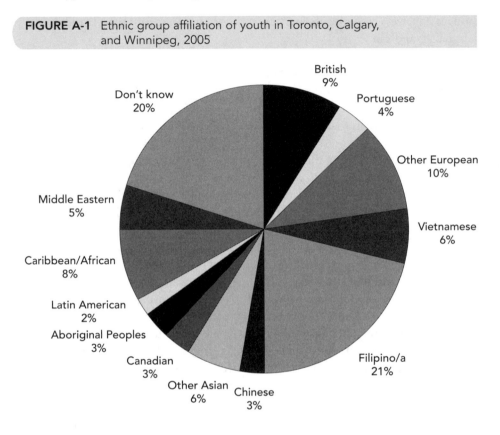

FIGURE A-1   Ethnic group affiliation of youth in Toronto, Calgary, and Winnipeg, 2005

- The parents of participating students are highly educated, with 26 per cent of fathers and 29 per cent of mothers having post-secondary qualifications. Only 11 per cent of fathers and 7 per cent of mothers had not finished high school, while 23 per cent of fathers and 26 per cent of mothers had a high school diploma. Nearly 10 per cent of the parents (7 per cent of fathers and 10 per cent of mothers) were still enrolled in post-secondary education at the time of the study. Surprisingly, a number of students could not tell us what level of education their parents had attained (32 per cent fathers, 26 per cent of mothers).
- The socio-economic status of the neighbourhoods in which the schools are located is important to contextualize the results of the urban mapping exercise. Tables A-1 and A-2 outline some of the major socio-demographic characteristics of each city.

Note the differences among the neighbourhoods and the cities. Some of these characteristics may influence how youths view their neighbourhood, the type of transportation they use, and whether or not they designate particular areas as safe or unsafe.

TABLE A-1   Toronto, Calgary, and Winnipeg neighbourhood socio-demographics

	WINNIPEG	CALGARY		TORONTO	
	NEIGH-BOUR-HOOD #1 (%)	NEIGH-BOUR-HOOD #1 (%)	NEIGH-BOUR-HOOD #2 (%)	NEIGH-BOUR-HOOD #1 (%)	NEIGH-BOUR-HOOD #2 (%)
Predominant ethnic group	Filipino/a (30)	American (15)	Vietnamese (22)	Portuguese (13)	East Indian (21)
Visible minorities	46	5	18	36	78
Home language (other than English or French)	55	2	21	21	16
Families with income less than $30,000	39	20	28	28	39

Source: Statistics Canada. 2004. *The 2001 Census of Canada: Neighbourhood Profiles*. Ottawa: Statistics Canada.

Youth were asked to identify the places where they preferred to spend time in their city. Table A-2 reveals differences in preferences among the youth. Youth in Toronto overwhelmingly prefer stores over other locations, with 53 per cent indicating them as their favourite place. While stores are popular in Calgary (25 per cent) and Winnipeg (30 per cent), they are not as popular as leisure centres among youth in Winnipeg (31 per cent) and Calgary (26 per cent). Spending time at home is also more popular in Calgary (27 per cent) and Winnipeg (23 per cent) than in Toronto (15 per cent).

Why is there a strong preference for stores among youth in Toronto? Perhaps the availability, diversity, and location of the stores in Toronto is a factor. Contrary to

TABLE A-2   Preferred places by city

	TORONTO (%)	CALGARY (%)	WINNIPEG (%)	TOTAL (%)
Homes	15	27	23	23
Institution	4	5	7	6
Leisure	11	26	31	25
Stores	53	25	30	33
Other	17	16	9	13
Total	100	100	100	100

our initial interpretations, the Toronto students mentioned that stores were used for more than just places of consumption. They are places where they can spend time with their friends and family. They are also locations where culture can be expressed. For example, students in Toronto are more likely to identify ethnic stores (such as grocery and clothing stores) as part of their shopping experience—more so than the youth in the other two cities. This could be an indication that shopping is a form of cultural maintenance. Students in Toronto also indicate that they use more public transportation than the students in Calgary and Winnipeg. That makes it easier for the students in this city to visit wider geographical areas. In the two prairie cities, students are more apt to identify problems with transportation, which may limit their mobility within the city. As a result, the youth in Toronto are more mobile than the youth in Calgary and Winnipeg, as witnessed in the next table.

Why are youth in Calgary and Winnipeg more likely to prefer leisure centres and homes than the youth in Toronto? One reason is the different cultures of the three cities. It is possible that youth in the prairie cities prefer to spend time in homes and leisure centres more than youth in Toronto because of a lack of youth-specific and youth-friendly places. Perhaps youth in Winnipeg and Calgary do not have as much disposable income as those in Toronto. The research team pondered this possibility, but the socio-economic status of the parents was examined and it was found that most of the Toronto youth come from lower-income families, so this would not explain the propensity of Toronto students to spend more time at stores. We examined other aspects of the data and determined that stores and shopping malls in all three cities are not primarily used for shopping. They are used for 'hanging out' and socializing with friends and family. Alternatively, leisure centres may not be advertised as effectively in Toronto as they are in Calgary and Winnipeg. Youth in Toronto might not be as aware of the facilities as youth in the prairie cities. This kind of information may encourage city planners in Toronto to better advertise their services to youth in that city.

Table A-3 indicates the geographic mobility of the students in the three cities with regard to their use of city space and their travels outside the city. Almost one

TABLE A-3   Travels within and out of the city

	TORONTO (%)	CALGARY (%)	WINNIPEG (%)	TOTAL (%)
Explores only within city	15	17	30	23
Explores city and beyond	79	76	56	67
Explores beyond city but rarely explores other neighbourhoods	6	7	14	10
Total (n)	33	46	71	150

in three youth living in Winnipeg (30 per cent) have only explored within the city. This compares to only 15 per cent of the Toronto youth and 17 per cent of the youth in Calgary. The second row refers to youth who travel both within and outside their city. Almost eight in ten youth living in Toronto (79 per cent) travel extensively throughout their city and beyond. The number is similar for Calgary (76 per cent), but only 56 per cent of youth in Winnipeg are as extensively travelled as their counterparts elsewhere.

Why is there a difference in travel patterns between Toronto and Calgary youth and Winnipeg youth? Perhaps families in Winnipeg are less interested in travelling. Perhaps Winnipeg families cannot afford to travel as much as those in Calgary and Toronto. As Table A-1 shows, 39 per cent of the Winnipeg youth come from families earning less than $30,000 per year. But this cannot fully explain the difference, since youth from Neighbourhood 2 in Toronto are just as likely to come from low-income families (39 per cent). Another factor is availability of transportation. Recall that youth in Calgary and Winnipeg are more likely to complain about local transportation. As well, youth from low-income families may not have access to private vehicles that would facilitate travel outside the city. Furthermore, evidence from other data collection activities in this project indicate that a number of youth in Calgary and Toronto have visited distant places in Canada and outside the country. While Winnipeg has an international airport, it has fewer flights to fewer places than the large international airports in Calgary and Toronto. That may also be a factor in the difference in travel patterns among the Winnipeg, Toronto, and Calgary youth. These are some of the possible explanations of the differences between Winnipeg, Toronto, and Calgary youth with reference to their geographic mobility.

The last row in Table A-3 is an interesting subset of the youth population. This group of youth has travelled outside their city at one time, but while in the city, they rarely leave the confines of their neighbourhood. In other words, these youth have very low geographic mobility. These youth have only been away from the city once—perhaps for a single family trip, or they may have immigrated from another country. After that trip, they have had very limited mobility in their city compared to other youth. In Winnipeg, youth with limited mobility make up 14 per cent of the sample. In Toronto and Calgary, fewer than 10 per cent of youth have left the city once and travel very little within their own urban areas. As a whole, they are more similar to the youth who never leave the city than youth who make frequent trips away from the city.

The following discussion examines some of the unique aspects of youth, space use, and mobility in the three cities.

Youth were asked to identify the places they prefer in their cities. We categorized the places identified by the students into four broad categories. Leisure places include theatres, sports complexes, zoos, galleries, and amusement parks. Institutional places include youth centres, community centres, schools, and churches. Stores include

TABLE A-4   Preferred place by sex, downtown Calgary

	MALE (%)	FEMALE (%)
Leisure	17	44
Institutional	0	11
Store	42	39
Other	42	6
Total	100	100

shopping malls, grocery stores, clothing stores, cafes, restaurants, and department stores. Other places include airports, bus stations, parking lots, and places of work.

In downtown Calgary, male and female students prefer different places. Nearly half of all the females (44 per cent) indicate their preferred places in the downtown centre are associated with leisure activities. For boys, there is equal preference for stores (42 per cent) and other areas (42 per cent). This observation contradicts an assumption that females prefer shopping more than males do. While we cannot dispel this myth because of the small sample size, we can encourage researchers to examine the consumer habits of young males more thoroughly.

A closer examination of the interviews given by the Calgary students reveals that while in the downtown area, youth prefer to spend their time with their friends and their siblings. As a result, the downtown becomes a place where youth can 'hang out' and socialize. Youth define downtown as a place to buy, eat, play, listen to music, read at the library, and have fun. In other words, the downtown is a multi-purpose space for consumerism at stores and malls, entertainment at the-atres and music venues, and social networking. These observations are similar to those made by youth in the United Kingdom and parts of Europe in describing their town centres (UK Local Government Association, 2002). City planners in these areas have redesigned their downtown centres for multiple uses, as centres of business and consumerism in the daytime and places of entertainment at night. It is clear from these data that a similar phenomenon is occurring in Calgary.

When interviewed, the youth in Calgary tend to describe the downtown as youth-neutral. They do not have strong attachments to the area because it is, for the most part, not designed specifically for youth. This is reminiscent of the *gessellschaft* concept described at the beginning of this report. Skateboarders, how-ever, feel more at ease downtown, at least when the police are not present. Time of day also has significant influence on youth's views of downtown. In the daytime, youth feel safe, while at night, they fear some downtown places. For this reason, the downtown becomes a place to avoid for some of the Calgary youth.

Youth in Toronto were asked the same questions as those in Calgary. This table shows their preferred places in Toronto Centre but compares the responses across immigrant generations. First-generation youth were born outside of Canada, while

TABLE A-5   Preferred place by generation status, Toronto Centre

	FIRST GENERATION (%)	SECOND GENERATION (%)
Leisure	16	0
Institutional	5	0
Store	47	40
Other	32	60
Total	100	100

second-generation youth are children of immigrant parents. As Table A-5 shows, first-generation youth are most likely to prefer stores over other places in Toronto Centre, while second-generation youth are most likely to prefer other places.

Both first and second-generation youth in Toronto express high preference for stores when compared to the youth in Calgary and Winnipeg. While Toronto Centre is a place where youth can purchase goods and consume food and beverages, the area is much more diverse than the downtown areas of Calgary or Winnipeg. It is a place where youth can 'hang out' and 'be seen'. This preference for the centre, particularly for stores, is facilitated by a good transportation system. Toronto youth indicate wide use of public transport, more so than youth in Calgary and Winnipeg. This information might be helpful to city planners in the two prairie cities. If they were to model their public transportation systems on Toronto's, there might be increased use of central areas.

At issue for the Toronto sample is the prevalence of shopping centres as preferred places. In a closer examination of the data, the places of consumption also include many ethnic stores and restaurants. This is not surprising, since Toronto is the most ethnically diverse city in Canada; well over half of the youth living there were born outside the country. As a result, besides being places of consumerism, stores represent links to their ethnic and national culture. They are places where friends and family can meet, and these spaces serve a form of cultural maintenance. They are places where food, music, and culture are shared and heritage languages are maintained. The ethnic stores and restaurants are generally places where families and members of the same ethnic community congregate, although they are also places where other youth can be introduced to cultures different from their own.

Ethnic stores are central to the identity of Toronto youth and provide many with a sense of community and a place in the otherwise anonymous *gessellschaft*. It also differentiates Toronto from Calgary and Winnipeg. While the two prairie cities do have a growing number of immigrants and a variety of amenities and services for them, the availability of ethnic stores and restaurants does not compare to that of Toronto's. For this reason, the identity formation experiences of Toronto youth, particularly immigrant youth, is likely very different from that of youth in Calgary and Winnipeg.

Hanging out in downtown Winnipeg

As Table A-6 shows, the downtown area is a significant place to spend time among the youth in Winnipeg. This is despite the fact that for other activities not discussed here, many of the students clearly indicate that downtown is an unsafe place and that they are afraid of becoming victims of crime and feel that they are unnecessarily monitored while in the area. Of the places defined as youth-friendly in the downtown area, the majority (79 per cent) are places of leisure. Private homes (12 per cent) and institutions (9 per cent) are other places defined as youth-friendly. Stores are overwhelmingly (100 per cent) described as youth-specific. It means that youth tend not to frequent stores that are not designed specifically to meet their needs. This is interesting and differentiates the Winnipeg youth from the Toronto youth. In Toronto, youth (in a table not shown) indicate equal preference for youth-friendly and youth-specific stores. This may be indicative of different attitudes in Toronto and Winnipeg towards youth frequenting stores.

TABLE A-6 Preferred place by orientation, downtown Winnipeg

	YOUTH-FRIENDLY (%)	YOUTH-SPECIFIC (%)	YOUTH-NEUTRAL (%)
Homes	12	0	0
Leisure	79	0	60
Institutional	9	0	40
Store	0	100	0
Total	100	100	100

Table A-7 examines area of origin differences in preferred places among youth in Winnipeg. The table shows that those from European backgrounds are likely to prefer their homes or school to an equal extent (46 per cent for both) over other places. Asian students, however, are much more likely to prefer school (63 per cent) over their home (18 per cent). Students from other backgrounds equally prefer their homes (40 per cent) and stores (40 per cent).

TABLE A-7 Preferred place by ethnic origin, Winnipeg Northwest

	EUROPEAN (%)	ASIAN (%)	OTHER (%)
Homes	46	18	40
Leisure	8	0	7
Institutional	46	63	13
Store	0	20	40
Total	100	100	100

While the sample is small (n=68), this is an indication of ethnic differences in preferred places among youth in Winnipeg. More research needs to be conducted to understand why. We can, however, contextualize these findings with direct comments given by the students themselves. During a follow-up interview, some of the students were asked why some groups of youth 'hang around together' more than others. A young second-generation Filipina female replied, 'I noticed that most people only stay close with those that go to the same school as them' (Ballhettawsomodd). She was not able to tell us why she felt this way, explaining, 'This is just what I see.'

Elaine, an immigrant Filipina female, explained when asked a similar question, 'I haven't lived here for a long time, but some people were [sic] respectful and kind to other people even though they were different from them. Some are racist and discriminating [towards] others.' This may explain why some of the youth in our sample prefer to spend time with others of similar ethnic background and why the preferences in places differ among ethnic groups. It may be their attempt to attain a *gemeinschaft* within an otherwise *gessellschaft* environment.

Students were then asked to reflect on how they fit in to their neighbourhood in comparison to adults and to other students. Kashmoney, a Canadian-born female of Scottish ancestry replies:

My values are simple, do the right thing always; [sic] always take into account who you may be hurting, and leave time for yourself. These are very similar if not the same values of those held by neighbours. I unfortunately cannot say the same thing for my city. It seems more and more this city is falling to 'kill or be killed' or 'survival of the fittest'. [Communal] values no longer [come] first, only people's own interests.

Still another student felt that socio-economic class affected their outlook on life and how they fit into their neighbourhood. She says:

My values are basically the same as all of everyone in my neighbourhood; we all have grown up in the shitty part of town and don't think before we act. I guess [neighbourhood and economic] influences are biggest factor in what you do or where you go in life (Spoofanie, third-generation female, German ancestry).

Spoofanie's comments underscore the importance of neighbourhood and place in shaping values and identity. She also prioritizes social class over other individual characteristics such as sex, gender, ethnicity, and immigrant status.

LIMITATIONS

Although 164 students participated in this research, the sample is very small and was not selected using random methods. This means that the results cannot be generalized to youth in Toronto, Calgary, and Winnipeg. We can only discuss the experiences of the youth who participated in the study. We can, however, use this study as rationale for applying for other research grants involving studies with larger numbers of young people selected randomly. As well, the data produced in this study can serve as a guide for academics who are interested in studying the land-use patterns of young people and may be of interest to city planners as a factor in deciding, for example, in which neighbourhood to situate the next skateboard park.

CONCLUSION

Youth in Toronto, Calgary, and Winnipeg experience their landscapes in different ways. In Toronto, stores are a preferred place for many youth. While we might be tempted to label the Toronto youth as consumer-driven, a closer examination of the reasons why youth prefer the store reveals several functions. The store is a place for youth to meet friends and family. It is a place to socialize and be seen. For some youth, however, the store is a place that fosters ethnic culture and language maintenance. Families and friends meet in downtown ethnic restaurants and cafes to enjoy one another's company in an atmosphere that reminds them of their homelands. In essence, these places become *gemeinschafts*, places of welcoming and relationships in an otherwise impersonal metropolis.

In Calgary, females prefer leisure activities in the downtown area more than the boys, who prefer stores and other places. Like the youth in Toronto, Calgary youth see the downtown area as a centre where they can 'hang out' with friends. However, the importance of ethnic restaurants and stores is much lower in Calgary than in Toronto. As well, Calgary youth are more likely to rate the downtown as youth-neutral, meaning a place that is neither welcoming nor unwelcoming to them. City planners may want to review the places and spaces identified by these youth in order to make them more inclusive.

In Winnipeg, despite overwhelmingly describing the downtown as unsafe, most youth spend time here. Their pattern of space-use is similar to that of Calgary youth, where a combination of youth-specific and youth-neutral places were identified in the downtown. Space usage and preferences differ by ethnic origin, with Asian youth overwhelmingly identifying institutional places as preferential compared to other ethnic groups. When this was investigated further, some mentioned the importance of ethnicity, while others felt differences related more to socio-economic class.

This study contributes a geographic analysis to the growing body of research on youth studies. Its innovative data collection strategies reveal unique aspects of how youth view their place in society. It helps academics to understand the connection between city and identity. It helps city planners understand how youth utilize and interpret the spaces they use in the metropolis. The information may be used to assist planners in making spaces more youth-friendly and safe. This research also contributes to a more positive and realistic view of the average youth in not focusing on negative stereotypes such as the bully and drug addict that permeate the media and academic discourse.

ACKNOWLEDGEMENTS

This study would not have been possible without the assistance of several student researchers. Charity-Ann Hannan and Carolina Greco, students at Ryerson University, assisted in the data collection and analysis in Toronto. University of Manitoba graduate students Rana McDonald, Fasil Demsash, and Temitope Oriola interviewed students and assisted in data analysis for the Winnipeg team. Sarah Baker, Sylvie Xiao Yang, Leanne Hildebrandt, and Bill Hartley provided research assistance from the University of Calgary. None of this research would have been possible without the kindness of the principals, teachers, and students who gave their time to provide us with the information needed to produce this research project. We thank them but will not name them or their schools so that the identity of all participants may remain fully anonymous. Funding for this study was received from the Social Sciences and Humanities Council of Canada, the Dean of Arts at the University of Manitoba, the University of Manitoba Arts Endowment Fund, and the Winnipeg Area Study.

BIBLIOGRAPHY

Biles, J., and H. Ibrahim. 2002. 'Testing "the Canadian diversity model": Hate, bias and fear after September 11th'. *Canadian Issues*, September.

Byrne, D. 2001. *Understanding the Urban*. London: Palgrave.

Cohen, Phil, Michael Keith, and Les Back. 1996. *Issues of Theory and Method*. Working Papers. Paper 1. London: New Ethnicities Unit, University of East London and Centre for Urban and Community Research, Goldsmiths University of London.

Cresswell, Tim. 1996. *In Place/Out of Place: Geography, Ideology and Transgression*. Minneapolis: University of Minneapolis Press.

Hébert, Y., L. Wilkinson, and M. Ali. 2008. 'New modes of becoming in three Canadian cities: Focus on second generation youth and implications for social policy'. In Xi'an Conference Proceedings.

Helly, D. 2004. 'Are Muslims discriminated against in Canada since September 2001?' *Canadian Ethnic Studies* 36, 1: 24–47.

Massey, D. 1998. 'The spatial construction of youth cultures'. In Tracey Skelton and Gill Valentine, eds, *Cool Places: Geographies of Youth* Cultures, 121–9. London/New York: Routledge.

Räthzel, N., A. Hieronymus, and D. Hoerder. 2001. *Safe and Unsafe Spaces: Young People's Views of Urban Neighbourhoods in Hamburg, Germany*. Paper presented at the 4th Canadian Metropolis Conference, Toronto, 22–25 March.

Schissel, B. 1997. *Blaming Children: Youth Crime, Moral Panics and the Politics of Hate*. Halifax: Fernwood.

Statistics Canada. 2004. *The 2001 Census of Canada: Neighbourhood Profiles*. Ottawa: Statistics Canada.

Tanner, J. 2001. *Teenage Troubles: Youth and Deviance in Canada*. 2nd edn. Scarborough, ON: Nelson Thomson Learning.

UK Local Government Association. 2002. *All Day and All of the Night? An LGA Discussion Paper*. London: Local Government Association.

Verkuyten, M. 1995. 'Self-esteem, self-concept stability, and aspects of ethnic iden- tity among minority and majority youth in the Netherlands'. *Journal of Youth and Adolescence* 24, 2: 155–75.

Watt, P., and K. Stenson. 1998. 'The street: It's a bit dodgy around there—Safety, danger, ethnicity and young people's use of public space'. In Tracey Skelton and Gill Valentine, eds, *Cool Places: Geographies of Youth Cultures*, 249–65. London/New York: Routledge.

Webster, C. 1996. 'Local heroes: Violent racism, localism and spacism among Asian and white young people'. *Youth and Policy* 53: 15–27.

White, R., and J. Wyn. 2004. *Youth and Society: Exploring the Social Dynamics of Youth Experience*. Auckland: Oxford University Press.

Wooden, S., and R. Blazak. 2001. *Renegade Kids, Suburban Outlaws*. Scarborough, ON: Wadsworth Thomson Learning.

Appendix B

A Table of Random Numbers

To use this table of random numbers, it is necessary to pick a starting point. One way of doing this is to ask someone to pick a number between 1 and 32 (in order to select a column in which to start) and then to pick a number between 1 and 50 (to select a row).

Once a starting point is selected, it is permissible to move in any direction (up, down, to one side, or diagonally) as long as the movement is systematic.

Let us assume that the task is to select a sample of 30 from a population of 90. The elements (persons, tests, laboratory animals, or whatever) in the population would be numbered from 1 to 90. The task is to randomly select 30 of the 90 numbers. Let us assume that your starting point was row 19, column 30. Since you are selecting two-digit numbers, it makes the most sense to use the numbers in columns 30–31. Hence, the first number is 06. If you choose to move down the column, the second number to be selected is 41. When you reach the bottom of the column, start at the top of columns 28 and 29 and work down until you have selected 30 numbers. This will comprise a random sample of 30 from a population of 90.

TABLE B-1 A table of random numbers

Row	1	2	3	4	5	6	7	8	9	10	11	12	13	14	15	16	17	18	19	20	21	22	23	24	25	26	27	28	29	30	31	32	Row
1	2	7	8	9	4	0	7	2	3	2	5	4	2	6	7	1	6	8	5	9	1	3	5	4	0	3	6	6	7	6	5	1	1
2	2	2	6	0	4	1	7	7	3	8	7	3	6	7	9	4	2	1	3	8	9	0	3	4	9	0	2	6	3	0	9	8	2
3	9	1	6	6	3	9	4	9	1	0	5	1	5	2	2	7	5	2	5	3	4	1	3	9	5	8	1	3	8	2	9	2	3
4	7	0	5	5	9	2	7	5	7	8	0	8	8	5	0	6	0	5	9	0	5	7	4	5	2	0	6	1	6	4	2	0	4
5	4	7	3	6	6	3	9	8	2	1	7	9	7	6	4	2	4	9	6	0	3	6	3	5	3	9	9	1	8	5	1	3	5
6	8	2	0	2	8	7	7	6	0	2	2	3	1	1	1	6	4	8	5	2	2	3	4	2	2	6	5	2	2	4	9	6	6
7	0	8	7	5	3	3	6	4	2	6	8	3	1	6	5	0	0	5	5	7	8	1	0	1	2	9	1	4	3	4	7	6	7
8	9	4	1	9	0	8	4	6	6	8	6	3	3	2	2	3	7	4	7	5	1	5	7	6	3	7	9	4	5	5	3	5	8
9	5	0	0	6	7	4	0	0	0	1	9	5	9	9	1	8	1	4	7	4	9	8	7	2	4	3	0	8	6	4	2	7	9
10	1	9	5	4	1	5	2	6	2	9	4	1	1	5	8	4	4	4	6	1	8	7	8	6	4	8	7	4	4	0	5	8	10
11	5	6	4	4	1	8	7	2	8	3	6	1	5	9	8	6	2	2	9	1	9	0	4	8	1	0	1	3	5	3	4	4	11
12	7	9	2	5	1	9	7	9	3	1	8	6	8	7	7	6	6	5	0	3	8	1	1	2	4	7	8	9	1	7	5	2	12
13	3	3	3	5	9	5	1	4	0	8	2	5	6	3	5	4	6	5	7	2	6	7	8	9	9	9	8	0	9	1	5	3	13
14	1	9	0	4	0	0	9	9	5	7	4	1	5	9	4	7	6	4	8	2	6	4	4	1	8	8	1	5	4	3	8	0	14
15	5	4	4	7	2	0	3	7	9	1	0	9	6	2	9	7	4	7	6	1	1	6	1	2	2	9	5	8	4	4	8	6	15
16	2	9	8	2	5	5	9	3	2	0	4	9	0	6	4	4	2	1	5	7	3	6	5	5	4	5	7	9	6	6	4	0	16
17	9	7	6	2	6	7	7	3	3	3	1	7	5	0	9	6	1	1	3	9	2	1	1	0	0	1	3	7	7	3	7	3	17
18	5	8	2	4	3	3	0	8	5	3	5	7	5	8	3	5	9	3	4	5	4	6	3	9	2	7	1	1	4	9	1	3	18
19	4	3	4	9	5	0	3	6	2	9	7	4	6	2	5	6	9	8	3	6	1	4	0	3	5	9	7	1	8	0	6	9	19
20	1	1	9	8	4	8	0	6	7	0	9	7	9	6	9	9	4	0	6	0	0	5	9	6	5	1	4	2	0	4	1	9	20
21	6	9	1	8	3	3	7	5	9	6	6	7	7	6	0	4	5	3	4	5	7	3	0	6	1	0	3	0	0	3	5	0	21
22	7	0	0	3	8	1	3	4	7	9	5	2	6	9	9	7	3	2	5	0	2	3	5	3	9	7	4	8	9	4	1	5	22
23	3	7	2	0	8	1	5	6	9	0	1	7	8	9	6	6	6	0	7	8	1	9	6	7	4	8	9	6	3	6	5	1	23
24	2	7	0	0	0	6	5	0	6	5	6	0	3	2	9	3	1	7	2	2	8	4	9	0	4	3	2	4	5	5	1	2	24
25	3	0	7	0	7	8	4	9	4	2	8	2	4	7	4	9	6	0	4	3	8	1	7	7	0	9	8	4	6	3	1	2	25
26	6	2	9	3	3	1	7	7	5	2	2	3	4	6	4	2	2	4	7	5	4	4	4	1	7	1	6	7	1	2	6	8	26
27	5	4	9	2	1	4	8	5	7	0	9	6	4	7	2	1	8	9	7	6	1	3	3	4	6	6	5	9	0	7	0	3	27
28	0	3	7	0	1	7	3	8	0	3	6	2	3	1	0	9	5	5	2	5	9	2	0	2	8	7	7	2	0	2	7	2	28
29	9	3	6	6	2	2	0	9	7	2	3	9	2	8	7	3	1	0	7	0	8	9	3	8	8	5	3	1	3	1	0	9	29
30	2	9	5	6	9	9	5	6	9	8	2	8	0	0	4	4	8	8	5	7	2	1	3	4	9	5	2	6	8	3	6	6	30
31	8	5	7	2	9	2	6	5	9	3	9	7	1	8	3	5	6	6	1	2	1	5	5	5	6	1	7	1	5	7	5	9	31
32	8	4	5	7	7	9	9	5	1	4	5	5	0	9	5	3	1	3	9	3	7	8	1	4	0	5	4	1	5	4	4	0	32
33	8	7	9	8	1	8	4	1	4	3	7	7	0	9	1	9	4	6	1	3	8	6	5	9	2	2	8	1	6	9	0	1	33
34	7	3	2	5	1	8	6	3	2	8	5	8	6	9	3	4	5	2	6	1	9	0	6	9	0	5	4	6	8	0	3	2	34
35	8	9	9	0	1	8	8	8	9	5	7	5	0	4	1	1	6	0	3	1	3	0	3	5	8	9	2	7	8	8	7	1	35
36	0	2	9	7	8	8	1	7	6	1	6	7	6	4	2	5	0	5	8	3	2	4	7	7	2	2	6	2	6	8	6	0	36
37	0	5	2	3	2	3	8	1	8	8	1	6	2	3	0	7	3	0	1	2	6	2	6	8	3	7	4	4	3	8	9	9	37
38	2	2	6	8	1	6	9	6	2	6	7	9	1	7	8	0	2	4	8	0	4	7	3	3	8	4	4	8	4	3	3	8	38
39	0	7	8	4	9	5	8	8	0	7	2	1	8	1	7	5	3	0	7	4	1	0	3	2	0	1	2	8	6	5	9	4	39
40	4	8	0	7	0	5	9	9	4	9	6	9	8	2	0	6	4	0	7	8	1	1	4	2	1	6	7	0	7	3	1	2	40
41	9	2	0	1	6	7	2	8	3	9	8	8	3	4	7	8	4	0	5	1	6	8	7	8	3	5	4	5	0	4	0	6	41
42	0	8	8	3	4	0	9	2	2	8	1	5	0	4	8	2	6	2	9	2	1	9	8	5	3	1	0	7	8	5	3	9	42
43	2	0	6	9	7	5	2	8	2	5	5	4	0	7	7	1	7	8	6	8	5	1	3	7	8	2	7	1	9	3	6	3	43
44	3	1	8	6	8	3	5	6	3	2	7	4	1	8	9	4	5	6	8	0	6	4	6	4	1	0	9	1	9	8	1	4	44
45	0	0	8	6	1	7	5	0	8	5	6	5	0	8	2	7	1	1	6	3	4	6	0	0	9	4	7	9	2	4	8	7	45
46	3	3	2	9	4	2	5	3	3	8	2	4	2	6	2	5	2	9	0	1	3	7	6	5	9	1	4	6	0	1	0	0	46
47	8	4	7	4	0	4	5	1	2	1	0	4	2	5	7	7	9	4	6	5	8	3	3	3	1	0	3	7	7	7	8	6	47
48	0	2	4	3	0	2	0	7	2	8	8	0	8	4	1	6	0	2	3	5	9	7	5	1	3	6	3	2	8	7	5	8	48
49	4	6	5	6	3	0	4	5	2	0	1	5	2	7	9	5	3	0	2	2	1	6	1	1	0	0	9	1	6	1	7	7	49
50	3	4	8	3	4	5	8	7	5	9	7	1	6	3	9	9	0	9	4	2	5	8	9	5	3	3	3	6	4	5	2	0	50

Index